# WANDERER FROM
# MY BIRTH

# WANDERER FROM MY BIRTH

b. 1910.

## C. C. Aronsfeld

JANUS PUBLISHING COMPANY
London, England

First published in Great Britain 1997
by Janus Publishing Company
Edinburgh House, 19 Nassau Street
London W1N 7RE

British Library Cataloguing-in-Publication Data.
A catalogue record for this book is available from the British Library.

ISBN 1 85756 355 7

Cover design Harold King

Photoset by Keyboard Services, Luton
Printed and bound in England by
Antony Rowe Ltd,
Chippenham, Wiltshire

A wanderer is man from his birth – born on the breast of the river of time.

Matthew Arnold, *'The Future'*

Dedicated to the Memory

of

my beloved wife

Helga Hanna

never to be forgotten

# CONTENTS

# PREFACE

This will be judged the story of a nobody. So it is. For when all is read and done, who am I? Just a scrap of flotsam that was whirled around bits of Europe, albeit in a crucial period, and my experience is that of those who survived the first half of the 20th century – no mean achievement perhaps if I may say so. I have been the plaything of history, and when I consider the sheer luck that took a hand in my affairs, guiding me safely so that I have come to feel great cause for gratitude, I cannot help remembering the received teaching of the philosopher Theodor Lessing that as we contemplate history, even our very own, we are driven to devise some sort of sense for something that essentially is (according to this 'friend of wisdom') devoid of sense. The significance with which I have invested the events that swept me along makes up that myth which, in retrospect, takes the place of history.

Memoirs normally deal with a life of action, adding personal views of events that may have general interest in the world at large. Mine are not of this kind. My life has not been one of action, of involvement in the world, but rather one of contemplation – of the world, not outside but rather inside – and such opinions as I have been able to form are strictly those of the dissident and at issue with commonly accepted thought. I like to hope that they can help to stimulate thinking, and where all agree or disagree I shall be satisfied if they will stop to reconsider. Such is a fruit of my wanderings along the river of time.

What it all amounts to, what I have learnt, what we can learn – frankly I do not know. Least of all, in spite of some effort, have I told the truth about myself. But then, who in attempting an autobiography, remembering our own past, can hope to be truthful? I should know. I have read several autobiographies when researching one of my favourite subjects, the story of the German Jews in Victorian England, my forerunners as it were. Among the most interesting things were those that were treated with discretion. But I may claim to have gone as far as in reason can be expected from an introvert and one living at some distance from the world. I can only hope I have told a worthwhile story and made the most of the Chinese curse 'May you live in interesting times'.

This quote reminds me that I should perhaps remark on my general inclination to quote opinions that helped me to broaden my mind much in the way travel is supposed to do. Though I spent a good deal of my time in libraries, I don't think I am a bookworm. I cannot claim to have read many books and much of such learning as I may possess was provided by browsing in and brooding over the thoughts I happened to encounter. I have been stimulated by them, especially those I disagreed with – of which there were many.

In fact when I was thinking of a suitable title for these reminiscences I hit on something like 'Against the Current' – until I discovered I had been pre-empted by Isaiah Berlin for his *Essays in the History of Ideas*, and although I cannot claim to be in any way akin to this great spirit, 'Against the Current' has always been my instinctive impulse when considering the opinions held by the majority. Dissidence happens to be part of a Jewish tradition and I would think it disturbing were my views ever seen in harmony with an (even Jewish) majority at any one time.

I was delighted when I discovered the confession of Socrates that he had 'gone through the treasures which the wise men of old bequeathed to us in their books and when we came across anything that impressed us particularly we excerpted it'. Something like this I have tried to do from my earliest youth, and part of my education was to enlarge on this practice. Later I came upon the idea of 'commonplace books' to which I was introduced by a writer (David Twiston Davies) in a newspaper article where he wrote: 'The prospect of copying out some favourite – and no doubt uplifting – passage from a respected author may have brought constant delight to the inhabitants of Victorian rectories, but why, it can be asked, would anyone today wish to save choice quotations?' I think I can answer this question, at least for myself: that delight is by no means confined to Victorian rectors.

It is still very much alive and I hope it will never perish, if only because it must help us to stumble upon some truth about ourselves. I have discovered that inward-looking truth among some of the finest English essays, and I am sure that those who earnestly try will also make that often gratifying, sometimes disconcerting, always stimulating discovery about themselves. I can recommend the effort which I have found invigorating whichever turn it takes, and if anyone reading this book will come to enjoy the effort I shall be happy to have suggested it.

# 1

# CHILDHOOD IN A VILLAGE

I was born in Exin (Kcynia) near Bromberg (Bydgoszcz) in the then Prussian (now Polish) province of Posen, not far from the Russian frontier, and the time was, incredibly, four years before the First World War. The tiny place had little claim to fame except that its history went back as far as 1262. In all that time the only distinction it appears to have achieved was in being (according to the reference books) one of those 'places of pilgrimage' with which the region is blessed. Gniezno, for example, or Gnesen, is another, better known; and of Roman Catholic churches in which legendary miracles have been wrought there is no end. Many of the miracles must be fondly regarded as so many plasters on the wounds that Poland has suffered in the last two hundred years or so when her body was mutilated by the rapacity of the big powers between which an unfortunate geography had placed her. So where the natural forces of history were cruel, the supernatural ones could not be other than compassionate.

Not least among the miracles was the undiminished vigour with which the Poles upheld their traditions and never ceased to believe in their nation's resurrection. The Jews surpass them only by the length of their exile, not by the fervour of their hope.

When Jews were mentioned in Exin's records for the first time in 1594, it was only to affirm the disabilities they were to suffer together with, oddly, the Scots, whom one would not normally expect to find in these parts and who have long since returned to more congenial regions. Though the presence of disabilities is not perhaps surprising when seen in the light of later events, yet in the preceding centuries, between 1350 and 1600, Jews had found refuge in Poland from Western persecution, even as early as the Crusades and especially at the time of the Black Death.

It is today perhaps a melancholy reflection that Poland, with Lithuania, was then one of the few European countries which would receive Jews fleeing for their lives and actually encouraged Jewish immigration. They came from various parts of Germany – from the Rhineland, Bavaria, Württemberg – but also from Bohemia and Austria, though Poland was then by no means immune from antisemitism as the Exin records of 1594 attest. It could be found mainly in two areas: first among the Catholic clergy and secondly among the generality of the German immigrants, for the most part traders and artisans who did not care for their Jewish rivals. Paradoxically, the Jews felt greatly attached to German culture and to none of its tokens more so than its language. As the Spanish Jews, after their expulsion in 1492, turned Turkey into a 'new Spain' by retaining the ancient language (now Ladino), so (says Heinrich Graetz, the 19th century Jewish historian) the German Jews turned parts of Poland into a 'new Germany' by developing their medieval German into Yiddish. They treasured it, according to Graetz, 'as a sacred memory'; it was to them a 'holy language second only to Hebrew'.

But this was perhaps the clearest indication that our family was not able to trace its origins far into the Middle Ages, for we did not speak Yiddish, hardly knew it and would regard it as little better than a fancy jargon, a sorry counterfeit of the German we spoke, the German of Mendelssohn and Heine.

This may also be the reason why I had no 'Jewish'

forename. Caesar (Casper), the forename of my father's father, was believed to be the civil equivalent of the Hebrew Yeheskel (Ezekiel); at least (so I was told) this applied to my first name, and as Caesar has frequently given rise to quizzical enquiries, I might tell a nice little story. After a meeting of the society to which I belonged, I was asked to see the speaker home. He was the local Minister, a worthy elderly gentleman of considerable classical education. In the course of some small talk, he chanced to enquire what my first name was, and when I told him he was visibly impressed. He had heard of many outlandish 'Christian' names, but it seemed this one beat the lot. One did not come across many people so named, he remarked, and he would definitely remember it, he was sure he would.

A few days later I had occasion to deliver a message at his home. The same slightly old-fashioned worthy with the ginger beard and now the heavy-rimmed glasses delicately perched on the tip of his nose, he looked at me, I saw at once he did not have a clue. I said: 'I don't suppose you remember my face, I am—' His face lit up. 'Ah,' he said, 'Julius, come right in!' He had promised to remember and he did.

My parents' families had been living in Exin and known each other for several generations. My father had inherited a kind of general store and grain business combined with a spirits and off-licence trade. I remember being told that 'we' had supplied Napoleon's army on its advance into Russia in 1812. I was told this as a kind of historical oddity, a little incident to be recorded in the family scrapbook.

Old Philip Cohen, Father's great-grandfather, who I believe was then in charge cannot have been very enthusiastic about this particular commission, for we were all good Prussians albeit of recent vintage like Prussian rule itself though not with the family roots which at least on Father's side stretched back far into the 18th century. As for Napoleon, whatever we may have thought of the ideas of the French Revolution, he was a foreign conqueror and I am sure we were anxious to be rid of him. We were, or fancied ourselves, enlightened liberals, and my father managed to be at once a partisan of the revolution of 1848 and an admirer of Bismarck (if only because of a shared contempt for the Kaiser). He was a faithful reader of the leading liberal *Berliner Tageblatt* whose eminently erudite editor-in-chief Theodor Wolff was a political pacesetter among German Jews who had long come to regard Napoleon with respect as the harbinger of civil emancipation.

Napoleon could have had no greater admirer than in my mother's mother as she was an ardent devotee of Heinrich Heine who of course worshipped the Emperor as an idol that would have been frowned upon alike by the Second Commandment and the Prussian historians. A portrait of Heine hung in her drawing room and she owned a fine edition of his works. Like most of her (Jewish) generation, she knew Heine's poetry largely by heart. She had been given a sound all-round education; her father, David Badt, went to the unusual trouble of advertising in the *Allgemeine Zeitung des Judenthums* for a governess to teach his three daughters English, French and music. They also were taught an unquestioning belief in the ideals of 1848 and in a progress which, having emerged from what used to be called the Dark Ages, was sure to be irresistible. Since the 19th century had shown so much promise, what would not the 20th bring by way of fulfilment?

My father shared this belief and in token of it he built, in place of his inherited rather run-down little cottage, a proud and spacious three-floor mansion which, standing prominently on the market square, seemed to proclaim its determination to last at least another hundred years. It did not occur to him that he might have built on shifting ground. The society in which we lived seemed secure enough.

We were relatively well off, as were most of the two hundred Jews in a total population of 4,000. They were assessed, in 1914, at anything between £1,500 and £30,000

4

(at the then exchange rate of 20 Marks to £1). Among them were twenty shopkeepers of various kinds, four cattle-dealers, three bakers, three glaziers, two butchers, two tailors, two hauliers, one solicitor (though no doctor), one stationer, as well as of course a teacher at the small Jewish school and a cantor.

We had a fine *Tempel*, about fifty years old, quite a stately building, but no rabbi, at least not in my time, though Exin once had the benefit of such talmudic luminaries as Akiba Eger and Wolf Klausner. There was in fact little religious life apart from the punctiliously maintained regular services, and only at rare intervals did a wandering minstrel appear, on behalf of an orthodox society in Posen, to treat those sufficiently interested to a more or less learned lecture. Nor was social life more effectively developed; one of the frequently changing Jewish teachers once tried his hand but the feeble effort soon petered out though an old-established Mutual Aid Society was conscientiously supported.

A traditional Jewish school of course existed, teaching Hebrew and prayers, and I was enrolled there a year before the general elementary school where I started Latin three years later. My upbringing at home was fairly strict. No manner of work was to be done on the Sabbath which was to be kept holy in accordance with the Fourth Commandment. I remember asking my father whether I would be permitted to whistle on the Sabbath. I no longer recall the learned opinion but I do know that when in doubt, the answer was No. Discipline was strict, in some ways almost Spartan. I was expected to do as I was told, and if the intensely unpopular barley soup was not finished for lunch, it was sure to be back at tea – until in the evening I had been sufficiently softened up to be ready for it.

During the Kaiser war, which left Exin largely unaffected, we met two foreign Jews, prisoners of war who were directed to work for local traders. One of them was 'ours', a Russian from Lublin, a most lovable, warmhearted man whom we soon were delighted to treat as one

5

of the family. The other was French, a sullen and defiant fellow, a worthy companion of Heine's 'Two Grenadiers'; when we, having heard that it was his *Jahrzeit*, asked him to the synagogue for *Kaddish*, Monsieur conveyed as intelligibly as he could that he would rather not join in prayer with Germans...

Our Jewish interests were particularly fostered by my maternal grandmother who ran a leather shop, taken over after her husband's death, also a stationer's and a lending library inherited from her father, which I suppose mainly served the predominantly West German seminarists at the local Royal Prussian Teachers' Training College. Grandma was a subscriber to the *Allgemeine Zeitung des Judenthums*, also to the *Alliance Israélite Universelle*'s German-language journal *Ost und West*, and through her we frequently received Jewish calendars and almanacs. I remember one in particular which impressed me with its impassioned manifesto by 'An Unknown Jew' at Konstanz am Rhein, 1840, calling upon his brethren to return to the ancient land.

We were no Zionists but of course we did not deny ourselves to the claims of charity, and when Zionist messengers visited the town offering for sale goods made in Palestine we would buy the picturesque souvenirs. I still have a magnificent little album bound in solid red leather and covered in heavy cedar wood containing 'Flowers and Views of the Holy Land' (Verlag A.L. Kahane, Jerusalem), with explanations in English, German, French and Russian – colour picture postcards and pressed flowers from Mount Zion, Mount Moriah, Mount of Olives, Mount Carmel, also from the Tomb of Rachel, from the Jordan Valley and from Jaffa, Hebron, Tiberias and Sfad. Under their veil of yellowing tissue paper, they must by now have reached their centenary, and I devoutly hope my daughter will treasure them well into the next century.

Living as we did in a kind of ghetto, we did not seem to understand the society into which we were cast. It was a divided society, to some extent a colonial society. For this

6

land had been part of the Kingdom of Poland as recently as 150 years ago, and the Poles were still there, much alive too. I regret I knew little of the Polish yearnings in the years when I was young and Exin was German. I heard of 'Russian Poland' – Kalisz, Radom, Wloclawek and far away Warsaw – but any such thing as 'German Poland' was unknown to us, even by definition: this was Germany, differing perhaps from other parts of the Empire in that here was a kind of triangular society – Germans, Jews and Poles, with a clear distinction between the three, certainly between Germans and Poles, if only because the Poles resented the foreign rule and the Germans looked upon the Poles as a backward lot that needed to be civilised in the tradition of the Teutonic Knights whom the Poles detested. The Polish language was regarded much in the way the British in their time might have regarded Swahili, one of the East African vernaculars. I never heard of Polish literature and culture that would have commanded respect.

I remember a lady teacher who I was told was Polish though she had the German name Fräulein Genau, but she never took advantage of her position to, as it were, 'indoctrinate' us. I, then seven or eight, was greatly attracted by her. I must have had something of a crush on her. I went to the trouble of finding out where she lived and, having discovered the door to her first-floor flat, I tiptoed along the spacious landing to venture a bold gaze through the keyhole though I don't think my gentle if fervent expectations were gratified. I didn't even catch a fleeting glimpse of her. So I sneaked away, a little deflated perhaps but content with having been (I felt) nearer to my beloved teacher than I had ever been before.

*     *     *

Ever since the 1880s the Germanisation policy was pursued by importing settlers from the West who, together with the reactionary civil servants and a conservative bourgeoisie, usually kept as clear of the more liberal-minded Jews as happened vice versa. There were of course exceptions. As I am thinking of the innocent delight with which I gazed at the pretty national costumes of the women from Bückeburg, Westphalia, I remember one of them in particular who was my nursemaid.

The Germans pushed forward by acquiring land for the exclusive use of the fast increasing settlers, and a tight network of sponsored cooperatives was designed to assure them of substantial advantages over the Poles who in turn developed their own cooperative defence.

In this struggle of the nationalities, the Jews held an unenviable middle ground. They felt drawn towards the Germans whom they regarded as rather more cultured than the Poles. This was no particular animosity against the Poles; in Russian Poland, for instance, they felt drawn towards the Poles whom they regarded as more cultured than the local Russians. In Exin too Jews could have met Poles who were by no means their inferiors either in culture or general education – if anything rather the reverse. However, as it was, they were met with sympathy neither by the Germans nor the Poles. In the circumstances, perhaps naturally, the Poles were on the whole no friends of the Jews whom they suspected of undue subservience to the ruling power.

The Germans again did not particularly care for the Jews except where they needed them, that is, in those areas where they were facing a strong majority of Poles. There the Jews would come in handy as a counterweight in the balance of power. There the Jews could be allowed a larger measure of those rights which the Constitution granted but which Government practice frequently withheld. Actually, not until 1869 – four years before my father was born – were the Jews in Prussian Poland fully (and reluctantly) emancipated, and where the administration was conducted in the spirit of the reactionary Eastern Marches Association (*Ostmarkenverein*) – popularly known as the HKT lobby after the names of its founders Hansemann, Kennemann and Tiedemann – antisemitism did not always trouble to be discreet. Certainly where German rule was held to be secure, no need was felt to treat the Jews as equals (except

8

on paper), and though Jews had once been allowed to hold office in local government – even the city of Posen once had a Jewish Lord Mayor and Exin a Jewish deputy Mayor – the trend was to keep them out. In 1906, a Zionist convention held in Posen found the Jews there 'suffering severely under the pressure of the nationality struggle and in serious danger of being ground to pieces between German and Polish antisemitism'.

In Exin we did not notice much of it, but then Exin was one of those areas in which the Germans depended on the Jews, who accordingly enjoyed some standing. The balance here was indeed precarious. The population of 4,000 in 1913 included about 3,000 Roman Catholics and 800 Protestants, apart from the 200 Jews, and the Catholics were virtually all Poles, the Protestants all Germans. The twelve-man town council – with its pseudo-egalitarian set-up of four Germans, four Poles and four Jews – was presided over by the Jewish *Justizrat* (roughly the equivalent of 'King's Counsel'), and in the 'executive' of six, two were Jewish and only one Polish. In all elections, general and local, Germans and Jews joined forces against the Polish candidate who could always rely on support from the Catholic Church then still very different from the one that produced a Polish Pope.

But this seemed to us a natural state of affairs, and we were not worried by the fact (if it ever occurred to us) that in the province of Posen, for example, in 1916, there were 60,000 Germans, plus 5,000 Jews, confronting roughly 90,000 Poles. The Germans were truly hostages to fortune. Little did we think how much like the whites in black Africa they were. It is only now that I suddenly recall the significance of the poem that grandmother often, movingly, read to me, 'Das Negerweib', by Johann Gottfried Seume, which was an American negro mother's lament over her baby's likely future; I can still hear the pathetic last line about those far-off days to come 'when the alligator will in peace lie with the lambs – when the Christians will turn human'. I heard it again later when I came upon William

Cowper's ballad almost identical in spirit, 'The Negro's Complaint', with its challenging last lines

> Prove that you have human feelings
> Ere you proudly question ours.

We in Exin had cause to appreciate this spirit – not so much as between white and black, a relationship we knew if at all only from hearsay. We were perhaps thinking of the antisemites, of any colour and nationality, who also had much to answer for, and the Polish 'negroes', with all the civil rights they had, could not help feeling the rule of *Herrenvolk* however relatively civilised when compared with the raving beasts that fell upon them in 1939.

Yet they never forgot the cruel partitions of their country, and though the spirit of resistance had aroused itself to no avail in the rebellions against Russia (1831, 1848, 1863), nevertheless the hope for a national resurrection was not crushed. I became early familiar with the strains (as yet subdued) of *Jeszcze Polska nie zgineta* ('Poland is not lost yet'). There were now rumblings in Prussian Poland too, even in Exin, and soon the rumblings erupted.

In November 1918, when the armed struggle began for the possession of the Province, we hoped the partisans of the German *Freikorps* would get the better of the Polish 'insurgents', just as in spirit we sided with the Red Army then fighting against the Tsarist White Russians and the Poles. Exin, with its great Polish majority, was taken over almost at once, without any ado, and we only heard relief-promising gunfire from a distance.

I cannot help feeling now the irony that we should have sided with these German partisans many of whom were to become the raw material for Hitler's storm troopers. Long after the war was clearly lost, they fought on fanatically to keep off the Poles trained and equipped by the archenemy, the French, and such was their fury at what they saw as the Western victors' callous and vindictive cruelty that they vowed, however impotently, to make common cause with the Bolsheviks and thus 'flood Europe', drowning the hated French alongside the detested Poles: shades of the Nazi-Soviet pact twenty years later.

Many Germans and Jews, known for their sympathies, were soon interned in the dreaded Szczepiorno concentration camp, and I remember some anxious talks being hurriedly convened both in our house and at the synagogue as to what action to take. My father eventually escaped internment; the reason must have been that as a confirmed liberal he never left any doubt of his unqualified opposition to the diehards of the HKT and always diplomatically managed to keep on good terms with the Poles.

But now the time had come for us to make a decision. All Germans were offered the choice either to adopt Polish nationality and stay, or remain Germans and go. Many Germans chose the first, but my parents and indeed the majority of the Jews decided otherwise. My father was a German patriot, he *could not* be a Pole, even if he had not heard as we now did of the insolent manifestations of a Polish antisemitism which, all over Posen, openly called for pogroms against the 'pioneers of Bolshevism', and 'allies of our enemies', 'the parasites no nation will tolerate', etc. He actually kept the text (which I have preserved) of some of the scandalous leaflets, little suspecting that we would soon be meeting another version of this murder-breeding hate further West. Freedom for those Poles merely meant (as it so often does) that slaves had broken their chains and suffering had in no way purged their minds.

So in 1920–21 we joined the trek that had been on the move for over two generations. In 1852 there were about 1,100 Jews in Exin – 34 per cent of the total; by 1871 they were down to 470, by 1906 to 220, less than four per cent. In 1920 there were still 210 (reinforced by arrivals from Eastern Poland), but by 1933 the number was down to eighty and now of course none have survived.

As my parents and their generation now left to escape from the upper German and the nether Polish millstones that were grinding them, they fondly hoped bigotry would

11

be less marked in Breslau or Berlin; some made a more resolute break by going overseas, to the Americas or England. For most of them it was of course no easy choice, and few could have been more profoundly attached to their ancient, hallowed homesteads than my parents. My father never again struck the roots that were now torn up.

Many years later he told me he once discussed the decision to leave with the (East European) cantor who was a bit of a kabbalist. Cantor Schmul could not understand why we wanted to go to Germany, even the fact that father's brother was well established in Berlin did not seem to him sufficient reason because, he said (in 1921), 'there are going to be very black times in Germany'. My father made a note of the forecast but of course did not, could not, believe it. Anymore than he believed the further forecast that there was only one country to emigrate to, the United States, and that is where the cantor himself went shortly afterwards, to join his son, a young doctor, who had gone there in 1920.

I saw the cantor's ghost, in the company of others, when I visited Kcynia in October 1987. In the climate of the Cold War it was a somewhat complicated journey. On a five-day visa, I had to fly to Warsaw (the only way, in those days, to get into Poland from Britain), over-shooting my destination by more than a hundred miles. I then took a comfortable fast train (four hours) in the opposite direction, to Bydgoszcz (Bromberg), the fare being 1,450 zloty, at the then rate of exchange less than £3 (in England I would have had to pay between £50 and £60). In Bydgoszcz I stayed at a good hotel, and a double-decker steam train, running once a day, would take me, in a leisurely one and a quarter hours, to Kcynia.

My father's house still stood, though it had come down in the world, not only withered by age but also neglected, scruffy, an ungainly sight. The cantor's house still stood too, almost unchanged, but the Temple had been destroyed by the Germans who murdered all the Jews when they broke into Poland in 1939 – until eventually they were overtaken by Polish revenge which drove out all those who had escaped slaughter. One of the symbols of a German presence, the old Protestant church, had disappeared too, and so had the picturesque windmill opposite the railway station, a most unusual sight here, which no doubt was also regarded as unbearably German. Some entrances to houses, including grandmother's, had been walled up, and looking at them I felt as if I were denied access to some of my most cherished childhood memories.

At the end of this ('High') street, which was also the end of the town, there still was the square which I had been told as a child was the horse traders' market. I did not now so remember it. I rather remembered it as something like the gate to the town, and whenever I thought of it as I often did, I could hear the lilt of Schubert's song about the lime tree – 'by the well at the gate' – and the 'sweet dream' that I might have dreamt there,

> and its branches rustled
> as if calling me – do
> come, join me, old friend,
> there is rest here for you.

And at this moment, while scanning my absence of sixty years, the very last lines came back:

> now I've stayed many hours
> far away, nowhere near,
> yet the rustling still whispers:
> there is rest for you here.

> (trs. S. S. Prawer)

I then tried to find the Jewish cemetery. I knew exactly where it had been but what I found was only a plot of open wasteland, covered with bracken, weeds and the leaves of autumn, where boys were gathering conkers and a neighbour kept his chickens, geese and ducks. And a sandpit was

13

there where playing children might delve into embarrassing depths. No memorial tablet indicated what kind of ground this was. But across the road a tall crucifix had been erected, as if to serve as a talisman against any thought of the evil that had been done.

I noticed the same at the small Protestant cemetery, at the other end of the town. It was still identifiable though heavily overgrown by all sorts of weeds. I could no longer make out the grave of my German teacher's brother, an airman, whose 1917 memorial I remembered was an aeroplane propeller bearing the words 'Love never ceaseth'.

Now facing the field of the Jewish dead, I said *Kaddish* – and I cried, a long time. Through a mist I seemed to be seeing the vision of the valley of the dry bones that were to be joined together, bone to bone, and arise again, and I heard, reverberating through my mind, the roll-call of all the Exin people whom I could at that moment remember – Badt, Buschke, Cohn, Dombrower, Haase, Herzberg, Jeruchim, Joseph, Leiser, Leszinsky, Loewy, Mamroth, Raphael, Rehfisch, Reich, Rosenthal, Salomon, Schimek, Seemann, Steinhardt, Süsskind. Where are they? What is man?

Am I being unduly sentimental? No more so than the famous Roman who came to little Arpino, his birthplace, and confessed: 'To tell you the truth, this is really my own fatherland, and that of my brother, for we are descended from a very ancient family of this district; here are our ancestral rites and the origin of our race; here are many memorials of our forefathers.' For this reason, Cicero confessed, 'a lingering attachment to the place abides in my mind and heart', and he remembers 'an exceedingly wise man' having 'refused immortality that he might see Ithaca once more'.

\* \* \*

I now (1920) left the place of my birth and it seems to me characteristic that I did so not with my parents but with my grandmother, who played an important part in my early life. I have mentioned her before and I should like to say a little more about her. My mother's mother was of a very

14

masculine nature but also of an aristocratic one that was at times bitter and could be harsh. Fate had not been particularly kind to her. She early lost her husband, she took over the business single-handed and she had two little children to look after. This was sad and what she felt was sadder still was that the two children were daughters. She had wanted a son and she visited the deprivation on the daughters. This bitter feeling, I assume after much thought, was occasionally compounded by the fact that both had married men who, however differing from each other, did not come up to her aristocratic expectations.

The daughters sometimes believed she did not have a true mother's love for them – which she did not deny, saying it was not in her nature, at least (something she did not say) in her feelings for the daughters. The younger one had been married early and when the first child was a boy (myself), her mother cast a jealous eye on him. Why was the daughter granted something that she had been denied? Why did not *she* have a son? She now coveted me as something to which she felt entitled and she determined to regard me as her son.

This was not too difficult as both Father and Mother were busy in the shop and particularly after a second child (a daughter) had arrived. Grandma then seemed actually to be rendering a welcome service by relieving the parents. I spent a great deal of my time in her house where I was spoilt but also educated. I was taught much poetry, mainly German but English too, for example 'My heart's in the Highlands, My heart is not here' – though I could not then fathom how weirdly appropriate this was for my separation from the world into which I was born. One of the earliest books I was given to read was *Gulliver's Travels* (in anticipation of my own if less exciting travels?). Grandma supervised my progress in Latin taught by a German teacher imported from the West, and she introduced me to a world far away from tiny Exin. I soon learnt all about the capitals of Europe and beyond, especially the one to which two of her half-brothers had emigrated, Lima in legendary

15

Peru on the other side of the moon which I knew to be real only because of the fanciful postage stamps that kept irregularly arriving.

She felt greatly attached to one of these brothers (Gustav) who had emigrated at the age of sixteen in 1865 when she was eight. She had never seen him again, but the family frequently received presents, and I remember particularly the little silver llamas which occupied a place of honour in Grandma's drawing room. Several photos arrived too, including one showing a well turned out country gentleman. He died in 1914 and the inheritance which she shared with two sisters enabled Grandma to lead a relatively comfortable, independent life.

So she was my companion when we began our emigration. The parents stayed behind for a while as father still had some business to attend to, selling the house that he had built in the very year I was born, a double token as it were of his trust in the future. I was thinking of him when I later heard Liuba's words in *The Cherry Orchard*: 'I was born here, you know, my father and mother lived here, and my grandfather too, and I love this house – I cannot conceive life without the cherry orchard, and if it really has to be sold, then sell me with it.'

This is how Father must have been tempted to feel, yet he went on his way, even as Liuba eventually went, and he at any rate must still have had hopes of planting a new orchard. As we took leave, he said to me: 'You will be crossing the frontier at Schneidemühl. When you get there, remember, son, put off thy shoes, for the place whereon thou standest is holy ground.' He meant Germany.

The year was 1920. Jakob Wassermann had just written his essay *Mein Weg als Deutscher und Jude* in which he said, as if paraphrasing Cantor Schmul, the Jew was an outlaw among Germans and likely to find justice there among the dead rather than the living. But we did not know about this, and, in fairness, had we known we would hardly have thought or acted other than we did. (Thomas Mann then thought Wassermann was 'immoderately exaggerating', and not until the Nuremberg Laws of 1935 did he realise that of course 'no sane reason could fathom' how 'immoderately true' that judgment was.)

In Berlin we joined the congregation of Jewish Posen expatriates whose newsletter *Posener Heimatblätter* was always eagerly awaited. We also belonged to the general association of Germans from Posen. I still remember their right-wing paper *Ostland* which prominently displayed the defiant motto: *Was wir verloren haben, darf nicht verloren sein* ('What we have lost must not remain lost').

Looking back I must doubt whether it was wise for us to join this crowd. But my father was a patriotic German, and there he seemed to see a hope, a faint but valiant hope, of a return to his roots, to Exin where he felt he belonged. I like to think that he would have been cured of this yearning had he seen the revival of irredentist craving, the attempts to resurrect the memories of the 'trans-border historical and cultural links between East Germany and its Eastern neighbours', those 'ancient merchant routes that emanated from Nuremberg' (of all places). He would have been, willy-nilly, resigned to his fate however cruel it might have appeared, for life in the impersonal vastness of Berlin was to him merely, at best, a counterfeit of life, an artificial plant. His home was far away. He would often speak about it, and the fond, pathetic hope of a return stayed with him almost to the very end, just as he fancied that all the money that he had lost in the inflation of the early 1920s, would, must, somehow be restored to him. In a special drawer he kept, as a kind of show piece, a big imperial 1,000 Mark (at that time £50) banknote which he seemed to regard as one firm rock in the new uncertainties, a promise that would not, could not be dishonoured. In the increasingly callous world, he no longer knew which way to turn, and it was only by the grace of good fortune that most of the family were saved.

# 2

# GROWING UP IN BERLIN

The Berlin in which we now settled was a dismal and desolate place. To me of course, then aged ten, it was an exciting experience. Little did I ever dream in the ghetto in which I had grown up that I would ever see, let alone actually live in, the city where the Kaiser dwelt. But in fact it was now the capital of defeat, and, for all its gay baubles and golden tinsel, a sombre city. All the imperial grandeur had gone. The Kaiser fled to Holland, a peace had been reluctantly signed at Versailles, and a National Assembly proclaimed at Weimar a lack-lustre workaday democratic Republic with a written Constitution which was hailed as the most modern in the world. It was resting on not too solid foundations, the letter of the law being so different from the spirit of the land, and it very nearly fell victim to a rebellion by armed gangs attached to the old regime. We were not greatly disturbed by these ominous events which happened before we arrived in Berlin. The Kapp*putsch*, named after the ringleader, an East Prussian Junker, was speedily suppressed and though clouds of brooding passions hung over the land, we could not yet hear the thunder rumbling in the beer cellars of the South.

Nor did we pay any attention to the wave of mainly

antisemitic propaganda (if we knew of it) that was sweeping over the defeated nation – often echoes of the Polish hatemongers we had just left behind. Pogromist incitement was commonplace not only in scores of pamphlets, leaflets and brochures but also in a number of daily papers (which we did not read), all obsessed with 'the Jews' share in the downfall of Germany'. These things were, as far as I remember, never mentioned in our family. No one ever recalled Cantor Schmul's prophecy of the 'black times' that would be descending on Germany. After all this was the homeland of *Kultur*, the land of Goethe and Schiller, our fatherland in which law and order could not really be at risk.

Yet the earliest thing I can distinctly remember – fittingly enough in retrospect – is murder: the assassination, in June 1922, of Walther Rathenau, the Foreign Secretary who happened to be a Jew. I still see the huge posters offering a reward for the capture of the killers, and for quite some time I could hear an echo of Chancellor Joseph Wirth's *J'accuse*: 'The enemy is on the Right'.

Those enemies were the forerunners of the Nazis, the miscellaneous bunch of *Deutschvölkisch* ('racialist') factions to the right of the German National People's Party which in itself was not above suspicion. This militarist, revanchist, monarchist crowd, had its fixed place of assembly, a café-restaurant in the west end, named 'Wilhelma', in honour of the runaway Kaiser. They probably knew, as we did not till very much later, that the Kaiser was (or had become) nothing short of a regular Nazi who, in a letter of December 1919, demanded that 'the tribe of Juda', 'these parasites', 'this poisonous mushroom on the German oaktree', be 'wiped out and exterminated'. I remember giving the weird haunt a wide berth, for this was a slough of iniquity where a Jew had cause to fear for his life.

There were of course different shades. Not all were killers, actual or potential, or aiding and abetting. I met some of them at the school to which I was sent. This was the *Prinz Heinrichs-Gymnasium* (PHG) which, in its way, could well serve as a mirror of much of the Weimar Republic. It was what was

19

called a 'humanist' school which meant that it emphasized education in the classics, teaching Latin and Greek rather than English and French. Apart from this, it was not conspicuous for a 'humanist' spirit, and the ideals of Greece were often obscured by the ambitions of a Prussian nationalism smarting under the recent memories of defeat. The school's war memorial was graced with the inscription *Invictis Victi Victuri*: To those who were never conquered (this stone is dedicated by) those now conquered (who however) will conquer (again). This smart Latin epigram, incidentally, was not the school's copyright. It appeared on other war memorials too, for example on Berlin University's where it intensely annoyed the French chairman of the Inter-Allied Military Control Commission, General Nollet, who reported it to the French Foreign Office.

German literature was taught by a devout Wagnerian, and though we read Goethe's *Faust* we never heard of his disdain for any national hatred. Virgil was presented as a warner against pacifism, and the verse of Horace 'It is a sweet and seemly thing to die for the fatherland' was raised to a kind of national credo. Homer was held notable chiefly for his praise of the absolute monarchy and democracy was deprecated by pointed reference to his lines 'It's no good for the many to rule: let there be one lord only, one king'.

Corporal punishment was accepted and practised as a matter of course. I am speaking from experience. I was once, at eleven or twelve, savagely beaten up by a teacher of German – and a Mozart fan – whose large and massive paws went far to confirm the theory of man's descent from jungle life. He later seemed, in a manner of speaking, ashamed of himself, but there is no telling how many more boys may have been maltreated by him and so perhaps turned into resentful bullies.

Life here went on as if there never had been a break in the tradition (perhaps there never was). France remained, now with a vengeance, the 'hereditary enemy' – an image that some of the French statesmen did much to perpetuate.

20

England was seen chiefly as the scheming manipulator of 'encirclement'; we never heard of her efforts to come to terms with the Kaiser (whose provocative follies were largely ignored). Nobody thought the worse of a history teacher who would refer to the Japanese, Germany's wartime enemies, as 'those yellow monkeys' – though he would no doubt take greater care ten years later in 1936 when Japan became a partner to Hitler's Anti-Comintern Pact. A large portrait of Prince Heinrich, the Kaiser's brother, in the uniform of an Admiral of the Fleet, dominated the assembly hall, and though officially now a 'state' school, inofficially the PHG continued to be known, defiantly, as 'royal'.

About humanism in the sense of the ancients, we were not taught very much. According to the letter, yes: man was the measure of all things, but in spirit that man was German, and I wonder how many of the parents and teachers secretly half agreed when in 1927 Dr Goebbels, recently made Gauleiter of Berlin, countered a Jewish appeal 'Humans, be human!' with the slogan 'Germans, be German!'

I must linger a little over this hideous cripple who was to become Minister of Propaganda and People's Enlightenment, first to corrupt the German people's minds and then to befuddle international opinion with the arsenal of brazen lies that screened Hitler's advance towards war. He knew how to dazzle the crowd both at home and abroad, making them see, as Swift puts it in his essay on 'The Art of Political Lying', 'their ruin in their interests and their interest in their ruin'. He it was who invented the Holocaust-fomenting sophistry that the Jew was a human being in precisely the way that a bug, a louse, rat or other vermin was an animal – existing only for the purpose of being exterminated.

His vile demagoguery had early caught my attention and I can hardly say how I detested this most evil product of the very dregs of hell, marked off only too visibly by the devil's own cloven hoof. He was in truth a degenerate replica

21

of Richard III, 'rudely shaped, cheated of feature by dissembling nature, determined to be a villain, subtle, false and treacherous.' I often thought whatever the punishment meted out to this scoundrel, if he were quartered and each quarter again torn to shreds, I would say he had been let off lightly.

But to come back to the largely unsuspecting fools of the Prinz Heinrich School. Of course they were no Nazis. Removed from humanism, they were committed to the kind of nationalism which is the half-way house on the road to bestialism. Certainly they were not free from what I may charitably call ambivalent feelings towards Jews. I remember an ugly scene when a teacher slapped a Jewish boy, saying 'Behave yourself, you aren't here in a Jews' school' – an antisemitic term of abuse of 'ghetto schools' where, according to centuries-old prejudice, neither discipline nor manners were known or taught.

This incidentally happened, if I remember aright, in 1926 when I was not yet sixteen. I have often thought of it and I am ashamed to say I did nothing to protest against the outrage which was directed against me as much as against my mate. I resented it of course but it never occurred to me to show my resentment. Later I wondered what right did I have to sit in judgement on those who failed to denounce the Nazi persecution of the Jews, especially when any such denunciation would have meant instantaneous imprisonment if not death? I was clearly the product of an education that frowned upon all rebellion against properly constituted authority.

Officially, on the surface, everything was correct. Jewish pupils were treated with consideration; Hebrew scripture lessons were given twice a week by a visiting, sadly ineffectual, rabbi, and in fact there were two Jewish teachers: one a distinguished Greek scholar and archaeologist, Professor Otto Rubensohn, and more especially my form master, Salomon Birnbaum, who through the vigour of his presence, the competence of his teaching methods and his authority as a mathematician and physicist, commanded unqualified respect. He never laid claim to any nationalist feeling nor did he ever do or say anything that might suggest he was a Jew except possibly when he showed himself particularly strict with his Jewish pupils. Ever since he singled me out, in front of the whole class, for a scene which I felt to be degrading, I confess I did not get on well with him. Whether in the general milieu he (in contrast to Rubensohn) ever felt at ease I do not know, though I cannot help wondering how happy he really was.

He was a native of Dubno, Poland. I don't know when he came to Germany. I imagine it was when his family escaped from the Tsarist pogroms either in the late 1890s or the early 1900s. Recommended by the brilliance of his professional qualifications, he joined the PHG in the early 1920s. In 1933, aged fifty, he was dismissed (under Nazi pressure); a petition organised by the whole school, for his reinstatement, was predictably unsuccessful. He then found a post at the Jewish school in Berlin.

Why neither he nor his wife (there were no children) made any apparent effort to get out of Germany I cannot say. It seems to me almost incomprehensible that this man, with his roots in the Eastern ghetto, whom I remember as one possessed of dour determination, energy and will power, was not eager to get out of this evil land which at the very least must have reminded him of some of the worst of Tsarist lawlessness. After all he did not, like us, belong to the German Jews who could dismiss any comparison with 'barbarous' Russia. But apparently he already was effectively assimilated, Germanised. In any case, he was either uncharacteristically slow to pursue emigration or vainly hopeful that, with his qualifications, he might be able to survive, for as he spoke both Polish and Russian (apart from his flawless German), in 1941, possibly through the good offices of a former pupil, he appears to have obtained a position as an interpreter at some army (Intelligence?) unit, but it did not save him for long.

One of his pupils (Hans Kuhnert) later told how, while

on leave in December 1942, he recognised Birnbaum 'walking like a ghost in blacked-out Berlin, wearing a light, threadbare little overcoat with the Jewish badge': 'I introduced myself. He remembered. He asked: did I know what was being done to the Jewish fellow-citizens? I said I knew everything. I tried to comfort and encourage him: he should try not to give up hope; things could not go on much longer. The war was lost and so were the Nazis, I said. There were people in the armed forces and elsewhere, I amongst them, endeavouring to do away with the regime. I had just had some talks along these lines in Berlin and Königsberg. He had reason to be confident, I said. He listened, but he could no longer believe. He said he and his wife would not last that long.

He proved right. Early in 1943 the couple was rounded up and on 12 March deported, presumably to Auschwitz. I wish to pay my sincerest respect to the memory of this most excellent man.

Very different was the story of Rubensohn. He did leave Germany, albeit late, in March 1939. It took him a long time to make up his mind. He was then seventy-two and he simply could not wrench himself away from the land of his fathers, even if he increasingly failed to understand it. He survived in German-speaking Switzerland, and when after the war the German Consul-General in Basle handed him the certificate of his restored citizenship, he was overjoyed at the thought of being acknowledged as a true German once again.

He was one of the generation of German Jews who put Germany above everything, *Deutschland über alles*, and if they were Jews too, they would regard the fact as what Heine had called a misfortune, at the very most an embarrassment. They would have liked to be accepted among the bourgeois nationalists who were then led by the relatively aristocratic Count Westarp. But even his company cannot have been an unmixed boon. In 1927 he supported the right-wing Government on the ground that there 'the Christian elements had joined forces against the infidel

Jews'. As the country squire did not think much of Berlin, he could find no more fitting word for his disapprobation than 'that New Jerusalem' (which to the faithful Christian might have been rather a cause for rejoicing). I myself heard him at an election meeting near the school abuse his political opponents as 'talmi- and Talmud-Jews'. It was a piece of irresponsibility for which he was to pay dearly. I believe he ended, like some of the more radical (non-Nazi) *Deutsch-völkische*, in a concentration camp.

His fate did not much differ from that of his spiritual counterpart, Superintendent General (later Bishop) Otto Dibelius who was chairman of the school's Parents' Association. His younger son Wolfgang was my classmate and I remember him sporting his badge of the nationalist war veterans' organisation *Stahlhelm*, presumably by virtue of his father's active service. The Bishop's unenlightened views were thoroughly representative of the Protestant ('Evangelical') Church which might well have been defined as the German Nationalist People's Party at prayer. As a confirmed diehard nationalist, supporting the callous lie that an undefeated army had been 'stabbed in the back' by traitors, Dibelius told the clergy of his diocese, even before the advent of Hitler, that he had 'always thought of himself as an antisemite',* despite 'the evil connotations acquired by that word', since 'in all attempts to subvert modern civilisation, a leading role was played by the Jews'. Thus so far from protesting against the evil spirit while there was yet time and the awful doom might have been averted by little more than vigorous stirrings of an outraged conscience, he, one of the foremost Christian leaders, was aiding and abetting the evil.

I knew of only one Protestant minister who was actually

---

* I am spelling antisemitism as one word, without a hyphen ('anti-semitism') which suggests the entirely misleading idea that antisemitism is something directed only against 'Semites'. Antisemitism today is (as I explain in Chapter 7) a propagandist weapon in the arsenal of those who seek to destroy democracy. I consider this a very important point.

a Social Democrat. In 1929 I went to hear him at his Charlottenburg church where he was preaching on the 200th anniversary of Gotthold Ephraim Lessing's birth. I remember he spoke of the author of *Nathan der Weise* as the 'lonely man' – himself – who had the courage to defy the Superintendents of the established Church by taking his stand on the Gospel teaching 'Love one another'.

Not content with the pulpit, Pastor Bleier entered politics. He joined first the Liberal, then the Social Democrats, and in 1921 launched a Society of Friends of Religion and International Peace. He never ceased to warn against those who were clamouring for 'revenge' and 'refusing to believe in reconciliation among men'.

Later, I learnt, he suffered much petty persecution, though compromise here and there saved him from the concentration camp. He tried to comfort 'non-Aryan Christians' by securing for them the right to attend services without any kind of restriction, but the many 'Jewish badges' among the congregation created an offence that would not be tolerated though by November 1938, after the nationwide pogrom, it became at least possible to turn the order of service into something of an anti-Nazi gesture by reading, instead of the normally prescribed lesson, the then all-too-topical story of the Good Samaritan.

Bleier by then had gone into an 'inner emigration'. He was no Niemöller or Bonhöffer. But in his own way he fought a good fight. He lived to see the fall of Hitler and I feel he deserves to be remembered with gratitude.

I also remember another, not a clergyman but in some ways also a nonconformist among his caste, the poet and essayist Börries von Münchhausen, who once wrote – rather unusual – a cycle of biblical poetry entitled *Juda*, published by the Zionist *Jüdischer Verlag* and illustrated by Ephraim Moses Lilien. This however was little more than a literary exercise, without much bearing on his views of the Jews of his time. Like many of his aristocratic clansmen, Münchhausen presented the contradiction which was to bring about their downfall. I have kept a little-known article by him, written in 1926, which characterises the best part of his generation. On the one hand, he agrees that 'the Jews who enjoy complete equality amongst us' have 'a right to exist' (which seemed to him by no means self-evident), and he 'would not dream of denying anybody the freedom of opinion'; on the other hand, he can think of 'German' Jews only in segregationist quotation marks.

He had been annoyed by a Gallup poll which showed that people were buying twice as many books by 'Jews and foreigners' as by Germans (possibly his own included). Nothing much wrong with the Jews on that score, he says, they only make use of their rights, but 'shame' on his fellow-Germans who were so 'lacking in racial instinct', so 'alien-worshipping', as to prefer Jews to Germans, who could not see that Heine's poetry was not really German or that Jakob Wassermann's 'master-hand' was able to portray only 'race associates', never Germans. It was not a question of locking Jews up in their ghetto – '*we* have long been locked up in a *Christian* ghetto'. In the best style of his ballads, he saw 'the German soul' on its 'death bed'; he even accepted the not otherwise acknowledged authority of a Frenchman who had referred to 'that Jewish land between Vistula and Rhine which backward geographers call Germany'.

He was not an antisemite, God forbid, indeed he declared he would have 'nothing to do with antisemitism whose father is envy and whose brother is murder.' Truly spoken, particularly about the brother, though *how* truly, Münch-hausen could not perhaps realise, especially when he called – long before 1933 – for 'the great *Führer*' who would 'forge the whole people into one unit'. Well, he lived to see him, and having mentioned the father and brother of antisemit-ism, he now came to know the rest of the tribe, the mindlessly abetting fools of whom he happened to be one.

He luckily escaped the consequences of his intellectual self-betrayal, unlike Dibelius who, having hailed the advent of Hitler, realised his fatal error too late when he – he of all people – was charged with 'treasonable attacks' on the Nazi Government.

Most of those associated with the PHG were readers of the Hugenberg press which regularly featured Dibelius's politicising homilies, and when in 1928 Alfred Hugenberg supplanted Westarp, the Nazis, then on the advance from twelve MPs to 107 in 1930, enjoyed the implicit good will of his vast and powerful press and film empire, far surpassing, in influence at home, the big democratic papers like the *Berliner Tageblatt* and *Frankfurter Zeitung* which international opinion chose to regard as the authentic mouthpiece of Germany.

That mouthpiece was much rather to be found off the beaten track, among the hosts of the provincial philistines who escape the attention of foreign correspondents. I remember noticing one such specimen somewhere in Westphalia early in 1930 and I jotted down this impression in my diary: 'Cultural activities of the Social Democrats will be reported only in inverted commas, but a Nazi meeting produces ripples of reverence and admiration.'

But if Hugenberg whose far-flung *Scherl Verlag* may well have owned that particular provincial paper, winked an eye at the Nazis, it was not because the diehard Conservative fancied himself to be one of them. Far from it. Though more radical than Westarp but purged of personal anti-semitism, he despised the upstarts who addressed their appeal to a socialism which, however phoney and nationalistic, was anathema to the double-dyed capitalist. Nor did he have any sympathy for the guttersnipes who revelled in revolting bouts of brutality. His eyes were on the expediency of a jingoist fanaticism which he reckoned would carry his own cause forward.

In contemplating and eventually concluding an alliance with Hitler, he did not understand that Nazis (like fascists) are not 'right-wing extremists', that is a political faction functioning (like his own) within a parliamentary system where 'right-wing' and 'left-wing' make sense. The old-fashioned reactionary did not grasp the new idea of an all-devouring totalitarian state now hovering over a country in which the drift towards totalitarian extremism, in the

Depression of 1929–30, threatened not only the 'moderates' but the entire system of which his own faction after all was a distinct and traditionalist part.

That drift towards totalitarianism was inevitably merging with a drift towards militant defiance – not yet in the uniform of Hitler's storm-troopers but rather in the spirit of a tempered nationalism. I remember attending, early in 1929, a lecture by the highly respected General von Seeckt on the subject of 'The Will to Fight' (*Über den Wehrwillen*). Seeckt, once C-in-C of the Reichswehr, was, both outwardly and inwardly, something like the prototype of the civilised Prussian aristocrat. He had commanded the force that crushed the Hitler Putsch in 1923, and if, up to a point, sympathising with Hugenberg, he wanted a foreign policy, as he put it, of 'reconciliation, peace, cooperation'.

His lecture now was organised by the German Students' Union. The 'creator of our Reichswehr', as the chairman introduced him, urged, in measured language and with an almost academic restraint, the imperative importance for every young German to be 'prepared for militant self-assertion'. Pacifism, he said, was all very well but there must be 'no dreaming in cloud-cuckoo-land'; one had to face the realities, and paramount among them was Germany's geography – her situation at the centre of Europe surrounded by the best armies of the world whose leaders were possessed of maximum fighting power and the strongest will to fight. A disarmed country like Germany, Seeckt said, was far more likely to be involved in war than an armed one, and if Germany was to maintain her neutrality she must, first of all, be able to defend herself. That was why she must insist on having arms. We must also remember, he told us, the example of J. G. Fichte, the philosopher, whose famous 'Addresses to the German Nation' had done so much to foster the spirit of defiance when Prussia was defeated by Napoleon. Those addresses were said to be as relevant now as they were then.

Seeckt was given a standing ovation when he had

finished. I too was impressed by the man and his transparent integrity. I noted in my diary that should I ever retain a pleasant memory of my student days, it would be of this moment. Those were the days of the false hopes raised by the foreign policy of that enlightened nationalist, Gustav Stresemann, who was unceasingly savaged by Nazi propaganda and eventually haunted to death but we were after all naively confident, and certainly I did not fathom (any more than any of those present, including the speaker) the hideous perversions which this sort of teaching could be made to serve.

I might have known better but now I realise how I myself was infected with nationalist feeling. I remember one of my fellow-students, one rather older than the rest, holding forth on the then (1930) ever topical theme of war and peace. 'For the time being,' he said, 'we were not likely to have another war – who was going to join in against France anyway? But if it's against the Poles, those dirty dogs, I bet each one of us will want to have a go!' None of his listeners disagreed, and I don't think I did either. Having been virtually expelled from my old home, I clearly was still unreconciled to my fate.

It is now commonplace to present the economic woes, especially unemployment, as a principal cause of Hitler's success, and there is warranty for it. As early as the 1850s, the English historian and statesman Macaulay warned the Americans that 'a demagogue' will arise, 'ranting about the tyranny of capitalists and usurers' and demanding that money should be taken from the rich to give the unemployed bread and jobs. Macaulay thought that 'when a society has entered on this downward progress, either civilisation or liberty will perish'. And sure enough, in Germany it happened, except that here both civilisation and liberty perished.

Yet it was not so decreed from on high. There were powers that could have barred the downward progress, and the German nationalists of the Prince Heinrich brand might have done it. They fancied they could play with the

Nazi fire without burning their fingers – and much more besides. How much, they hardly could know, like the students I later met at Berlin University who greeted with rapturous applause the matter-of-fact remark by Professor Ernst Heymann, the jurist, that in medieval German statutes, 'Jews were regarded as aliens and outlaws'.

No doubt here were some of Himmler's budding accomplices in the Final Solution. Yet it was not they whom we seemed to fear. They were, in our eyes, disgustingly absurd freaks deserving none but a psychiatrist's attention. I took little more than a collector's interest when I found my visiting card which reserved my seat in a lecture hall besmeared with the message 'We'll get you yet', plus an ink-drawn gallows (gas chambers were then comparatively unknown).

The problem seemed to lie elsewhere, and it is here that I find the most poignant and the most lasting of my recollections of the Weimar Republic – the role of what I might call the Prince Heinrich crowd, the people who were to determine the fate of a society which appeared on the face of it so hopeful an experiment. For the issue was not really one between the friends and the foes of democracy. It was settled, strange though it may seem, within the bosom of the foes. The friends, the democrats of the various hues, were little more than a veneer that could easily be scraped off. They lacked the passionate conviction, certainly the militant resolution, to stand up for what they believed in. The determined Nationalist-cum-Nazi aggression was granted all the privileges of an undiscriminating democracy, notably unbridled freedom of expression, so that Hitler could confidently boast, three years before 1933, that 'democracy would be destroyed with the weapons of democracy'. Later he and his propaganda chief, Dr Goebbels, frequently jeered at the 'democratic imbecility' which 'allowed itself to be exploited magnificently'.

The stunted democrats were indeed no match for their brutally ruthless enemies, and inevitably, when the chips were down, they without ado turned tail. They were the

shadows, here was the substance. The bourgeois nationalists of whom the PHG was a symbol held the scales of
power, and they again abused their office because, in the
last resort, they lacked all sense of moral scruple and the
strength of conscience – quite apart from an anything but
firm grasp of the realities. For by agreeing, however guar-
dedly, to make common cause with Hitler (whatever the
reservations), they first provided him with a majority, then,
having been cheated of their foolish miscalculations, covered themselves with unutterable shame until at last they
perished in unknown graves all over the East – if they had
not already suffered the vengeance of the hangman's rope
after the attempt on Hitler's life in July 1944.

This is by no means a story of merely historical interest,
and I feel I must tell it in some detail. It has immediate
topical relevance at a time when again 'extremists' challenge an established democratic order. It must carry a
warning lesson wherever moderate nationalists are then
tempted to make common cause with immoderate ones
and/or Nazis, as for example among Frenchmen sympathising with Le Pen's 'National Front' or in South Africa
where 'Conservatives' are attracted by the Afrikaner Resistance Movement, or in Israel where strictly orthodox Jews are
impressed by 'at least religiously observant' followers of
the late Rabbi Kahane.

The German Conservatives organised in the National
People's Party were an element of the established order, of
the 'Right', middle class, bourgeois, elitist aristocrats too,
however *déclassé*, and when they beheld the proletarians
among the 'National Socialists' they felt little more than
contempt. They opposed force and rejected terror, and to
that extent they were prepared to regard Nazism as 'destructive'. At the same time, they were sufficiently blind to give
Hitler credit for his 'patriotism', for the 'transparent honesty
and sincerity with which he served his and Germany's
cause'. They could not help noticing 'ill-considered out-
bursts' but these, they felt, were all too 'human failings'
which did not stop them from lending Hitler that support

which alone made it possible for him to obtain a legal majority – adding their 8 per cent of the vote to his 44.

It was then not very long before they found themselves labelled 'hopeless reactionaries' and sneered at as 'apostles of the past'. Soon the Nazi demagogue-in-chief, Dr Goebbels, the Minister of Propaganda, asked the 'bourgeois so-and-so's' who they thought they were? Were they trying to pretend that they too had 'a stake in the Nazi revolution'? In that case (they were told) they were nothing better than 'hyenas' prowling around for their 'share in the booty', 'camouflaged as our friends'. Their fate was seen as one more illustration of an 'old story' – 'radicals will always gobble up the less radical': it was 'not the jackals that were feeding on the lions but the other way round – the lions were swallowing up the jackals'. Such was the reward the 'respectable' nationalists got for the services they had rendered the Nazis.

These shamefully (though deservedly) deceived fools were among those too many who chose to ignore the warning addressed to the German public by the spiritual leader of German Jewry, Rabbi Leo Baeck, more than a year before Hitler was installed in power. In an appeal entitled 'End the Silence', he spoke of 'a history of man's speech and a history of man's silence'. If crimes were able to spread, he said in 1931, it was nearly always because 'the consciences were locked and the lips dumb of those who ought to have opened themselves to a word of righteousness and morality. Guilt is upon those who perpetrate evil, he said, but guilt, especially in the sight of history, is also upon those who see or know about iniquity done and keep their peace. They are those who, without wishing it, prepare the path for evil.'

'Only where there is no freedom,' he went on, 'can violence have its way, and no one is more unfree than he who stays mute when he ought to speak and warn. When the burden of such silence oppresses a country, the only hope can be that some merely keep silent because they do not know what is going on, and therefore it is our bounden duty to tell all those who wish to be counted among the free. It is our duty towards our people and our country.'

The appeal went unheeded. Those to whom it was addressed were proving Dr Goebbels right when in 1943 he boasted of 'stepping up our antisemitic propaganda so that no enemy statesman will dare to be seen at the side of a Jew without being immediately discredited among his own people as a stooge of the Jews.'

I will dwell a little on Rabbi Baeck's impassioned plea 'End the Silence'. The appeal was made before Hitler was in power, and of course the challenge returned with a will when he was. One of Baeck's colleagues, the then hardly less famous Rabbi Joachim Prinz, later confessed: 'The most important thing that I learned under those tragic circumstances was that bigotry and hatred are not the most urgent problems. The most urgent, the most disgraceful, the most shameful and the most tragic problem is silence. A great people who had created a great civilisation had become a nation of silent onlookers. They remained silent in the face of hate, in the face of brutality, and in the face of mass murder.' Thereafter the challenge began to confront the whole world which for too long remained silent, and even when the world at last began to speak, one voice was not heard, the voice of God.

I am making this point because it has become part of the debate on the Holocaust. We are now authoritatively told (I am quoting from an address given in 1986 by Chief Rabbi Jonathan Sacks) that 'God is powerful not through his interventions in history but through his self-restraint' – a self-restraint which is interpreted as meaning that 'He sees the suffering of his children and remains mute.'

Are there then circumstances in which we can justifiably stay silent as so many did? According to Jewish theology (we are told), God has given man freedom to be either good or evil, and we can choose – he neither forces us to be good nor stops us from being evil, and when we do evil, no matter how unutterably evil, he will not intervene. He may, as some theologians put it, weep with the victims, go with

34

them into exile, but he will not do what we may feel entitled to expect from the 'Sovereign Lord' who, according to the Prophet Ezekiel, assures us that he 'will rule over us with a mighty hand and an outstretched arm and with fury poured out'. One might well wonder how a God of this power and fury can remain mute in the face of suffering as vast as that which we have seen, especially as he is known to have inflicted exemplary punishment, on the whole world, at the time of the Flood for example, or on Sodom and Gomorrha, or on ancient Egypt where he delivered the Hebrew slaves 'with great judgement'.

It must seem strange that he did not so act in Auschwitz where the suffering was infinitely worse – not slavery that allowed for survival and liberation, but calculated and indiscriminate mass extermination. I know of no argument sensibly accounting for this phenomenon except one according to strict logic. If God did not act in Auschwitz, we have every reason to believe – *a fortiori* – that neither did he in Egypt where the deadly threat was so much less. If the ghastly carnage in Auschwitz did not move him to intervene, why should the cries of the slaves have done so? His reaction then was merely in the minds of devout scribes and a very good story they made of it.

I will return to the period immediately preceding the advent of Hitler. I have already remarked that in Exin we did not seem to understand the hazards of the society in which we lived. Now again, in Berlin, we had no inkling of the force that was gathering to destroy us, and come to think of it, why should we? It is true the would-be destroyers told us, – all and sundry heard it from the very roof-tops – 'Perish Judah', and Hitler later (1941) had every reason to boast: 'More often than I, no one ever explained what he really meant'. But what we heard was such that the normal mind refused to believe it. Neither Germans nor Jews nor the rest of the world would think it feasible; they would in fact brush it aside as utterly inconceivable beyond the whims of certified lunacy. Never, never would it be possible for Jews to be treated as Hitler threatened, seeing

35

they were so interwoven with the German social fabric, and
even if the Germans were such fools as to permit it, I can
still hear some of my elders say, 'the world' would never
stand for it.

Yet Hitler, the prince of liars, had told the truth, and it
was only much later that I thought of his murderous
threats when I read the lines of Byron's

The Devil speaks truth much oftener than he is deem'd:
He hath an ignorant audience

– an unsuspecting one, much like the crowd drawn by the
Pied Piper and other demon-ridden charlatans of whom
Goethe had said 150 years earlier: 'All the moral forces combined are powerless against them ... however much the
more enlightened among men may expose them as frauds:
the masses will be attracted by them.' Revealed by the
psychological probe of projection, 'a phenomenon in which
(says Anthony Storr) characteristics belonging to oneself
are attributed to others', Hitler drew a perfect portrait of
his own listeners (as well as of himself) when he wrote in
*Mein Kampf* about the objects of 'Marxist' propaganda:
'Considering the diabolical skill of these seducers, who
could condemn the wretched victims? How great indeed
was my own difficulty in realising their dialectical men-
dacity!' Germans disbelieved the implausible, unbelievable
truth – just as later a whole world believed Hitler's believ-
able, plausible lies.

I remember reading at the time in the early 1920s that
Hitler had sworn: 'I shall keep on pouring oil into the fire
all the time and there would have to be a miracle if there
were no explosion.' I made a note of it, but in that respect
we were all believers in miracles. Those who occasionally
worried were assured they were overrating the danger, and
the powerful Social Democratic Party as well as the highly
influential Roman Catholic Centrists were thought to be
'immune against the siren songs of the Nazis'.

Some Jews, even among their own leaders, were slow to

36

perceive the looming threat. The Heine lovers may or may not have been familiar with the poet's famous vision in 1834 of the time when the Teutons' 'Berserk rage', in contempt of 'the taming talisman; the Cross', would 'stage a play that will make the French Revolution seem like a harmless idyll'. But that was regarded as the playful, somewhat extravagant figment of poetical fantasy dwelling on such abstract themes as 'Religion and Philosophy in Germany'.

Besides, Heine could be remarkably fallible as he demonstrated the unusual phenomenon that while able to look into the future the prophet can be ignorant of the past. When he, a devout admirer, indeed lover, of France then living in Paris, noticed the French people's, even the French Government's, unfeigned belief in the lies then spread about a 'Jewish ritual murder' in French-controlled Damascus (1840), he thought, and actually wrote down, it was worse than in Germany where 'the knowledge of history' was 'so well inculcated among the people that not even the grimmest anger will dare to revive the ancient blood fables'. Even he was incapable of imagining monsters like Julius Streicher and the half-million circulation of the pornographic *Stürmer*.

A more realistically inspired voice was raised, half a century later, in the very year of Theodor Herzl's booklet 'The Jewish State', 1896, though this prophet also went without honour. In a slender 57-page print entitled *Vor dem Sturm* ('Before the Storm'), the otherwise little-known author, Dr Bernhard Cohn, a physician, declared things had reached such a pitch of 'moral savagery' that 'the voice of reason, justice and truth is no longer heard'; the 'total extermination' of Jewry was being preached as 'the infallible cure for all the ills besetting the world'. Dr Cohn knew of no section of the people who were immune – the civil service, the business community, army officers, the Junkers, the clergy, the teachers, the farmers, and as for the academic youth, they 'regard it as the only true patriotism to ensure that the Fatherland be purged of the Jew "intruders"'.

37

It seemed that 'only a spark is needed to blow up the store of explosives'.

When the spark was supplied a generation later, after the defeat in 1918, the German-Jewish historian, Ismar Elbogen, in 1926, found that 'the theory of the inferiority and iniquity of the Jewish race' had 'thoroughly poisoned people's minds', even 'beyond all expectation', and according to him, 'a premeditated racialist campaign was designed to bring about the Jews' economic isolation and destruction'. But again the implications of this persistent campaign were not regarded as an immediate threat in practical terms.

Baeck was fully aware of an 'epidemic of antisemitism raging in the land' at that time, but he felt it was merely a 'literary and "spiritual" one' (he may have been thinking of people like Börries von Münchhausen); it was, he held, 'much exaggerated by friend and foe alike', certainly 'not the expression of any widespread popular feeling'. Two years later, in 1928, he felt sufficiently confident to declare: 'The era of the Ghetto, in terms of history, is past', and soon afterwards he thought that 'on the whole, Jewry today is more solidly established, more sure of itself and its future, than a century ago'.

As late as 1930, after Hitler's tremendous success in the September elections, Jewish leaders were, on the whole, unruffled, comforting themselves (and us) with the old adage that nothing was eaten as hot as it was cooked. Some would assure us that antisemitic movements had a way of coming and going. Georg Bernhardt, MP, editor of the *Vossische Zeitung*, thought things would sort themselves out – a little more fighting stamina, a little more pride, a little less fear would work (yes) wonders.

The well-known German-Jewish author Emil Ludwig presented his own sophisticated theory to explain why the Germans' 'love of order' would accept only a 'dictatorship of their Princes and Kings', but not of 'men who come from the people'; Germans simply were not yet sufficiently 'democratic' to believe this possible. Consequently, he wrote in the London *Sunday Times*, 'a Hitler who was a painter could not in Germany attain chief authority through inherent genius'. Ludwig went so far as to wish the Nazis should be forced to govern; then it would be seen that though these 'idealists without ideas' could 'make rousing phrases about chains of slavery and bondage to the Jews they could not long hold leadership in the Reichstag', etc.

In my family we certainly were not seriously concerned. We were neither Zionists nor members of the *Central Verein* (CV) of German Citizens of the Jewish Faith. We were middle-of-the-road Jews, committed Jews, taking our Judaism as much for granted as our Germanism. We belonged to a moderately orthodox synagogue which, in Anglo-Saxon countries, would go by the name of 'Reform' or 'Conservative'.

I still see the distinguished-looking, black-bearded rabbi who confirmed me at thirteen, Arthur Levy, who was proud to wear his smart army (Lieutenant's) uniform when father and I visited him to discuss details. It was he who had been appointed to translate into Yiddish the famous proclamation by the (later antisemitic) General Erich Ludendorff, commander of the German armies invading Russia in 1914, 'To my dear Jews in Poland', promising them freedom from Tsarist oppression. Rabbi Levy's synagogue was destroyed with the rest in November 1938, and he died an exile in far-off Brazil.

The memory of the Münchener Strasse synagogue is preserved by a brass tablet let into the pavement near its former site. I saw the ruins when I visited Berlin in February 1953: the gaunt shell was still there, all burnt out. It was winter, the rubble and the ruins all around covered in deep snow, and after I had made my way through the eerie silence of a wholly deserted street, I glanced through one of the small windows, now gouged like a blind man's eye, and I saw, or thought I saw, among all the savage debris, the seat where we used to sit, somewhere also, in the distance, the shadows of the altar, and up there the ghost of the choir, and suddenly there came back to me the

39

tune of my favourite Psalm 92 about the righteous who shall flourish like the cedars of Lebanon.

I vaguely felt like one of the Babylonian captives who had perhaps escaped for a while and now beheld the sorrowful sight of the desolate Temple in Jerusalem. I thought I was hearing the voice all over again. Of course I heard nothing except the crunch of the snow I was treading and the croaking of a crow overhead. But I saw, all of a sudden, the painting by Samuel Hirszenberg, *Golus* (*Exile*), the trek of the Russian Jews as they wander across the wintry wastes – without a home, almost without a hope. The painting had hung in my parents' home as long as I can remember. I then probably thought little of it, but now I seemed to be one of them, on a trek without end.

We were faithful readers of the non-party paper *Israelitisches Familienblatt*. It so happens I have kept the front page of 5 September 1929, commemorating the 200th birthday of the philosopher Moses Mendelssohn, and the ideas expressed on it were broadly our own. Mendelssohn was the great champion of equal rights for Jews in Germany, and today, said the distinguished writer, former Privy Councillor Cohn, 'what he had hoped for in his invincible, truly Jewish optimism, has been accomplished: the German Jew is free in the eyes of the law and enjoys equality of rights'. Jews had done much in the service of the fatherland but, alas 'the true practice of equality leaves much to be desired'. German Jews were seen threatened by political parties, boycotted in economic life and unwanted in better class 'society'. It was 'truly a difficult situation', said *Justizrat* Cohn, 'but not a hopeless one', so long as we 'while appreciating what has been achieved, do all we can to fight for our good cause', even as Mendelssohn did, 'faithfully upholding our Judaism while finding our place with the German branch of mankind'.

In practical terms, the author advised German Jews who had hoped for an easier life in the big cities to return to those smaller places where alone it was still thought possible to start independent businesses. Ironically, the trend

40

later was in the very opposite direction – those left in the smaller places moved into the big cities where they could hope to find not just an easier life (if that) but quite simply greater safety from physical attack.

*   *   *

When my father came to Berlin he remembered that though in Exin he had a general store with a kind of off-licence and specialising in grain and cereals, the trade he had really learnt was the manufacture of liqueurs and he now sought to establish himself in that line. He would probably have done well to find himself a position in one of Berlin's big liqueur businesses where his expert knowledge would have been most certainly useful, but he had an all too independent mind – unfortunately so because, away from the small trade, he was not cut out to be his own master, he was at best a second-in-command, not the boss but the manager, and it was his misfortune that he either did not realise this or could not adapt himself.

So, with financial help from his mother-in-law and assistance from his well connected brother, he started, in a suburban basement, a small-scale liqueur-manufacturing business which depended largely on private recommendations. It was a one-man enterprise in which the children were employed for most of the menial work including not only bottle washing and label sticking but also delivering the goods (by tram, though with the prospect of an occasional inflationary 500 Mark tip). Father never went in for advertising; it might have meant expansion and this would have been beyond his power to cope. Not surprisingly it was not long before he decided (or was forced) to fold up: it literally did not pay – quite apart from the galloping inflation.

I remember I was having piano lessons at the time, and I see myself trudging along to Mr and Mrs Zickel, carrying not only my music but the much heavier load of bundles of bank notes – the fee – which, on arrival, Mr would grab, pass it on to Mrs so that she could do the shopping before the money lost more of its value.

41

But to return to my father. Having chucked the liqueur manufacture, he found himself something else: he would handle the mother-in-law's money in a different way – investing it by financing mortgages. This was something of which he also had some (albeit limited) knowledge, and it allowed him to operate in circumstances more congenial to his temperament. He made some little money that way though we never rose above the level of lower middle class.

He was operating on the same small-town level as he had been in his liqueur-manufacturing enterprise. No doubt he was constitutionally incapable of doing better, but his limitations which no self-criticism ever examined also proved destructive when he spoilt a chance of improving the family's fortune (and thus his own) by salvaging Don Gustavo's inheritance in Peru. There was a plan in the 1920s that Grandma and her two sisters would send a representative to Lima, the son of one of the sisters, a lawyer well fitted for the assignment, but father, either feeling unqualified to take the mission on himself or suspecting the man's competence, advised Grandma to withhold her agreement. The result was, apart from a family split, that a local man was appointed, the general manager of the German Transatlantic Bank, a friend of the deceased, over whose actions the family, while never doubting his competence or integrity, had little control, and though some of the estate was saved, much of it was lost. Ignorant of what to do with his own life, father knew only too well how to embitter other people's lives, even his own.

With the modest money she received from Peru, Grandma was able to provide for my education. My school fees were paid by her and she also enabled me to see parts of Germany which I would never have seen otherwise. I was her companion when she visited watering places like Wiesbaden; I travelled with her even to far off Piestany in Slovakia (where King George V had just sought healing). She would have granted me any wish I cared to make. It was the fancy she had for me from the very beginning, but some of the old resentment also still seemed to rankle when she appeared to be less liberal towards my mother – or was it because she suspected Mother of being unable to handle money judiciously (as she, Grandma, understood it)? I once, late at night, watched Mother count the pennies for next day's budget and I know she struggled to make ends meet by getting herself casual jobs such as addressing envelopes. I tried to help a little by giving coaching lessons in Latin, Greek and maths, and she accepted gratefully the pittance I could offer.

I felt I had to do this, rather than spend it. If I was able to make that little money (at fifteen or sixteen) then it seemed to me I had to put it to the best possible use and that was to repay where it was due and obviously needed. Certainly I did not wish to spend it on myself and, oddly enough, it would have seemed reckless to spend it on a girl friend.

*     *     *

There was one whom I did my best to please but not by trying to show off and appearing something I was not; I have always detested the very thought of such phoney behaviour. But if in this respect, it was also in others a less than satisfactory or desirable relationship. For one thing, Ruth was fourteen years older and she was a Roman Catholic. I saw her every day on my way to school. She worked in a newspaper shop where I was permitted to look up all the different magazines in which I took an early interest. She also allowed me to be her escort when she cycled home to a backyard flat where she lived with her unmarried mother. We loved each other. She was my first love and a strictly platonic one it was (and remained). We went out, occasionally, on a *bummel*, not too far and in the most modest way. She did not care for a razzle nor did I. She, having come from Silesia, was as provincial as I was. There was a touch of melancholy about her as if she felt marked by the fact of her illegitimate birth which in those days was considered a blemish, and as a Catholic she must have been particularly pained by it. When she confessed it to me, she burst into wild tears, and it took me a long time to reassure her that I was attaching not the slightest importance to it.

But if she thought that illegitimacy was her blemish, then mine was, in her eyes, that I was a Jew. She belonged to the generation whose ambivalence towards Jews was responsible for that moral indifference with which the rise of Nazism was viewed. She tried to relieve me of the blemish by taking me frequently to her Church which was to me as novel and therefore interesting an experience as were later my attendances of spiritualist meetings. Once she agreed to come with me to a synagogue, and when she had seen the Scrolls of the Law she enquired what those 'dolls' were for.

From time to time we separated as if to reconsider our unbalanced relationship, but we always found each other again, and when I left Berlin for good in 1933 she wrote me a most moving farewell letter which I have treasured to this day. Thereafter we did not hear much of each other because at that time it was dangerous for a German woman to have any kind of contact, if only by way of correspondence, with a Jew. I remember reading in a London paper how women in German towns were chased through the streets with a poster round their neck: 'I am here the biggest pig in town – I carry on with Jews'. I can still feel the horror this caused me, and after I had just sent off a letter I immediately stopped and of course I never heard from her.

Now this may seem all too humdrum business but to me it had a crucial significance. For though the relationship was, on the whole, tolerably harmonious, in spite of our differences and occasional quarrels, a deep shadow fell upon it when my mother discovered it and now did everything within her power to break it up. The whole thing was in her eyes an abomination, and I had to be rescued as it were from the clutches of what she regarded as an unprincipled hussy intent upon corrupting an inno-

44

cent youngster. There was no stratagem she would recoil from to destroy my feelings. It was, to her mind, an unutterable shame, such an awful thing to happen in our family – who could tell where this would end?

I no longer know what it was that most aroused her: the fact that Ruth was not Jewish, that she was much older or that she belonged to a class considered not on a level with ours? Eventually Mother made something like a constructive, certainly intelligent effort to stop the rot: she put my name down at a Jewish dancing school where she must have hoped I would find a counter-attraction. I was not enthusiastic but I acquiesced, without suspecting any ulterior design. In fact I enjoyed the dancing lessons and attended regularly. Nor did Ruth seem to be disturbed; whatever she might have thought of it, she never showed any fears that she might be crowded out; perhaps she even regarded it as something perfectly natural. However, the purpose of the exercise was not achieved. I did not make any acquaintance of the kind Mother had in mind. The only partner who lasted for the duration of the lessons was a wallflower who happened to be not Jewish. And my relationship with Ruth remained as before.

Except that I was now badly split in my emotions though I was determined not to be put off; psychologists now might tell me this youthful rebellion was a sign of growing maturity. Anyway the affair went on in great secrecy. I managed to jog along by telling my parents all sorts of lies. But I suffered of course by having to live as it were underground. How happy I would have been if I could have brought Ruth home and introduced her – as a friend, just that, not at all a prospective, even a potential marriage partner. The thought never entered my mind nor, I am certain, Ruth's. We were both fully aware of all the insurmountable impediments. Even if I had been of marriageable age, I would have considered any mixed marriage of this kind to be as basically undesirable, as I do still.

Even a visit was out of the question, unthinkable, taboo.

45

Mother was not to be reconciled: this was a matter only to be settled by fire and sword. Ruth knew about it but did not seem unduly concerned; perhaps because she felt she had a clear conscience. But my emotional life was damaged – something I did not begin to realise or suspect till very much later.

I might have enjoyed my youth and grown up in spiritual freedom and undisturbed self-confidence, but now everything seemed grey and gloomy, and I was locked up in the frustrations of a bad conscience. I could have lived in a world of harmony but now it was like a house divided that could not hope to stand. My first love could have blossomed, now it was vegetating and withering. In saying this, I do not wish to blame my mother, treating her as a scapegoat, for one thing she could not help it and then I believe that however young at this stage, I must be responsible and in command of my life.

Oddly enough, also, I never felt any resentment against Mother. Subconsciously I must have granted her a right which I only opposed with a right of my own. She later showed an exemplary concern for my well-being and I have retained an immaculate memory of her. In her behaviour towards Ruth I can now – up to a point – understand my mother much better and I would not wish to criticise her intentions entirely though she pursued her legitimate purpose with inadequate means not least because of the damage that was wrought in my soul.

That damage was grave because it was inflicted at so early a stage of development, and I have often wondered whether I was not perhaps like one with a mutilated, stunted limb. How different everything would have been if, with a little psychology, Mother had been able to show some understanding and trust. But she was a product of the Victorian age where such ways of dealing with people, especially young people, were entirely unknown. The generation of my parents often seems to me like the generation of those who lived before the discovery of America, and most likely we shall be regarded by those who come after us as those who lived before man's settlement on the moon.

Eventually the whole story fizzled out. Fate intervened and I was spared a decision. I did not entirely forget Ruth, and some time after the war I discovered her again. She was now teaching scripture at her Church, we corresponded and at my first visit to Berlin twenty years later in 1953 I saw her. Many of my old feelings had died away. I had now been married eight years and I wanted to be home. She seemed to be disappointed that I had not as it were waited for her, and the letters which I now received from her caused me to break it all off. Years later I heard from her again: she was now in an old people's home and I visited her there. Since then all trace has been lost. I would like to speak only well of her but unfortunately I cannot, and this too is doing me no good.

*   *   *

Meanwhile I had made steady progress at school. I excelled in Latin and Greek. I positively enjoyed learning these classical languages, translating from and into them. I seemed to have a gift for languages, both ancient and modern, and could enjoy the finer points of them. I much relished the little story about that French (almost German) professor who while about to expire remarked 'Je meurs' but did not forget to add the important rider 'On peut également dire "Je me meurs"'. I did not unfortunately make the most of my talent, and of course the full benefit of much of the classical reading did not appear till many years later. When I mechanically recited as I did whole chunks from the Odyssey, what could I know of the meaning of that story, which was to be something like a *leitmotif* of my life? I too was to travel from land to land, though unlike Odysseus I could not hope to find my home. Is it a comfort to hear from a modern Greek poet (C. P. Cavafy) that 'when you start on your journey to Ithaca, then pray that the road is long' – because of the wisdom we shall reap? Yes, but who will not also wish to listen to the song of Tennyson's Lotus Eaters that

47

surely, surely, slumber is more sweet than toil, the
  shore
than labour in the deep mid-Ocean.

Of course, the thought that Greek, if not Latin, was still
alive and spoken by people of our time, never occurred to
any of my teachers. We were told about 'the golden years'
of Hellas but never saw an Athens newspaper.

Nor did we hear of the modern pronunciation of Greek. I
once wanted to buy a copy of the daily *Eleutheria* ('Freedom')
which I pronounced as I was taught Eloitheria; I was not
understood until I pointed to it and was enlightened: it's
Elefteria. Another little thing that might amuse the Western
visitor. I had learnt that *idiotis* means 'private individual', it
does still, and when we visited Delphi and had dinner at
the very modern restaurant there, I could not help seeing
my classroom Greek in action when I read the notice 'For
Idiots Only', i.e. a private car-park.

      *    *    *

Much of my knowledge of Latin and Greek I owed to one
of my father's brothers, a classical scholar of the old
German school who knew the theory of those languages
inside out. He was a most peculiar character, and I feel I
should say something about him.

He had a scantily furnished room in a fairly slummy
district of Charlottenburg where I was told he had been
living in solitary confinement for the past twenty-odd
years, since about 1903, when he was thirty-nine, and the
same landlady was looking after him. It was never intelligibly explained to me why he had so locked himself up.
He was apparently a kind of skeleton in the family cupboard which had to be accepted as one of the never
fathomed facts of life or what may pass for life. I gathered it
was something to do with a protest against a family dis-
agreement over some plan or ambition of his. He had
resented it and as he could not be, or make, good, he
decided he might as well be the recluse he became.

If this is a correct explanation it was perhaps an example

of that 'passive aggression' which Karl A. Menninger discusses in his book *The Human Mind* (1947) where he cites the case of a man who, having been scolded by his wife, said: 'All right. If that's the way you feel, I'm going to bed. I'm going to stay there the rest of my life', and he did, up to a point: 'He got up when the bed started to feel uncomfortable after seven years'. After seven years; but Uncle Philipp stayed indoors for thirty-odd – very odd.

Be that as it may, he was an accepted part of the family tree, and no one ever devoted a critical thought to the incredible fact that here was a man enjoying good health and endowed with great gifts (he might have made an excellent teacher) who was permitted to live on the charity of his brothers, themselves not too well off. This was probably in keeping with 19th-century ideas of philanthropy which tolerated unfruitful lives rather than create opportunities for their productive development.

His relatively well situated brother in Berlin wrote home to their widowed mother in 1900 that he was 'not seeing much of Philip' and 'would have to wait until the first of the month when he almost certainly will show up' (to collect his alms which he presumably regarded as his due). An oddity also was that the similarly seclusive mother, while still in Exin and able to travel, never once visited the virtually lost son, if not out of natural interest or affection then at least to see what influence she might bring to bear.

So far as I know, no one ever urged him to earn his living; nor did he himself make so much as an effort to live by his own labours; neither – the most amazing thing – did he seem to feel a primitive obligation to make such an effort. Possibly, charitably, he might be said to be earning a little, a pittance, by giving lessons to a few relatives like myself and some of my cousins. I confess I had never heard of a similar condition and am still unable to understand how this was possible except perhaps on the assumption of some sort of moral insanity known to psychologists as seriously irresponsible anti-social behaviour, though this does not imply any defect of the intellectual faculties.

It certainly didn't in Uncle Philipp's case. He was not only an expert on classical languages: he also knew much about classical philosophy, century-old tomes on which covered the best part of one wall. He had shown an interest in philosophy and a certain talent for it already at school though his teachers also had some reservations. While noting the interest and ('possibly') talent, their final report, in 1883, remarks on the 'pretentious manner' in which he was said to be approaching the subject, 'showing that he was trying to tackle notions which he was incapable of coming to grips with.'

Certainly none of his philosophy, any more than the Hebrew teaching with which he was familiar, taught him what a man's duty is in society. He would occasionally acknowledge on postcards, his 'gratitude' for 'the many and heavy sacrifices' that the family had made on his behalf but he never showed that gratitude by attempting to offer any sacrifice himself – not in the latter days when I knew him and it was too late, but much earlier when it was still time, and he might have been able, to change course.

He lived as Heine says of Immanuel Kant, the philosopher, 'a mechanically ordered and abstract old bachelor life in a quiet retired street', except that he did not even leave his home to amble down Kant's Lime Tree Avenue nearby, and no wonder all his reading of many philosophers (like Duns Scotus whose works I was asked to obtain) never suggested to him any Critique of either Pure or Practical Reason, least of all his own.

Perhaps, though unattached to any organised religion, he was a monk *manqué* and – in a manner of speaking – should have taken advice as to which particular order or monastery to join. On the other hand, he might not have found here much in the way of salvation, for he also took a lively interest in politics although, from the window of his back street cell and separated from the world by an upheaval like the Kaiser war, he was apt to misjudge situations. Actually, confinement to his cell need not have barred understanding, but, alas, he had nothing of that 'genuine poet' who, according to Goethe, has 'an inborn knowledge of the world and does not at all need a great deal of experience or a large stock of empirical observation in order to be able to depict it'. Nor would he have been much wiser even had he read a newspaper more enlightening than the equivalent of the *Daily Express* or *Mirror*, his landlady's choice.

As it was, Uncle Philipp lived in a fancy world in which for example the point about Hitler was that he was a Roman Catholic and thus a tool of the (supposedly anti-semitic) Vatican. Like so many others, even now, he had not yet moved out of the Middle Ages – or perhaps this was another symptom of his general, possibly 'schizoid' condition which separated him from reality.

He died in 1936, aged seventy-two, by inadvertently committing suicide: an attempt to extract a tooth caused a fatal blood poisoning. I say 'inadvertently' because so I was told. It may well have been otherwise, a thought that was suggested by Albert Camus's observation: 'Dying voluntarily implies that you have recognised, even instinctively ... the absence of any profound reason for living ... Suicide is a solution to the absurd.'

Actually there was a suicide in the family, and it bore out Camus's definition almost to perfection. The victim was a cousin of Philipp's and my father's, though I never heard of him until I as it were unearthed the body in the course of my researches. Robert Jaffé (1870–1911) was in fact a by-no-means unknown author in his time. He was a gifted and prolific essayist, a confirmed and knowledgeable Jew, also, rather remarkably in those early years, a dedicated Zionist. But the running sore in his soul was revealed in what he called a 'modern novel' characteristically entitled *Ahasver* (1900) where he described the despair of a German Jew – himself – who, despite all his love and longing, will not be accepted but is harshly, indeed cruelly, rebuffed by his fellow-Germans.

He was actually anticipating Jakob Wassermann who was writing at a time – the end of the disastrous Kaiser war

51

– when all the laments of Ahasver were glaringly shown to be only too well founded. Wassermann was more securely rooted in his Jewish convictions, while Jaffé was wayward, easily swayed by the dark moods that passed over him. He would warn the 'many Jewish antisemites' who, he said, fancied they could 'separate themselves from their own people's path of suffering' – and yet that was precisely what he did. He suddenly converted to Christianity and, as frequently happened in those days, he joined not the good Christians but the very worst, the veritable anti-Christians, the antisemites. He actually misused his talents by writing for one of their leading ideological journals, *Hammer*, edited by the notorious Theodor Fritsch.

I still do not know what produced this grisly change, a true self-mutilation. Some have blamed his physical disabilities, a deformity: he was in fact partially paralysed. I am inclined to believe it was, beyond that, the utter, extreme despair at what he felt was the irremediable hopelessness of his Jewish existence. Whatever it was, he became an unperson in the family who did not as much as mention his name. He apparently remained in contact with the then already immured Philipp; I have a postcard he sent him in December 1910 on which, after the suicide, Philipp scribbled the resigned words: *Involuta veritas in alto latet* (Baffling truth rests hidden up on high). To us today the truth is not so firmly hidden. The suicide was almost inevitable, 'the last link in a chain of confusions' it was called already at the time, branding the absurdity of a life that was bound to founder on its own glaring self-contradictions.

*  *  *

When Philip died, father lost the last of his three brothers, and with them more of his roots, as he was deeply attached to them personally, if not to their families for whom he does not seem to have cared a great deal. I cannot remember any get-together of the families; they never met, at least not with father (or his brothers) present. Nor would he join the family on any holiday or any other family outing,

52

though he once took us all to the Cecil de Mille film *The Ten Commandments*, an occasion for which we had to dress specially as if for a dinner party.

The three brothers formed their own fraternity, the fourth, the permanent absentee, being the odd one out. Keeping strictly to themselves, they would meet more or less regularly once a week over a game of cards when matters of general interest were discussed. Private affairs, I am inclined to believe, were treated as strictly 'private'. None of the three was very literate, reading books or good journals or visiting the theatre; for the topics of their conversation they must have relied chiefly on their daily papers, Father still clinging to the liberal *Berliner Tageblatt*; one brother, a family doctor and orthodox Jew, subscribed to the Communist paper, while the third was a strictly non-political businessman (with a zeal for stamp collecting from which I profited).

Philipp was present as the skeleton in the cupboard; his views, canvassed from time to time (when he received his family 'pension'), were considered authoritative because (weirdly) detached and 'independent'. It was an odd, almost unworldly quartet, each one in his own way separated from and at issue with reality.

While Philipp coached me in the languages of the ancients, Latin and Greek, also in Hebrew, in all of which he possessed considerable theoretical knowledge, my special interest was French which, at that time, was the first foreign language taught at German schools if only because it was considered essential when Europe was widely thought to be pre-eminent in, if not virtually identical with, the world at large. Whatever we might have thought of France, Germany's 'hereditary enemy' whose 'civilisation' was sometimes contrasted with German *Kultur*, it was popular among liberal Germans, certainly Jews, and a visit to Paris was deemed all but indispensable to good education.

At least this was so in the second half of the 1920s, after the chauvinist Raymond Poincaré had been succeeded by the enlightened Aristide Briand who in 1926 welcomed

Germany into the League of Nations. The earlier harsh policy culminating in France's occupation of the Ruhr in 1923 was strongly opposed by such Jewish liberals as Theodor Wolff, notwithstanding his French sympathies. The British ambassador in Berlin at the time, Viscount d'Abernon, was in error when he believed that German Jews generally 'prefer Paris where they have been maltreated both before and after the Dreyfus trial'. They took a firm stand against the scoundrels of that *affaire* but they also felt France had emerged from the trials with credit. D'Abernon, a little unduly preoccupied with what he termed 'Jewish influence', is equally wrong in charging 'the leading Jews, particularly those in the press' with being 'definitely', 'temperamentally anti-British', feeling 'little gratitude for the relatively generous attitude of England towards their race as shown in the absence of antisemitism in England'.

Antisemitism, at least the social variety, was never absent from England – certainly not at that time as was demonstrated in John Galsworthy's much-discussed 1922 play *Loyalties* – and as for anti-British feeling among German Jews, it was so little popular that for instance the notorious 'Hymn of Hate' by the Jew Ernst Lissauer was treated with contempt by us and most of our friends. In my family I remember England was held up as a model democracy; the ideal of a 'gentleman' was made our own, and when I as a boy of two or three received a new smart outfit I was greeted as a 'little Lord'.

At school I started English three years after French (1925), and my beginnings were hard going. When I read my first English piece, the teacher was not amused; he asked me not to treat him to a 'Chaucer pronunciation'. I did not then appreciate the sarcasm of the comment but it seemed sufficiently remarkable to be noted. Things improved a little when we later read Macaulay's 'Clive of India'. Still even then my preference was French. I remember reading, under a French tutor's guidance, Romain Rolland's *Vie de Beethoven*, the story of a man (I wrote in my diary) who, while reacting to events of history (for example the

54

rise of Napoleon whom he first admired then hated), was withdrawn from the world, in contrast to Goethe who was very much a man of affairs and a commanding figure in society. I daresay when the time came to emigrate I would have chosen France. But something happened to bring about a providential change, one that I may well claim saved my life.

In 1929, when Grandma took me with her to Wiesbaden, I went on a hiking tour of the Rhineland. From Mainz I travelled north, via Rüdesheim, crossed the Rhine, having paid due respect to the Lorelei, and hoped to spend my first night in Boppard. I went to the Youth Hostel, only to be told that they were full up – except possibly for one room which I could, if I wanted to, share with two men. I did not mind, especially as there was no choice and night was falling. In due course, I met my room-mates, one a German from Thuringia, the other a Londoner, John Nilson. We soon made friends and agreed, as they were travelling south and I north (as far as Koblentz), that we would meet in Bacharach next day. So we did and we stayed together for a day or two when it was time for me to go back. We exchanged addresses and promised to remain in touch. We actually met again after a few months in the Thuringian's home town. I had by then established a close pen friendship with John, a representative of the General Electric Company who was visiting his German friend on business. He wrote in German (of which he had a near-perfect command) and I in straggling English.

John, by the way, was no ordinary *commis voyageur*, a traveller wedded to his business and caring for nothing else. I have already mentioned his command of German and he also knew at least French and Flemish – quite an achievement at a time when the command of any foreign language, among British business people, was (and is) by no means as widespread as might be expected. When Prince Charles once made the point in a speech to the Royal Society of Arts, a Sunday paper featured it under the headline 'The monoglot businessman must be taught a lesson'.

But John's interests in German went further. He had read a history of German literature, he knew all about *The Sorrows of Young Werther* though I don't think he was quite as awkwardly in love as young Goethe then was, and he assisted my English education by sending me such books as Galsworthy's *Forsyte Saga*, G. K. Chesterton's *Short History of England* (not perhaps an ideal choice for the uninitiated), Disraeli's letters from his Eastern travels, a much treasured volume of English essays (in Everyman's Library), also a collection of Edna St Vincent Millay's poems after I told him I had come across the following of her lines in German:

Ich liebe den, dem eine Hyazinthe mehr bedeutet, als ich ihm bedeuten werde.
Wenn in den Nächten draussen die Fledermäuse kommen, kann er nicht schlafen.
Er hört ihre feinen Zähne an den Zwiebeln seiner Hyazinthe,
Aber das Nagen an meinem Herzen hört er nicht.

Unfortunately the slim little volume he promptly sent did not say anything about that hyacinth. It was only much later that I discovered the original:

I am in love with him to whom a hyacinth is dearer
Than I shall ever be dear.
On nights when the field-mice are abroad he cannot sleep:
He hears their narrow teeth at the bulbs of his hyacinths.
But the gnawing at my heart he does not hear.

I no longer remember (if I ever knew) what attracted my intense attention when I first came upon these lines. Did I perhaps have a hunch that I too was one of those who could hear field-mice setting their teeth upon the bulbs of their hyacinths and yet are never aware of the pain they

56

cause to other people's hearts? I was certainly, beyond my age, immature.

*   *   *

I was still at university, studying law – or supposed to be. I don't think I ever really did. Law and medicine were then a routine choice for young men and women of the Jewish bourgeoisie. You might not eventually practise it but it was considered a sound foundation on which to build a well ordered, respectable life. Unfortunately, my heart was not in this study. I did not have a lawyer's mind, even though the logic of law appealed to me and I could enjoy the neat, sometimes tortuous constructions of a legal argument.

Perhaps, therefore, I have drawn some benefit from my study, however casual, of the law. I hope I have. Among the notes I have carefully preserved is one that has meant much to me from the very moment I set eyes on it, and I treasure it to this day, indeed particularly today. It is a passage from a book by one of the great German jurists of the 19th century, Rudolf Jhering, dealing with 'the rule of passionate emotions in law':

> Contradiction is the test of self-control, passion cannot endure it (Jhering wrote in 1867). Savage man will be irritated by the mere difference of opinion, and he will justify his violent reaction by accusing people of knowingly telling the untruth. To tell the untruth is to the savage, as it is to a child, tantamount to lying. This applies to nations as well as to individuals. A nation passionately embracing any idea will punish even a mere difference of opinion; errors, i.e. truths which the masses don't like or don't understand, must be crimes ... The surest mark of a truly educated mind is the freedom from passionate emotion, the self-control of judgment.

These words have stayed engraved on my mind. I saw their truth demonstrated in the age of totalitarian tyranny, and I see it again in the rampant intolerance infesting our present age.

However, the fact remains, I knew that, as a profession, law would not satisfy me, and I was in no way surprised when I failed in my first exam, as I had just done. My interest was history, on which I read far more than ever on law. But in the opinion of my parents (to whom, in this respect, I listened perhaps rather more than I need have done), what was history likely to do for me? They did not realise that it was doing quite a bit for me. I had, at nineteen, come to understand some of the essentials of our situation. I had learnt from Ferdinand Lassalle, the social reformer in the 1860s, that 'Constitutions are of value only where they correspond to the actually prevailing constellations of power'. Otherwise they are no more than 'scraps of paper'.

Judged by this standard, how much could the Constitution of the Weimar Republic claim to be worth? Assuming (I wrote in 1929) that a Jew were to be proposed as Chief Justice – an utterly fictitious conceit – what prospect would there be for him? Well, according to the letter of the Constitution, 'all Germans' were 'equal before the law', but the fact was that, according to the constellations of power (and the state of the public mind), Jews were not considered equal to all Germans. This much I had learnt by then though the full implications, actual and potential, were not as yet clear to me.

Another landmark in my mind was the words of Friedrich Schiller, the philosopher and historian (as well as poet), at the time of the French Revolution, that 'those are not yet fit for civil freedom who still lack so much in the way of human freedom'. As I remembered these things and often thought on them, I found history was doing much for me.

But perhaps what my parents meant was how would I make a living out of history? Uncle Philipp was a warning example; was I to bury myself in bookish studies as he had done? The question was not asked. The uncle was an unperson who was never discussed. But quite possibly the thought of him was present on occasions like this. Was I perhaps to be a professor of history? Some hope, some prospect. Or take the journalism I was talking about on and off. Who were those journalists, anyway? The German 19th-century novelist Gustav Freytag had written a still remembered play *The Journalists* in which he had satirised those people as unprincipled opportunists. Also my father knew: Bismarck had once said 'journalists are people who have missed their vocation in life', and anything that Bismarck had said was regarded by my father as second only to Holy Writ, regardless of the fact that whatever may have been true in Bismarck's time much had happened since – if indeed he had not really meant journalists critical of him.

I was advised by a professional guidance consultant to study journalism, combined with history and literature, at Leipzig University, then apparently the only place which made provision for such studies. Actually journalism was not a recognised discipline, you did not 'study' it, even in those days; by far the best way of learning it would have been practical work on a newspaper. Immersed in my legal chores, I did not get this chance – as a Jew I could not even hope to get it, and so I swotted away at law until the time came when I realised that law under Nazi rule was a contradiction in terms.

Meanwhile my correspondence with John continued until one day, in spring 1933, I received a letter from him saying they knew what was going on in Germany and should I at any time wish to come over to Britain he could offer me the hospitality of their home, at least for a week: it would then be up to me to make my own arrangements. Few letters I ever received so excited me. It struck a chord deep down in my mind. Had anybody ever asked me, 'How did it happen that you came out of your country?', I would have had to say like the Pilgrim: 'It was as God would have it, for when I was under the fears of destruction, I did not know whither to go; but by chance there

59

came a man, even to me, and he directed me to the Wicket-gate which else I should never have found, and so set me into the way that has led me.' For some time past I had been thinking of how to escape from the increasingly oppressive and degrading atmosphere, getting away from this unutterable evil of Nazi tyranny, and now I was offered this most welcome chance, truly a Godsend.

Boycott Day, 1 April 1933, the tear- and blood-stained mockery of All Fools' Day, left me devastated. In this slough of Satanic infamy I had to save my soul. That was how I felt. Some years later, in a published article, I recalled my feelings: 'And then the day came, inevitably, when every Jew was an outlaw, abandoned to the unclean spirits of a maddened mob, when the honour of a good name was thought nothing, when the love of the dearest friends failed, and shame and burning anger consumed the souls of those who (they solemnly swore) "before God and men stand free from guilt".'

At one time I was vaguely planning to go to France, which had long been uppermost in my mind. Now all thought of this disappeared, and as I look back upon that moment, it strikes me as some sort of odd premonition that made me think of England even before I met John. Out of the four subjects set for my written final exam in 1928, I chose the one dealing with Anglo-German relations: 'The growth of England's Enmity against Germany before 1914'. I was now to be a living witness to much of the same story for the years leading up to 1939. In choosing England I was choosing my survival. Had I gone to France I most probably would have stayed there – and been lost. Truly a sheer accident had saved my life. A new world seemed to be arising before me: the shadows of the past and the horrors of the present seemed banished for the moment.

I answered John's letter at once, expressing gratitude for the offer and saying I would be only too glad to do as he had suggested. So I immediately prepared to leave 'home' – for the second time. Having lost my Prussian home when it became Polish, I was now about to lose my German home when it was turned into a Nazi death camp. I did not have the courage to tell my parents that I would leave never to return: it seemed a cruel thing to tell them. I said that having been invited by John to visit him, I was accepting the invitation.

Later I was reminded of the story of my forefather Abraham who was told to leave his country, his kinsmen and his father's house, and this then appeared to me an essential human experience. I had yet to come up against the other side of that experience – the very stuff of tragedy when you wander about as an alien whose label usually is 'undesirable', when you yearn for rest, when you wish you were not asked how you spell your name and where do you come from, and when you wonder how long you may be able to stay before having to move on. I have sometimes felt so when I began to look upon myself as the Wandering Jew, the one Byron heard speak:

> I must wander witheringly
> In other lands to die,
> And where my fathers' ashes be
> My own must never lie.

I had not yet seen those less fortunate than myself who later found the world divided into countries in which they could not live and countries to which they were not welcome. Where was I between past and future? It seemed beyond my understanding. But if this is my destiny I must make the best of it. I must wear the badge which is a timeless distinction.

I did not *have* to leave. I was in no personal danger, I was not a politician. I had not come to public notice. I was as inconspicuous as I have remained, and some of my friends wondered why did I 'run away'? This must now sound an absurdly rhetorical question, but the fact is that even after the outbreak of the Third Reich, even after Boycott Day, people (not only Jews) would not believe that a supposedly

61

civilised society could, in the long run, tolerate lawlessness of any kind, let alone aid and abet, indeed inspire and instigate, crime. This utter incapacity to credit the apparently impossible is of course at the root of all the bestialities that eventually were perpetrated.

It was not they that Germans, disillusioned by all other parties, had in mind or could have had. I can still hear people say, before the Nazis were in power, Things cannot go on like this. Apart from the economic misery, there was no stable Government, no resolute authority, only rule by emergency decree, from hand to mouth as it were. People wanted all this to be changed, and if there was some rough handling, well, they would shrug their shoulders, you cannot have an omelette without breaking eggs.

At all events it was to be a change within a conceivable system to which they were used. This might have been unreasonable, but they did not, could not, see that the Nazi system was not just fundamentally but inhumanly different, and this was the trap into which they fell. Theirs was the case that Mephisto puts in Goethe's *Faust* – 'at the first go you are free', but thereafter, having made your choice in free elections, 'you'll be slaves', and then another dispensation takes over, Omar Khayyam's:

> The moving finger writes; and, having writ
> Moves on: nor all thy piety nor wit
> Shall lure it back to cancel half a line
> Nor all thy tears wash out a word of it.

Here, it seems to me, is a solution to what is often described (by, among others, a reviewer of Francis King's novel *Punishments*) as 'our century's most defeating historical riddles' – why so many decent, cultured folk could allow Hitler to perpetrate such evil in their name. They did not allow him: they first allowed themselves to be made unfree by the wiles of Mephisto who did not seem to threaten evil but rather promised much longed-for relief which then turned them into slaves – one of those things between

62

heaven and earth that are undreamt of even in the philosophy of decent, cultured folk – anywhere.

So much for the Germans. There were also quite a number even of Jews prepared to appreciate what they liked to fancy were 'positive features' of Nazism. There were representative orthodox Jews who actually welcomed the Nuremberg Law for the 'Protection of German Blood' as a bar to the 'apostasy' involved in mixed marriages; the enforced segregation of Jewish children was hailed as in harmony with orthodox demands for Jewish schools, and a good word was put in for the degrading ban on Gentile maids in Jewish households. Others again were willing to appreciate Nazism as a 'necessary reaction' against Germany's foreign enemies; it caused Max Warburg, the banker, to rejoice in the thought that 'the German nation, after years of suffering, has gathered so much strength in this [Nazi] movement.'

Fortunately there were others, standing out in the crowd. I shall never forget how stirred I was by the defiant spirit of Professor James Franck, the Nobel prize winner, who, in April 1933, resigned a professorship which as an ex-serviceman he would have been graciously allowed to keep (until further notice). He point-blank refused to be treated as 'an alien and an enemy of the Fatherland' though he appreciated the position of those who 'thought it their duty to carry on'.

One of these, regrettably, was Sigmund Freud who was most reluctant to leave his native Austria in 1938. Whatever analysis he may have made of the Nazi psyche, it did not help to speed his departure, and on his arrival in London he confessed he had 'greatly loved the prison from which he was discharged'.

Another, one I happened to know personally, was the famous professor of civil law, Martin Wolff, a veritable Teutomaniac who never missed an opportunity of extolling the Teuton heritage and was probably troubled only by his remarkable un-Teuton dwarf-like appearance. He enjoyed an enormous popularity among students; the Auditorium

Maximum at Berlin University was barely capable of holding the rapturous crowds. The Nazi revolution did not seem to affect him. He was teaching as late as summer 1935, long after the Bartholomew's Night of 30 June 1934, when wholesale murder had become the law of the land. I heard about it in England, I – even I – could hardly believe it. As so many others had long gone, did he not feel he ought to be off? He actually stayed till the Nuremberg Laws put an end to the spook, and he was fortunate in escaping to Oxford in 1938.

There were people in those days of whom it was said they had six good reasons for staying – a wife and five children. But this defence could not be claimed by Wolff. This was a man of genius and well-founded reputation. Others perhaps could not afford to go, but this one ought to have set an example, not by his teaching of civil law which was a nonsense in those days, but by upholding the freedom of man that could have no truck with the abomination of Nazi tyranny. But of course if people like Wolff did not set such an example, what could be expected from lesser lights, and so it must seem only natural that when I left, ten days after the burning of the books (May 1933), people wondered why?

All I can say is I fled because I was persecuted, not in body but in spirit. I did not leave because I foresaw what was going to happen; I foresaw it no more than anybody else. Had I been told then that within three years German Jews would be deprived of their civil rights, I would have hesitated to believe it; had I been told that within ten years tens of thousands of my fellows would be murdered, I would have considered the informant unbalanced if not downright mad.

I left because I was an outlaw, abused, degraded, sickened to death. I felt I *could not* remain. I could not bear the shame and horror even then. I simply found it, quite literally, impossible to breathe the polluted air of the accursed land – everything seemed unclean, untouchable, I felt positively choked as if about to be asphyxiated, yes, about to be gassed. Now I remembered, dimly, what once struck me as the rhetorics of the famous champion of German-Jewish civil emancipation, Gabriel Riesser: 'Those who challenge my claim to my fatherland, challenge my right to my own thoughts, my feelings, to the language I speak, to *the air I breathe*, and for that reason I will defend myself against them – as I would against murderers'.

The words seemed to me melodramatic when I read them as a youngster: now they came back to me in their full force: that was how I was feeling now – and again later when I came upon Christian's words in the *Pilgrim's Progress*: 'I was driven out of my native country by a dreadful sound that was in my ears' – *Juda Verrecke! Perish Judah!* – 'to wit, that unavoidable destruction did attend me if I abode in that place where I was.'

Even then, while still in Berlin, I had already copied from a tattered edition of the Letters of Junius, the anonymous and mysterious critic of the ministries of England's George III. I copied some passages that seemed to me strikingly relevant, carrying warnings that I felt I must heed: 'We betray ourselves, we contradict the spirit of our laws, and we shake the whole system of English jurisprudence, whenever we entrust a discretionary power over the life, liberty, or fortune of the subject, to any man or set of men whatsoever, upon a presumption that it will not be abused' (1771). If this was true of England, even 150 years ago, how much more relevant was it now in the face of the Hitlerite abomination? and even though Junius seemed to be reassuring – 'We owe it to the bounty of Providence that the completest deprivation of the heart is sometimes strangely united with a confusion of the mind' (1769) – nevertheless what he had said was more than enough to make up my mind. I could not be in any doubt: I had to go – now.

When I decided to leave Germany, at this crucial turning point in my life, aged twenty-two, what sort of a person was I? I wanted to find out, and I consulted a modern equivalent of the Delphic Oracle. I sent a specimen of my handwriting to a graphologist who had advertised her services in a daily paper. She had an academic ('Dr') degree which seemed to indicate that she was not a charlatan though I even then attached importance to graphology, distinguishing it carefully from the pretensions of such wise gentry as palmists, star gazers and fortune tellers, some of whom I had watched at pleasure grounds.

The learned lady's verdict began with a notable flourish: I was 'intelligent', even 'highly' so, possessed of an 'acute mind' and specially gifted for research where I would excel in the purely scientific variety. I would be very good at meticulous blood tests or research into bacteriology. With my 'logical mind' I would also make a good mathematician. 'Painstaking skill' would drive me to 'go right down to the bottom of any proposition'.

So far so good. 'On the other hand, unfortunately' my 'mainly intellectual mind' also resulted in a 'lack of contact with the environment'. There were signs of an 'egocentric disposition' which caused 'compulsive inhibitions'. I was 'unmistakably scared of life' so that I 'did not dare make direct contact with people and open myself to them'. While always willing to help others, I was 'relentless' in my 'demands on myself' and would be capable of experimenting on myself, simply to ascertain any reactions, etc.

Such was, in broad and somewhat disconcerting outline, a portrait of the person about to enter the arena where theory would be tested by practice.

It was a few days after the burning of the books, the bonfire facing Berlin University, when the newly appointed Minister of Propaganda, Dr Goebbels, spoke the memorable words: 'The soul of the German people can again express itself'. Börries von Münchhausen must have rejoiced over this resurrection of that 'German soul' which he had already seen on its 'death bed'. He lived long enough to witness the unacknowledged truth of Heine's saying almost exactly a hundred years earlier: 'Where men burn books it won't be long before they burn human beings too.'

Before I now leave Berlin, I feel I must pay tribute to the man who in those days aroused and comforted the hearts

66

and minds of those now facing persecution – Rabbi Joachim Prinz, then a young man of thirty. Those who, like myself, heard him, in the burning upheaval of outraged passion after the Jew-baiting Boycott Day (1 April 1933), will never forget him. This was truly one of the great men of our generation, a beacon in the tempestuous seas. He preached at the *Friedenstempel*, the Temple of Peace, and his message, delivered with a heart-stirring power of oratory, gave comfort and balm to those who had been cruelly insulted by the enemy and callously abandoned by those who were considered friends. He revealed, in however naturally limited a sphere, a spirit of defiance but even more a spirit that gave hope of a better Jewish life. He attracted countless numbers from far and near, people too who had never known they were Jews. Here a prophet seemed to have arisen amongst us, a genius that seemed to be gathering strength and spreading it in nothing so much as in the teeth of adversity, and the call went out from him, unceasingly, that Jews need by no means be dismayed if only they 'embraced their fate with passionate devotion'.

He was wrong perhaps, up to a point, when judged in the larger perspective of history, but then, at that moment, he appeared like the spirit that would arouse the dry bones. I still remember how he fiercely rebuked those who sought to strike a bargain with the enemy by claiming the privileges which were at first treacherously allowed to some categories of Jews. He held up as a shining example the action of Professor Franck who on no account would have any dealings with a Nazi Government and of his own free will left the country at once.

Prinz himself did it four years later and perhaps the light that had been kindled had by then grown dim. Perhaps he should have spent his inspired energies on urging his people to seek emigration regardless. But this is the wisdom of hindsight, and certainly nothing will detract from the honour of the place Prinz won in the fire of a great revolution and will hold for ever in all the hearts that, through the fire, received his message.

As for myself, as a young fellow, I was unburdened by responsibilities, so it was easy for me to go. Yet looking back, I cannot help wondering whether perhaps some more might not have shown the foresight due to nothing but passionate resentment. They knew they had lost their honour, they were yet to learn that thereby they had in fact, even then, lost everything. They were enjoined by their leaders to 'wear the Yellow Badge with pride', but none explained how so contradictory a feat was to be accomplished. (The reference to the Yellow Badge was of course only figurative. The medieval Badge was not actually introduced, by law, until 1941.)

The man who coined that slogan, Dr Robert Weltsch, then editor of the Zionist *Jüdische Rundschau*, himself illustrated the conundrum. In the summer of 1935, after two and a half years of Nazi rule, he attempted gently to criticise the official Nazi view that the Jew was human in the same way as a flea is an animal, existing only for the purpose of being exterminated. He thereupon received from the Ministry of Propaganda a communication which said: 'Your paper has been banned because of this article. The ban will be lifted, but in view of the polemical nature of the article I have to reprimand you most severely and expect to have no further cause to object to your publications.'

When Dr Weltsch related this episode thirty years later, I wondered: was he right in carrying on, as he did, or should one feel that in submitting to such 'authority', he could not wear his yellow badge with pride? This question is not intended to imply any criticism of Dr Weltsch who later pointed out that 'the ghastly atmosphere in Nazi Germany at that time ... often appears almost incredible'. My question is asked precisely from the vantage point of today, for our values must be assessed anew in each generation.

As it was, many German Jews followed an all too human urge to pretend things were not really as bad as they seemed, and however nasty the shock of Boycott Day, they would get over it. They refused to admit that the absurd reversal of the most enlightened belief in progress could

68

last. 'How could one expect,' one of their leaders later exclaimed, 'that a Government could even think of abrogating the idea of the equality of all men?' The famous scientist Professor Richard Willstätter, who as far back as 1925 had resigned his post at Munich University because of the academic authorities' antisemitism and now of course was deeply disturbed, would not believe that the Germans could go any further in their antisemitic antics; in 1934 he returned from Palestine saying: 'I know that Germany has gone mad, but if a mother falls ill it is not a reason for her children to leave her. My home is Germany, and I must return.'

It is true that the thought of emigration was not neglected. People were 'retrained' and youngsters fitted for life in Palestine. It is also true that if the number of emigrants was negligible, the reason was the daunting prospect of economic hardship caused by the ruthlessness of Nazi robbery devices. Moreover, the world was virtually closed against them. Everybody pitied the Jews, nobody wanted them – a fact that provided grist to many Nazi jeers.

But the main reason was that the majority of Jews were of two minds, halting between fear and hope, never far from hope, however battered and degraded, a hope pinned on the magic powers of an international opinion which Arthur Koestler later summarised thus: 'There were those who said, "They cannot be as bad as all that". And those who said, "They are too weak, they cannot start anything". And those who said, "They are too strong, we must appease them". And those who said, "You are frightened of a bogy, you've got a persecution mania, you are hysterical". And those who said, "Hatred doesn't lead anywhere, one must meet them with sympathy and understanding". And those who said, simply, "I refuse to believe it".'

This probably was what most of us did, finding comfort in the thought that antisemitic subversion had never scored any lasting success: in Germany the Stoecker movement, in Russia the pogroms, in France the Dreyfus affair – incidents that were regarded as major failures from the antisemitic point of view; so it seemed quite wrong to dramatise the threat posed by the Nazis.

This we believed even when we heard an emphatic warning, in June 1930, a few months before Hitler's spectacular gains at the polls. An (as yet unnamed) German-speaking Jew from Alsace ('G.H.': Gaston Heymann) asked the weirdly prophetic question, addressed to the German Jews: 'What are you waiting for? For the year 1940, when the young generation that is now being incited to a veritably insane degree will be in office?' The question was asked in a general political magazine, and the answer was weary resignation.

The warning was by no means pooh-poohed. Things were bad, yes, it was said, but most Jews simply didn't see, didn't want to see, in fairness could not see, *how* bad things were, and so did little to support those actively engaged in the struggle. If 'rational enlightenment' had proved pointless, then the utmost, indeed a desperate effort was required to restrain, even so far as possible prepare to resist, the lawless 'feeling' that was bent on crime. Orthodox Jews, while acknowledging that the virtually impotent Government ought to act, put their trust in God.

Again, if the Government was impotent, if (according to the historian Golo Mann, the son of Thomas) the democratic leaders must be charged with 'lack of imagination, lack of an understanding of power in a situation where naked power had become decisive', then one also should not forget the impact of another important factor, the policy of the victors of 1918. In his memoirs, Churchill describes how the French, by their fear-born intransigence, helped to 'breed the martial curse' and fanned 'the passions of the mighty defeated but substantially uninjured German nation', etc. In so doing they deprived the democratic leaders of much of the authority needed to strike at the Nazi subversion.

However, even the Alsatian warner could foresee nothing worse than an official boycott which would confine Jews in a ghetto where they would be left to their own devices. Others foresaw a repetition of the Tsarist pogroms. As late as August 1932, a Russian-born Zionist leader, Leo Motzkin, cited this example on the strength of his 'thorough knowledge of pogromist atmosphere', although mere pogroms were of course not what the Nazis had in mind as their 'final solution'. At all events, any idea of large-scale violence, of organised mass killings, let alone planned extermination in gas chambers, was far beyond the horizon even of this earnest warner, and those who might have hinted at anything like it would have been dismissed as irresponsibly alarmist if not deemed downright unbalanced and in need of a psychiatrist.

This was true even in Russia. Motzkin recalled 'the biting sarcasm with which the pillars of Jewish society had pooh-poohed all those who could see signs of threatening violence'. Such also was the way Theodor Herzl was received when he published his book *The Jewish State* (1896), for what was to be thought of a man who, a hundred years after the French Revolution, would not believe in the promises of Jewish emancipation? Was he at all in his right mind?

On the feast commemorating the story of Esther (*Purim*), in March 1933, Rabbi Joseph Lehmann, of Berlin, in a printed and widely distributed homily, discussed not Haman the Jew-hater, but Balaam, the pagan prophet who spoke in praise of the Jews. Haman is dismissed as 'something ludicrous', because 'what Judaism really thought of its enemies and how it desired to conduct the disputation with them, is shown by Balaam, a story 'of the highest topicality', of a man whose mind may be 'clouded by prejudice' but 'one day the veil before his eyes must be torn away', and Balaam will 'speak nothing but what God puts into his mouth'. As Jews protested their centuries-old German *Kultur*, their faithful ties with the German people, their love of Germany, they recalled Goethe's maxim, 'If I love you what's that to do with you?'

When I say 'Jews', I mean leaders who had every right to be regarded as representative. They were prepared to show

71

that they 'willingly and cheerfully accept any form of Government that will grant them dignity, work and freedom'. They proved the point made at a big Queen's Hall, London, protest meeting in June 1933 that 'the great majority of Jews, like the great majority of Gentiles, are most anxious to accommodate themselves to the State in which they live, and naturally they take on the tone of society around them. In a Marxist State, they will be Marxist, in a Fascist State they will be Fascist.' By the spring of 1934, in spite of the never relenting, unappeasable hate, German Jews had sufficiently recovered to take something like a detached view of their troubles. Jewish humour, even black humour, determined to laugh in spite of all, came into its own with such jokes as this: Hitler ordered Rabbi Leo Baeck to compose a prayer asking God to grant him 'eternal youth', whereupon Baeck replied: 'We cannot do that, but we can ask that you shall not grow old.' Some were actually bewailing their fate of being denied a share in the Nazi May Day celebrations.

Any idea of 'resistance' – and I am passing no opinion as to whether it should or should not have been – was far removed from their minds. They were no revolutionaries: most of them were old-fashioned liberal bourgeois, perhaps tending towards the left of centre; they would also have tended towards the right of centre had they been made welcome there, and some were in sympathy with the Catholic Centre party (which once sported a Jewish parliamentary candidate). Certainly the idea of 'resisting' lawful authority was alien to them; they as a body were no less willing to 'be submissive to the Powers that be' than any disciple of the New Testament, though there were of course individual Jews who played their part gallantly in such general resistance activities as were possible. But as men and women of action they were no more representative than were any individuals of the (non-Jewish) German resistance. I once came across a problematical specimen – but about this later.

When I had been in London three or four months, I

received a letter from a Jewish friend in Berlin saying in effect, Foolish boy, you ran away too soon, come back, everything is settling down nicely. I heard the same message even later when the persecution seemed, for a tactical moment, to be abating, for example, at the time of the 1936 Olympic Games in Berlin. I confess I didn't understand, and of course I didn't argue. I was determined that never would I, of my own free will, go back to Nazi Germany.

In this I differed from many of my fellow-refugees in London. I remember we attended Hebrew classes run by Dr Ernst Simon, the well-known disciple of Martin Buber, and when the class was much reduced in size at a bank holiday, he caustically remarked: 'The refugees seem to be distinguished by frequently returning to Germany.' No doubt they were longing to 'go home', especially at Christmas, and *Heimweh* was not something from which I was entirely free. But Nazi Germany was not my home, and as for my family, I could not persuade them to follow my example. I was struggling to establish myself, and I did not yet understand sufficiently the wisdom of Ecclesiastes: 'Man knoweth not his time; as the fishes that are taken in an evil net, and as the birds that are caught in the snare, even so are the sons of men snared in an evil time, when it falls suddenly upon them.'

# 3

# REFUGEE IN LONDON

I landed in England on 19 May 1933 at Parkeston Quay, Harwich. It was a somewhat drab and prosaic sight, and the first human being I espied happened to be a policeman, but to me the view seemed hardly less bright, romantic and dramatic than the White Cliffs of Dover on which my mind saw emblazoned the word *Freedom*. 'Freedom all solace to man giffith' – this 14th-century poem was among the earliest I had learnt, and now I came in search of the reality.

I walked up to the Immigration Officer, remembering I had been advised not to mention politics. So when he asked, somewhat gruffly, what I had come for I said (which was also true) that I wanted to improve my English. Strangely enough (or so I thought) the information did not seem to satisfy the guardian of the stringent law. He sternly looked at me as if he had at last debunked a typically undesirable alien, and he said: What did I mean? Did I think they did not know what was going on in Germany?

I was faintly glad to hear he knew and indeed HM Government had already been warned by their ambassador in Berlin about the ruling gang of 'unscrupulous fanatics, hooligans and eccentrics' who were 'notoriously

74

abnormal cases'. But if the Immigration Officer knew of this (as he must have done) and could have no doubt about the youngster facing him, should he not have been, I mused later, a little less harsh and a little more compassionate? In the event, having gravely consulted two of his colleagues, he announced that I could come in on one month's probation, and my Aliens Registration Certificate reminded me, in bold red print, that I had no right to enter 'any employment paid or unpaid'.

The treatment accorded me was no exception. This was the rule. Aliens are, almost by definition, undesired – in Britain no less than anywhere else. The late Alan Herbert once noted 'the ancient tradition' to 'discourage and irritate the foreign visitor by every form of inconvenience ... and so dispose him to return to his own country.' I began to see new meaning in the biblical reference to the aliens as 'the terrible of the nations'.

There were of course good people exerting themselves in Parliament on behalf of the newcomers. Commander Oliver Locker Lampson who was host to Albert Einstein; Eleanor Rathbone who became the virtual patron saint of the refugees, and Colonel Josiah Wedgwood who occasionally overdid it as when he referred to the Palestine administration as 'the most antisemitic Government in the world'.

Even so, while there was no lack of voices denouncing the Nazi cruelties, practical fellow-feeling for the victims was distinctly underdeveloped. There was a strong anti-alien lobby. Already before landing I had heard of one Edward Doran, MP, urging 'steps to prevent alien Jews entering this country from Germany'. (In the time-pilloried tradition of the numbers game, he alleged that 'hundreds of thousands of Jews are now leaving Germany and scurrying from there to this country.') He was later disowned by his local Conservative association who told him that 'the man who could side with the persecution of the Jews was nothing less than a cad'.

I remember also press reports, in my very earliest days in London, about a Jew, one of the Rothschilds (the budding, later famous, scientist) having been refused service at a road house, and a Leeds City coroner declaring a jury of eight to be 'overweighted' with five Jews (of whom he promptly dismissed three). These incidents, however, like my encounter with the Immigration Officer, did not seem to disturb me much at the time, as they might have done, like a kind of sheet lightning, but I made a note of them just the same.

I arrived at Liverpool Street Station, and I still see the dreary, ill-lit platform lined by sturdy young men all wearing a white armlet with the Star of David, ready to take care of the homeless. It was a pathetic sight that profoundly stirred me, even to tears. It was like an eagerly longed-for balm, and hope, however faint, seemed to be rising over the cruelties and infamies that were fiercely burning in my mind.

I soon forgot my Immigration Officer. He seemed as it were the odd man out, much like Mr Doran, and I wanted to see in England the head of a world-encircling proud and powerful Empire that could well be compared to the Roman one. It still had a Government that could boast a Secretary of State for India, as an earlier England had known a Secretary of State for America. Those days of course had long since passed, but Elgar was still alive, the composer of 'Land of Hope and Glory', of that spirit which Schiller had extolled in his poem on England's victory over 'The Invincible Armada', *Der Unterdrückung letzter Felsendamm, Tyrannenwehre, grossherzige Britannia, glückselige Insel* ('rock-built dam against oppression, rampart against tyranny, great-hearted Britannia, blissful island').

This was the England I wanted to see, and so I was not really concerned with such signs and portents (if indeed I noticed them) as the somewhat ambivalent reaction to Hitler's first speech that week on foreign affairs. He (he of all people) was complaining of the unjust treatment allegedly accorded to Germany which in fact he, by the 1 April boycott, was imposing on the Jews: 'It is not wise', he said, 'to rob peoples of the economic possibility of existence without taking into account the fact that human beings demand the right to live.' But then of course he did not regard Jews as human beings.

*The Times* was impressed by his 'moderation' which seemed to suggest that he had learnt the truth of Bismarck's saying, 'Politics is the art of the possible'. (Actually, in his book, Hitler took pains to avow his aim of 'achieving seemingly impossible propositions' and explained how this could be done!) Though his words now had to be examined against 'the background of his own doctrine of force elaborated in his remarkable book' (*The Times* said), he was to be regarded as 'sincere in his desire to collaborate with the world.'

The first example of Hitler's treachery in action was, much to the amazement of all the world, not least the Germans themselves, the 'Non-Aggression Pact' with Poland, a country most Germans (and certainly the Nazis) deemed fit only for slavery and worse. Now Hitler did what no democratic German statesman would have dared: he ostentatiously made friends with them, saying 'Germans and Poles will have to accept the fact of each other's existence. Hence it is more sensible to regulate this state of affairs which the last 1,000 years have not been able to remove and the next 1,000 will not be able to remove either, in such a way that the highest possible profit will accrue from it to both nations.'

Such was the kind of Big Lie which Hitler mentions in *Mein Kampf* – only to impute it to his enemies.

The Poles (and Germans) were not the only ones who were then fooled. The British ambassador in Berlin thought the German Chancellor had now proved he was a statesman by sacrificing some of his popularity to a 'rational foreign policy'. That's how we all were fooled.

Now Hitler made much play of 'equal rights' for Germany because 'the disqualification of a great people cannot be permanently maintained'. Few saw through the brazen falsehood by simply asking, What about the Jews?, though admittedly on the day I arrived *The Times* had a letter about the Nazis' 'incredible insanities' which 'created a danger of war'.

But then there were so many other things that claimed attention, though reminders of the Nazi experience often impinged on them. There was the latest American film *Gabriel over the White House*, the story of a US President who, as a result of a car accident, suffered brain damage and from that moment appears to be of unsound mind. He seeks to enforce Prohibition by 'exterminating' the alcohol smugglers, to cure unemployment by raising 'construction armies' (à la Nazi Labour Service) and uphold world peace on the racial basis of an alliance of all English-speaking peoples. The parallel to the events in Central Europe was not difficult to draw. When I saw the film an organist, playing 'Songs of the Nations', chose as a sample for Germany the *Tannhäuser* aria 'Oh thou sublime sweet evening star'.

I frequently reported home what I thought would give comfort to my family – about the way great German Jews were honoured, among them Einstein and that 'most famous German actress of today', Elisabeth Bergner. The well-known journalist Carl von Ossietzky who later (while in prison) received the Nobel Peace prize was quoted as having requested a book on 'German history during the Middle Ages'.

I noticed, much to my amazement, women using make-up in public, smoking in public too: this was never done back 'home'. Altogether everybody seemed to be smoking here so much more, even in the cinemas, and when a man did twenty cigarettes a day it came to 150 a week. I was much struck by the posters of Players, the famous tobacco firm of Nottingham, and it occurred to me that they might wish to use as an advertising slogan the lines (from *As You Like It*): 'All the world's a stage, And men and women (smoke) merely Players'. I actually submitted the idea and then waited eagerly for the effect of what I considered would prove an inspired scoop. I did not have to wait long.

A reply came almost by return: I 'may not be surprised to learn' that they had used the quotation more than thirty-five years ago. 'Not surprised'? Why, the Greatest Expectations collapsed, turning into the Bleakest Houses, and since no reason was given I could only speculate on why Shakespeare should make no permanent appeal to English smokers. Clearly the Bard was not without honour except among his own. Not even the consolation prize of a de luxe packet could soften the cruel blow – to me, a confirmed non-smoker.

I noticed with special interest the posters frequently displayed by churches. One said 'Love your enemies', while another, not too far away, added 'Drink is your greatest enemy'.

Before long I was in touch with the Jewish Refugees Committee at Woburn House where I was registered as No. 562, which did not mean that 562 German Jewish refugees were then in Britain. There were actually believed to be 2,000, but 562 had been registered; many no doubt never troubled to register, others probably left again – for a variety of reasons and destinations, including return.

The Committee obliged me with a number of names and addresses of people willing to let rooms to refugees and I got myself fixed up in north London (Stoke Newington) where I discovered prices were very much more reasonable than in Hampstead and other parts of the north-west. I have always been rather fond of this sort of discovery which I shared with a surprising number of others especially Scots. Gauguin's 'flights', I later read, were 'always from a place where it costs little to live, to another where it will cost even less'. Anyway I was able to relieve John of my presence within a week.

I now also remembered the distant relative of ours that Grandma once told me we had in London – Trude, the wife of Sir Albert Levy, head of the Imperial Tobacco Company. I frequently heard Trude's name mentioned. Grandma had actually kept among several postcard photos received from London before 1914 one of Trude surrounded by a whole tribe of relatives, old and young, happily settled in the then fashionable neighbourhood of Maida Vale, some too assembled in front of their stately home at 134 Goldhurst Terrace, West Hampstead, in September 1908. I believe one of the gentlemen was Sir Albert Levy.

Anyway, I wrote to him while still in Berlin but received no reply. Now Grandma wrote, with the result that Sir Albert's Secretary informed me that the great man was prepared to see me. It was really very good of him for I understood that the Levys over many years had held their German relatives virtually responsible for the loss of a son killed in the Kaiser war. Even now he took care not to arouse undue expectations. He told me over the phone that he was afraid he would not be able to do much for me, after all I knew what the general situation was, didn't I? Well, yes and no. I knew all about the economic situation and there was that ever-present immigration reminder about 'no employment paid or unpaid'. What I did not know was the financial standing of Sir Albert. In 1929 he had established the Albert Levy Benevolent Fund of £250,000 for the support of hospitals and other charitable objects. The total amount available, including the interest, was calculated to be £400,000 (the equivalent today of several millions). Well was it said by the *Jewish Chronicle* at the time: 'While such fine altruism as that displayed by Sir Albert exists ... there is no room for despair of human nature.'

His fears that he could do nothing for me were amply confirmed when I saw him in his princely mansion at Devonshire House, Piccadilly. He explained that he was now retired from business but, as I probably knew, he had given to the Refugees Committee a large amount (£2,500) and asked them to devote special attention to my case. This, so far as Sir Albert was concerned, took care of the situation if not necessarily of me. Lady Levy also was at a loss how to find a satisfactory solution but made a personal contribution by ringing for the butler to serve lemonade and biscuits, the symbolic equivalent of tea and sympathy.

The Committee conscientiously lived up to its purpose, which was to provide advice and assistance for the refugees. Its top priority, due to the widespread unemployment, was an urgent concern that we should be no charge on the economy. Its *Helpful Information and Guidance for Every Refugee* contained the passage; 'The Jewish Community would rather pay out of its own pocket for the maintenance of refugees, until they can find their own permanent home overseas, than have it thought that work was being taken from British workpeople.' The best advice that they could offer therefore was to prepare for further travel, and no effort was spared to assist those who might wish to see the attractions of other parts of the world. No Israeli emissary could have been more persuasive in singing the praises of *aliyah* (immigration to Palestine) though other countries were by no means neglected. In 1934 openings were detected even in Germany where Jewish firms were thought to be urgently wanting private secretaries. In all these efforts, both stick and carrot were evenly and discreetly applied.

Relief of course was generously organised. The Central British Fund for German Jewry collected substantial sums, and the Temporary Shelter in the East End stood always open. But it would have been strange if there had not been those who felt like the Labour leader Ben Tillett thirty years earlier who told a band of hopeful arrivals from the Tsarist pale: 'Yes, you are our brothers and we will do our duty by you. But we wish you had not come.'

Actually we know from James McDonald, the then League of Nations High Commissioner for Refugees, that English Jews who, he said, had given him £500,000 in 1933 were 'not enthusiastic and did not wish many German Jews to enter England'; in America too, he confided to a friend, there was 'much interest in limited circles but no enthusiasm for taking persecuted Jews into the country.'

On several occasions I was told by a high official of the Refugees Committee that our prospects were pretty dim and anybody thinking of coming to England would be well advised to seek his fortunes elsewhere. He was anticipating, by roughly ten years, the no less thoughtful, if perhaps more original, envoy from the War Office who conveyed to a body of Alien Pioneers the hope that 'the adventurous spirit which had brought them to this country would take them far afield at the end of the war'.

Jewish reluctance could claim ancient precedent. This was another chapter of the *Ostjuden* story, and the German Jews were now tasting the medicine they once dispensed to their fellows from Russia and Poland, as the Italian Jews had done to the Spanish Jews fleeing from the Inquisition in 1492, or the Sefardim of the Stuarts to the Ashkenasim from Hamburg. Lord Reading made the Anglo-Jewish position perfectly clear at the 1933 Queen's Hall meeting: 'We have well in mind, in our duty as British citizens, that we must take care that we do not add to the burden of the great unemployment existing in this country.'

Nor was fear of unemployment the only force militating against the alien; there also was the dread of antisemitism. Oswald Mosley was as yet at the beginning of his Fascist career, but by 1938, after the Nazi November pogrom, the Home Secretary confessed he had to take notice of 'an underlying current of suspicion and anxiety, rightly or wrongly, about alien immigration on any big scale' as otherwise the already existing 'definite anti-Jewish movement' would 'inevitably' be growing.

The anti-Jewish feeling was organised by Mosley, but, to a large extent, it was, unorganised, much more widespread, and the dispatch of Lord Winterton as Britain's delegate to the ill-fated Evian Conference (1938) was one conspicuous symptom. Soon after my arrival I met a civil servant of HM Patent Office who, in exchange for some German conversation, enlightened me on conditions in England. He was educated, had been to university for three years, knew a great deal about German history; in fact he thought that when retired (he was now not quite fifty) he would like to settle in Germany though he said he did not admire the Nazi Government. Hitler's general prospects seemed to him literally poor: being without experience, he would find no friend or customer in the world, and how could a country prosper without exports? (Such views appeared to have been fairly widespread among his colleagues.) My friend was well informed on the history of Anglo-Jewry, about their expulsion in 1290 and their return in 1660. Broadly, he told me, the English did not care very much for the Jews but they did not object to them going about their business here. He confirmed Heine's observation a hundred years earlier that Jews here were tolerated with good humour so long as they kept within certain limits. In the Patent Office, for example, the staff of 300 included one Jew – this was as much as they would think the right proportion, my friend remarked with innocent candour.

Such was part of the atmosphere in which refugee relief had to operate, and I remembered it at a meeting specially convened by the Committee where an eloquent plea was entered for Brazil whose 'booming economy' would guarantee us a bright future, whereas here, with no chance of finding a job, we could hardly hope for our permits to be extended and so would most likely have no choice but to go back where we came from. I don't know how many chose Brazil but shortly afterwards we learnt that the necessary labour permits were refused. Here was a stage on which many a drama was played out, tragedy and farce, and the decor was a map of the world such as once inspired a caller to enquire: Is this *all* you have to offer?

There was much despair, even and especially among the youngsters, and thoughts of suicide were never far from their minds. I remember one I knew personally: he could not bear the idle, aimless life any longer – 'lying around in the streets'. How often have I not heard this, in so many words or in weird hints. It is a pity no statistic has ever recorded these victims of Nazism. Some were quietly resigned, others tempted to go berserk – they would have liked to blow up the whole of Woburn House (the Committee's HQ).

Another man I remember was a Jewish aristocrat, a

83

middle-aged, well established barrister in a big provincial German city, conservative to the bone, a supporter of the Hohenzollern. He would go around telling us that if only the Kaiser were still in power, all these things would never have happened, and then the refrain to all his lamentations: Oh, the shame, the shame of it, the utter shame...

One morning in September 1933 eight of us were summoned before the Committee to receive the news that the Hebrew Congregation of Nairobi had asked for young people like us, up to the age of twenty-five and with some legal training, to serve as overseers of black labour on local Jews' coffee plantations about fifty miles outside the city. We were of course eager to consider this unusual project which seemed to offer a chance of settling somewhere permanently, even if the initial permit was to be for nine to twelve months only. It was definitely preferable to the Brazilian venture if only because we would be within the British Empire, and if the worst came to the worst, we could come back. I was however warned by my acquaintance in the Patent Office who obtained some information about conditions in Kenya: the coffee business was by no means having bright prospects, he had been told; unemploymeant was not unknown and there was no shortage of local people able to do the job we were offered. Not all of my friends were impressed when I told them this; they preferred to rely on the 'guarantees' we were given by the people in Nairobi: surely they would see to it that we were securely employed.

The Committee of course urged us to accept the unusual, challenging – indeed, we were assured, 'ideal' – offer, and some at least began, if only for lack of other occupation, to tackle basic Swahili. Eventually only one, together with five others not of our group, took the plunge, and after a few weeks he reported the very friendly welcome he had found, praising the public spirit of Nairobi's Jewry whom he had quite wrongly suspected of searching for eligible sons-in-law. Later, shortly before Britain's withdrawal, I was to meet him, a lawyer from Mainz, now indeed a well turned out Kenyan son-in-law, wearing the uniform of a captain in the Queen's Own East African Rifles.

He had been lucky. When the original project produced meagre results, it was repeated in May 1934. The chairman of the Committee, Otto Schiff, then enquired whether the people in Nairobi could 'absorb' twelve good refugees. One of them who spent some time in Nairobi, Julius Carlebach, later remarked on this incident: 'In a country with a tiny European population, where every refugee had to be found a post on a farm as a "farm manager", which more often than not involved paying the farmer to keep him, it was difficult to accept even batches of twelve.'

\* \* \*

While the efforts of the Committee were viewed by some of the refugees with a certain reserve, others were full of unstinted praise. I have kept part of an 'ode' (by one of us) that was recited at a party held in 1934 under the Committee's auspices, and I feel I must try and preserve the extract from oblivion (whatever its poetical merits):

> In other words, we feel and see
> That spell of hospitality
> Which fills this house with golden sun
> And tries to give us joy and fun.
>
> And thankful are we rising here
> Now all of us to hail and cheer
> All Woburn House, its Committee
> And spirit of Democracy.
>
> We owe them deepest gratitude
> For all their sporty attitude
> Which represents the deal so square
> Of English Jewry, proud and fair.

Gradually we tried to organise ourselves. We met regularly in the atmosphere of a spiritual dosshouse, hatching more or less naive ideas which we hoped the Committee would

85

take note of. Since the recently launched Central British Fund had, by July 1933, raised as much as £150,000, it occurred to us that some of the money might be used to buy from HM Government a small territory, anywhere in the British Empire, where we could form something like a workers' settlement. It was an absurd idea and must appear so perhaps not only in retrospect though to us, at the time, it seemed perfectly within reason. We might have pondered the remark that had then been reported of an Arab leader about the Jews buying land in Palestine. 'It is not enough that they should buy their earth,' he had said, 'they must fight for it. Then and then only can they win it and hold it.'

Anyway, nothing came of the hare-brained scheme and more attention was fixed on Palestine. This was done mainly by the *Gruppe Junger Zionisten* under the chairmanship of Dr Josef Cohn, later secretary to Dr Weizmann and director of the Weizmann Institute's European Committee. These Young Zionists offered a well-designed programme of regular lectures, and discussions were always on a high level; attendances, never less than sixty, included sometimes some very strange non-Zionist freaks, descendants of Rupert Brooke's *'temperamentvoll* German Jews' enduring an utterly incomprehensible 'exile'. and those Christian 'non-Aryans' who felt they had been raised from the valley of the dry bones.

Among the lecturers I remember Hans Jonas, the distinguished scholar, then a budding philosopher, whose elaborate thought systems impressed even (and especially) those who tended to lose their way in the learned maze. He was respected as an intellectual luminary and found himself particularly popular among the young lady listeners. As I did not always concentrate on the essentials of the occasion, I only remember the inessential fact that one of the ladies had cast a rather bold eye on him and seemed intensely peeved when another, plainly not without skill, also tried her eye in this black art. I am not sure whether Jonas was aware of the dramatic situation which must have flattered even his abstract philosophical ego had he noticed it. It is quite possible he had already grown into a bit of an absent-minded professor, but among his less philosophical listeners the situation was notorious and a topic of much animated if discreet discussion. I don't know how this drama developed. I soon left London for a more matter-of-fact environment where I lost contact with this exciting spectacle of 'stratagems and subterfuges'.

\* \* \*

The more social life was to be fostered in a London Jewish Club 1933. This was the brainchild of a few people, refugees and others, who realised the demand for a club but also the need to be discreet as they feared a suspicion could arise that a club of this kind might wish to compete with the powerful Committee. Such a suspicion, however unwarranted, would have been disastrous, and so the great thing was not to attract possibly undesirable attention. As irony would have it, we managed to attract attention that was at once welcome and embarrassing.

Before we had moved very far, a hand was taken in our affairs by a remarkable woman who decided to help us in every way she could and that was not the way of bureaucracy but personal initiative, care for the individual and the charity which is the companion of faith and hope. This stocky, youthful, eminently serious-minded woman, who might easily have been mistaken for an Indian student, was Emmy Büchler, daughter of the famous principal of Jews' College, and we all thought the world of her.

She soon became the life and soul of the club. She set up an Anglo-German library, organised a reading circle, lectures, English and Hebrew classes, also entertainment and refreshments, etc. I still treasure a generous testimonial with which she obliged me, stating (if I may so blow my own trumpet) that I 'undertook any work required in the club' and was able not only to do the English correspondence but also to 'draft and print notices artistically'. (After all, it is good, if idle, to reflect on what one was once able to do.)

I might also perhaps mention that about this time I managed to get my first letter published in the *Daily Telegraph*, no less; it was on the then foremost subject of unemployment, and though I forget the particular point I made, I remember a few days later a reader taking me up on my 'un-English and un-Christian' ideas.

This 'literary success' emboldened me to try and go in for journalism. I had already discovered a School for Journalism and on application I was asked to submit a specimen of my talent. I promptly did – with the result that I was advised first to learn proper English. This rebuff might have shaken my linguistic ego but, curiously enough, it did not. I just disagreed and somehow was impressed by what seemed to me the school's commendable, scrupulous interest in its prospective customers, even if it was not perhaps to be admired from a business point of view. For I did not think (and still don't) I was so underdeveloped – after barely four months in England – as to hold out no hope of gradual growth if competently tended, which might have been to the school's benefit as well as my own. I have kept that specimen and should like to reproduce it for the record as well as for the flickering light it casts on the London of sixty-odd years ago.

RELIGION IN ENGLAND

I often heard and read that the 20th century is hostile or anyhow indifferent to religion. If there is something true in it, it seems to be so only as far as Continental Europe is concerned. The outlook apparently differs greatly in the British Isles. I do not mean of course to say that in England the customs of the middle ages prevail, that historical period when religion was the supreme problem not only of any private person but in public life as well, when e.g. the question whether the wine and the bread given during the Lord's Supper was really Jesus' blood and flesh or only represented it symbolically, was far more interesting and essential to the world than even the latest and more thrilling prophetic novels of H. G. Wells possibly could be to the literary public today.

No, religion in England is certainly not more important than business, greyhound racing and cricket. It is on the other hand no less widespread and popular. As well as you see the big business advertisements at the corner and the posters of the newspapers announcing cricket results and 'Latest from the stables', you will often find placards with pious and moralist inscriptions, especially quotations from the Holy Bible, and if you walk attentively through Whitechapel you will probably be surprised by the great number of quotations from the New Testament, to say nothing of the variety of the Christian club-houses built up in this very district. Every evening you might also listen to religious speeches in Hyde Park and in all other quarters of London. There will be hardly any speaker without a big crowd round him and they are all very interested and have remarkable discussions which often are absolutely adequate to the best entertainments the finest non-stop varieties the West End can provide.

Moreover riding by bus you can occasionally get a ticket with a religious sentence printed on the back. There is a special Tram and Bus Text Mission. It apparently is its task to look after those who cannot or won't go to church. They undoubtedly do real good. Suppose a man has an 8d ride every day, he's got plenty of time and opportunity to learn by heart the religious part of his ticket, and by daily practice he will never in his life forget it, even if he occasionally rides to go to an atheist or communist meeting, he will be able to enjoy verses from the psalms and other religious ethics.

This shows however that religion in England is not treated indifferently, you will meet it everywhere. I should not like to discuss now whether it always appears in an adequate form or whether the frontier between the sublime and the ridiculous always is watched very closely. The fact remains that religion in England exists not only in the churches but is really bound up with public life. And this, I think, is one of the very many phenomena which – more deeply and more clearly than the Channel does – separate England from the 20th century Continental nations.

Admittedly this essay could not claim to qualify for a literary prize though it might have been worse *considering*. But then of course English has its pitfalls which can easily be the foreigner's undoing. My friend in HM Patent Office once told me about a German acquaintance who meant to describe to him an experience that made his mouth water but emerged as one that 'made water in his mouth'. I also remember how, on one of my early outings I was approached by two boys, street urchins, with the query: 'What's the right time, Gov'nor?' I told them and at once made a note of the encounter: you ask not for 'the time' but for 'the right time', and when you speak to an elderly worthy, you address him as 'Governor'. I am glad to say I never had an opportunity of applying this specimen of the King's (or Fowler's) English but it stuck in my memory and I was distinctly impressed having been looked up to as a member of the ruling class.

On the other hand, I was badly confused one day when I came out of my local public library where I had asked for a certain book. The very friendly assistant promised to check, disappeared behind a curtain and came back with the announcement: 'I am afraid we have not got the book.' I didn't quite understand: what did he mean, *he was afraid*? I wanted to know: do they or don't they have the book? Apparently the man had made a very superficial search, he could not say for certain, there was room for doubt, being afraid he cannot have made sure. I was most disappointed. This was poor service. I was not then, linguistically speaking, in a position to argue (which was perhaps just as well),

90

so I walked away, disgruntled and dissatisfied. Clearly I still had much to learn.

So, for that matter, had the English (yes, the English). For this little incident is not quite as innocently amusing as it may appear. Correct English is liable to mislead foreigners, sometimes (as in my case) in a harmless way, but sometimes with disastrous consequences. If Hitler had been addressed in a language that did not have the vagueness and refinement of English he might have taken more notice of British policy than he did and a great deal of trouble might have been saved. As it was, he was told what Britain may or might (not) do and that in certain circumstances we were 'afraid' a 'grave view' would be taken of this, that or the other. Hitler may well have thought that if this was all we were prepared to do, he need not worry: this sort of language did not impress him. What he should have been shown was the banging of a table of good old English oak. *This* was the thing he respected because he understood it. Yes, the niceties of English can be gravely misleading.

However, to come back to Miss Emmy Büchler of the London Jewish Club. Though some of us occasionally liked to smile at the sheer intensity of her concern, I think we owe her more than has been publicly acknowledged. She was originally one of the teachers of English at Woburn House, and I believe it was through her exertions that the refugees were enabled to consult certain doctors and dentists free of charge. She also secured for us, away from the often depressing Committee atmosphere, the use of the annexe to St John's Wood (now New London) Synagogue, Abbey Road, where we spent many relatively carefree hours.

I remember the genial Revd Gustave Prince, our neighbour, who frequently dropped in and once told us this amusing little story. He had been Army chaplain in France, and one day a German Jewish prisoner was brought to him who promptly stood stiffly to attention and, saluting, introduced himself as 'Gefreiter (corporal) Moses'. Prince was a little taken aback, he said; he was familiar enough with the

91

name of Moses but *Gefreiter* he only knew as an ingredient of *Gefreite* (fried) fish – and how did this here make sense?

Now with all the great benefits she conferred on our club, Miss Büchler had, from our point of view, one drawback – she went in for that publicity which we sought to avoid. She arranged for a formal opening of the club in the presence of Hampstead dignitaries including several rabbis; she was thinking of a club magazine called *Unterwegs* ('The Wayfarers'), and she began to canvass support outside the Jewish community. She approached for example the Quakers who agreed to lend a hand; as a first effort they were to send us a speaker on the subject 'The Unemployed and the Wasteland', the idea being to stimulate greater interest in agriculture.

However, the lecture was never given. The Committee got wind of it and they would not have it. Miss Büchler had not informed them of this sort of activity, or for that matter of any of the club's activities, and they were not going to tolerate what they regarded as interference in their affairs. To the best of my recollection, Miss Büchler was summoned to Woburn House and in effect ordered to conform to Committee policy, which she did, and shortly afterwards the club was 're-opened' with Committee blessing. Among the clients some deep-drawn murmurs were heard though, and the then novel and soon fashionable term *Gleichschaltung* (enforced coordination) was freely applied to the procedure.

All this took place in Hampstead because that was where most of the refugees lived. As I lived in north London, near the East End, I had a chance of meeting fellow-Jews who remembered how, thirty-odd years earlier, they passed through Germany on their way from Russia. They thought that in some respects I was in their position then, for (they said) they were not really wanted by the German Jews whose main concern was to get them a ticket for the crossing from Hamburg to England (or America). There was occasionally an undertone of *Schadenfreude* but of course the essential historical justice of the comparison

92

could not be denied. Some too understood the tragedy that was engulfing us all. I can still hear dear old Mrs Marks, a childless widow, who could not do enough to look after me, how she would often sigh: 'The world is made only for the *goy*,' adding after a while as was her custom, 'Absolutely'.

Now also memories of the Kaiser war were revived. Some were talking about the spectacular Zeppelin raids, and my doctor friend Joshua Zeitlin related how awful it was for him during the war when his classmates at school twisted his already provocatively un-English name into 'Zeplin'; he nearly went up into the air, in a manner of speaking.

At the great Jewish ex-servicemen's march in Hyde Park in July 1933, big banners proclaimed 'In 1914 we defended freedom against the Huns, in 1933 we defend the Jews against Hitlerism'. But, said my landlady, 'What good will it do? The English have already forgotten the war.' In fairness, they had not quite forgotten. When the Nazi 'philosopher' and foreign policy 'expert' Alfred Rosenberg, on his official visit in May 1933, had the *chutzpa* to lay a swastika-draped wreath at the Cenotaph, it was promptly removed and flung into the Thames as 'a protest against the desecration of our national war memorial', perpetrated by the emissary of a Government that was 'contriving to do those very things and foster those feelings which many of our fellows suffered fighting against in the war.' Hitler's effigy at Madame Tussaud's was daubed and, with notable perception, marked 'Mass Murderer'. Even some notorious antisemites were 'appalled by the Hitlerite atrocities'. G. K. Chesterton, quipping as usual, declared himself 'quite ready to believe now that Belloc and myself will die defending the last Jew in Europe. Thus does history play its ironical jokes upon us.'

Naturally, there was a strong anti-German feeling among Jews. Even before leaving home I had read in a Berlin paper about a 'Whitechapel mob' being led by what was made to appear as a particularly obnoxious rabble rouser called

Barnett (later Lord) Janner, Labour MP and later President of the Jewish Board of Deputies. The *Jewish Chronicle* in those weeks seemed to be providing new chapters for Foxe's *Book of Martyrs*.

Protest meetings were held, especially in the East End, and the Chief Rabbi, Dr J. H. Hertz, composed a special prayer for German Jewry. At a service of intercession, he clearly perceived the 'satanic idea of mass massacre' which (he said) showed that 'nothing less than extermination of the Jews would satisfy the wilder spirits among the Nazis' (Hitler's of course being among the wildest). This address must have been heard by Pandit Nehru, the Indian leader then in London, who shortly afterwards wrote to his daughter Indira: 'On the Jews, one and all, a death sentence has been passed'.

An anti-Nazi boycott was (haphazardly) organised by the gallant Captain Webber who conducted a private if luckless campaign, and later, with greater energy though not much greater effect, by a Jewish Representative Council under the inspiration of the dedicated Alfred Goldstein, a textile trader, who claimed a success rate of 75–80 per cent while admitting to me in 1938 that in England, in contrast to the USA, the organisers of the boycott had to proceed with considerable caution, despite support from both the Labour Party and the TUC.

Many took pleasure in contrasting the two countries – Britain's 'self-assurance' which could match the Jews' any time, and Germany's 'inferiority complex' which clearly could not. I remember making a note of one of Prime Minister Stanley Baldwin's speeches referring to 'the spiritual unity of the British Empire', with its 'ultimate goal – the Kingdom of Heaven on earth'; its ideal of equality and freedom too was being pointedly reaffirmed at the time of Nazi Germany's first open act of defiance, the withdrawal from the League of Nations.

Many too fancied that Hitler was not likely to last long; this Nazi business really seemed too bad to be true. Yet there was also a feeling that what had been possible in

Germany, 'the land of *Kultur*', was not altogether impossible in England.

A highly individual campaign was conducted at the Progressive Synagogue in Stoke Newington which I attended on Saturday mornings. Its Minister, Revd Maurice Perlzweig, adopted a very special order of service. Whereas normally rabbis concentrate on the prescribed portion of the week which should suggest a subject for their sermons, Perlzweig did it the other way round: he would choose a topical subject and then find a suitable text. And since the most obvious topic in those days (and in that part of London) was Germany, the posters outside the synagogue advertising the sermon often read like the posters of daily papers except that, I regret to say, they did not sell as briskly: the large, barn-like hall was, in that respect no different from other synagogues, more than half empty.

*　*　*

I did not often talk about these services when I visited the very orthodox family which kindly invited me to spend the Sabbath afternoons in their house. I was introduced to them by one of the sons whom I had met at Jews' College where he was studying for the Ministry. It was a fairly large family, and one of the daughters, a quiet but determined and businesslike woman, took an interest in me. She was employed in her father's business – printing and stationery – and it occurred to her that they might be able to offer me an opening there. Daddy was actually looking for somebody he could take into the business, she explained, someone he could rely on and who might perhaps eventually take over. His two sons were not eligible – the one was studying, the other had a business of his own. So, she said, it would be somebody he could regard as a third son, and he thought he would find him best through her, his daughter.

She had prefaced her story by hinting, gently, discreetly, that I might not at once get the idea, and she was not entirely wrong as she had in fact been at first (shall we say) a little vague, tentatively groping. But now there was no doubt and she added she would be very happy if I consented. She had not mentioned the matter to Daddy, she said – I might wish to approach him, though perhaps if I preferred her to do so, I 'only had to command'.

I did not command and I made no move. I sounded out some of my refugee friends by telling them the story as that of a third person I had heard of, and most were agreed: 'That man now has nothing to worry about.' But I, perhaps oddly, had – a great deal too. I did not like the idea of mixing sentiment and business, and though I knew there was nothing unusual in marriages being 'arranged', I did not want mine to be. Basically, while Judy loved me (and confessed her love to me), I was not sure I loved her and perhaps was frightened by the prospect of the responsibilities which I would not be able to discharge, for I was and am not a businessman and looking back I am surprised none of the family realised this. But I must have subconsciously felt that I was bound to be letting myself in for grave disappointments. Even if I had won some prosperity I would have bought it at too dear a price and in one way or other, sooner or later, I would have gone – materially, intellectually and emotionally – bankrupt.

Also I would have entered a social world that was vastly different from mine and in which I might well be a misfit. We were all Jews, yes, but we are not on that account akin (except in the fate that might and/or did overtake us). I was of the West, the world before me now was of the East, and tradition and upbringing had implanted greatly differing values in us. Judy was strictly and naively orthodox, of a religion where (it seemed to me) the letter of the law might easily cast a shadow on the spirit of the practice. Had she been a Roman Catholic, she would have missed no mass and unfailingly attended confession. I was (and remain) 'progressive' in the widest sense, and the ritual of religion has little appeal for me. It would have been virtually a mixed marriage with many of its appointed seeds of failure. I distinctly felt I was not the one this Solveg was waiting for.

96

My parents were sorry to hear of my reaction. They thought I was too much of an idealist and too little prepared to make those compromises which, according to them, were in such situations acceptable and customary. I was not convinced nor was my mother discouraged. She came over and we all met face to face. The differences were then made clear, and though I would have been free to go on enjoying the great-hearted family's hospitality, I broke off. I have often thought about this quasi-romantic episode, especially when I once chanced upon Wilfred Thorley's lines

> In this world he lives amiss
> That letteth love go bye.

Yet, strangely perhaps, I have never regretted my decision – the second, within a year, at a crossroads of my life.

I was now soon to leave London, moving north to Yorkshire, where I stayed for a couple of years. The farewell was in some ways sad for I had made friends, among them that civil servant whose ambition was to read *Mein Kampf* in the original which I am glad to say I was able effectively to interpret for him. But the saddest parting was from my landlady's eight-year-old son Albert, a quiet boy with a mind of his own. His dearest desire was to engage me in a round of rummy – any time of the day, preferably over breakfast. There was nothing quite like it for him, and sometimes when we had to stop because Mother urgently reminded him it was time to be off to school, he after a while would come back, announcing he had thought better of it – he *much* preferred another game of rummy with Mr A. And no wonder, whatever the odds may have been at school, here he (nearly) always won.

# 4

# MECHANIC IN LEEDS

After almost exactly a year, on 6 June 1934 – memorable because it was Derby Day and my favourite 'also ran' – I left London for Leeds. It was not entirely of my own choosing. It was rather part of the Committee's policy of trying to provide for its clients' future overseas. I was to learn a trade that would qualify me for what was then known as a 'certificate for immigration into Palestine'.

Like a number of other youngsters in my position, I received a list, compiled by the Committee, of trades to make a choice from, and I had indicated, for lack of anything more congenial, a preference for engineering which included sewing machine mechanics. My training was scheduled for one year at the end of which I (like the rest) would be required to leave the country.

Leeds as a centre of the clothing industry seemed an ideal place in which to acquire such undoubtedly useful knowledge. Since I wanted to be 'retrained', which in those days was considered essential as a move away from a disproportionate Jewish share in the academic professions, it did not perhaps much matter which trade was chosen though I might have preferred typewriter or car mechanics. At all events, I was now embarking on my new voyage into the unknown with considerable enthusiasm. I believed I was duty-bound to make the effort as the spirit of the times seemed to require it.

About Leeds I knew next to nothing. I had read somewhere that the historian and poet Macaulay, when MP for the city, once delivered a speech about 'the loveliness and intelligence of Leeds', but that was in the far off past and perhaps said to suit the occasion. More recently Bernard Shaw had been reported as saying that 'the whole place wants burning down', and a possibly all too dramatic critic, St John Ervine, considered the Leodensians to be 'corpses looking out for their coffins'. So I was rather prejudiced, and indeed people were sorry for me when they heard about my destination. Clearly not all of Leeds was substandard. Yet I can remember at the time of my arrival seeing human habitations which would have been disapproved by the Royal Society for the Prevention of Cruelty to Animals. They must have been built in the early 19th century and might have served as a background for some of the Brontë stories.

I heard it said that the new housing policy was 'an attempt to civilise people who had not had a decent chance of being civilised'. Even now the country was thought to be 'suffering from the evil legacy of the haphazard development of the industrial revolution' with its two 'outstanding evils' – the slums and overcrowding. Actually it was not very long before we heard tales of the coal being kept in the bath tubs of the new tenements.

There were other houses open to different criticism, and I regret to say one of them was chosen by the local Committee as a lodging for young fellows like us, even if we soon cleared out. It was a kind of boarding house in an otherwise genteel residential quarter, where we shared accommodation with a frequently changing company of theatre folk (and/or what passed for them) – actors and actresses, comedians, musicians and other migrant minstrels who appeared in local shows. The greatest star, however, was the lady in charge who, in conducting the business, was ably assisted by the Prince Consort who served as a never

99

failing witness as soon as called upon to bear out the lady's unsubdued self-praise. When the radio was blaring its canned music, she would accompany it with a voice that could tear your heart and make your hair stand on end. As soon as she returned to her libretto, she was sure to amaze her listeners not only with the rapidity of a Dickensian landlady's utterance but with the sheer strident vulgarity.

I was not unfamiliar with swearing. I had picked up a little in London though the full flower of this sort of social intercourse, the sheer grinding monotony of it, was growing on the shop floor although, even there, not without discrimination. I remember using it once in an argument with an elderly colleague who appreciated my effort with this qualification: 'I don't mind you swearing but I do mind you using obscene language.' So I was not exactly a greenhorn. But this toothless shrew of a land'lady' really was as disgusting in her manner as she must have been efficient in her business. She would refer to people known to us in terms which even common labourers used to swearing – my mates – would keep clear of. She did not mind enquiring of boarders in the presence of her husband, strangers and the maid too, 'Would you care to sleep with me tonight – the Old Man's out.' One probably would be prudish now to object to such scenes but in those days and in this neighbourhood it was (I thought, perhaps naively) revolting, and even as a 'joke' liable to make you vomit, especially when the Prince Consort, a willing butt, was braying in approval like a superannuated ass. I was glad when I managed to extract myself from this filth.

When I told the Committee's chairman about my new address and passed on a message from the brothel madam that she did not want him to send her any more people like us, he replied: 'D'you think I will, to a mad woman like her?' Well, the madness was not so hidden as not to be noticeable in the first place.

The firm that had kindly agreed to train me was the

Bellow Machine Company in the main Jewish business quarter of North Street. My employer was Mr Abraham Bellow, A.Inst.P.I., M.Inst.B.E. (late First Aircraftman Belovitch, Royal Flying Corps) whose letterheads proclaimed him 'the largest employer of labour in Europe in this particular type of business'. This was probably no exaggeration and I am prepared to believe there was no one like him anywhere in the ironmongering North of England. The firm's logo was an ornamental bell which seemed to be giving a joyful sound though I had already learnt that bells could also 'toll for me'.

My weekly 'wage' was what I believe was the legal minimum amount of 30 shillings gross, or at the present rate £1.50, i.e., after deduction of insurance, 28 shillings and five pence, which paid for my lodgings and full board (£1.10) and left the rest for savings and occasional entertainment (a theatre seat one shilling, or 5p). I could have supplemented my wage by collecting from the Committee a weekly bounty of ten shillings (50p) but foolishly never did as I felt, with no thought of the future, that I could manage without it.

Bellow, who had founded the company in 1919 with the now modest capital of £100, succeeded greatly by his enterprise and drive. I later learnt from F. P. Godfrey's *International History of the Sewing Machine* that 'in order to keep abreast of the latest developments in the field of garment-making machinery', he 'travelled abroad extensively', and coming from Germany, I was particularly interested to hear that in 1927 he acquired the agency for a Munich firm.

I was almost at once joined by another young fellow, also hailing from Berlin but with a more practical, technological turn of mind enabling him to make faster progress in repairing 'the finest machines in the world for sewing, cutting', etc., for which Bellow had established a sound reputation. We were both soon taught how to dismantle the heavy factory machines and put them together again, but if the firm promised '100% results wherever

101

installed', it was not I who was chosen to honour the promise.

Even so, after a while we both were allowed, under due supervision, to embark on outdoor operations. Sometimes we found no more than two or three machines tucked away in a dismal, dilapidated habitation above some grimy backyard. More often we called at those forbidding relics of the industrial revolution where crowds of 'hands' were harnessed to bleak rows of benches which we had to tackle either on the spot or by taking machines back to the shop. Then we would be conveyed on a horse-drawn, not too steady cart, looking (and feeling) like passengers on the once fashionable Parisian tumbrils, especially on Saturdays when we were on those wildly detested moving jobs dismantling gear and installing it again over the weekend so that the never-tiring owners might finish at one place on a Saturday and start at a new place next Monday. But for the irrelevant technical changes, the seamstresses swotting in these melancholy surroundings were the women of Thomas Hood's poem

> Plying her needle and thread –
> Stitch! stitch! stitch!
> In poverty, hunger and dirt.

Many of them, both English and of immigrant stock, had been used to this kind of work for years. Some, indeed most, would now work for a Jewish master. But that was not always so. When John Barran introduced the band knife for mass production, a strong force of Jewish immigrant labour was recruited for him by Hermann Friend, himself a Jewish refugee. Some 10,000 Jews then came to Leeds, into that 'Old England' which the nationally famous Revd Studdert Kennedy, affectionately known as 'Woodbine Willie' from his work handing out Woodbine cigarettes to the troops in France, once wrote 'were a curse':

It were sleepin', sweatin', starvin',
Wearing bootsoles for a job,
It were sucking up to foremen
What 'ud sell ye for a bob.

But the Jews worked their way along with a zeal and an efficiency that persecution was powerless to impair. One of them was Michael Marks – later St Michael – who came from Poland and in 1884 hired a stall to sell soap, sponges, brushes and combs in the Market Hall. The price was one penny, here and in all the northern towns whither he soon dispatched his stuff on barrows, until he met Tom Spencer, the sales manager of a Leeds textile firm. With him he went into a £700 partnership, to launch the Marks & Spencer Penny Bazaar.

Others established entirely new industries, manufacturing caps, slippers, furniture, and they had no small share in the more than 400 firms which by 1934 were engaged in the production of ready-made and wholesale bespoke garments, giving employment to many tens of thousands. In due course, they made considerable progress, and that meant, for a great many, considerable money.

Inevitably too they encountered much prejudice, especially among those who sadly failed to do likewise, in spite of devoted efforts. For the people of Yorkshire were by no means without an appreciation of that eager spirit, as (in Charlotte Brontë's *Shirley*) Joe Scott says to the foreign newcomer, the Belgian Robert Gérard Moore: 'Onybody may see ye're akin to us, ye're so keen o'making brass and getting forrards' (which did not necessarily endear him to the natives). Dr Johnson once thought that 'there are few ways in which a man can be more innocently employed than in getting money.' What angered him in rich people, Boswell explains, was their 'lack of ideals' and the 'torpor of their self-satisfaction'. I frequently had occasion to ponder this timeless remark.

Among the 30,000 Jews in Leeds (in a population of 500,000) very little was available in the way of cultural amenities. There was not one Jewish bookshop. Mr Levy's messy stationery shop, later under the management of his son, Mr Lee ('Levy' and 'Leeds' combined) was selling such food for literary thought as the *Jewish Chronicle* and the Yiddish paper *Die Zeit*. Leeds Jewry's affairs or history (such as it was) had never attracted the attention of a researcher. A noteworthy local talent was Dr Ipshen, a medical man, who wrote plays in some of which (under a pseudonym) he gently satirised the more patent of the community's failings. These plays would be staged at the Young Men's Institute where a great deal of Jewish social life passed off. Lectures of not too heavy a calibre were delivered here and usually, often in contrast to many functions of the Zionist Society, fairly well attended – even if not always from love of the subject alone but rather more in the manner of Miss Jenny Simper who, as readers of Addison's essays will remember, attended divine service for the purpose of making conquests.

There was of course scope for entertainment generally. As Leeds at the time had no permanent theatre, performances were given by visiting repertory companies. Considering the city's prominence, even if not in the cultural sphere, I was surprised to read that nearby Huddersfield, of no greater cultural standing, was establishing a municipal theatre. So I wrote to the *Yorkshire Post* saying that 'what is possible in Huddersfield should not be altogether unimaginable in Leeds'; the Lord Mayor had already given a hint that a subvention might be granted, but had there been any response? I soon found out. My letter was printed and the response was nil.

I frequently went to the theatre – as often as my weekly wage permitted (there was 6s net after I had paid my full board of 22s 6d) and this was to cover my companion, one of my landlady's nieces who was interested. She was herself a budding actress, shy and withdrawn by nature but a *grande dame* on stage, and she frequently appeared at the Jewish Institute where my assignment was to take her home, on a moon-lit walk, both as an esteemed 'dramatic critic' and a discreet fan and admirer.

Weekends were usually reserved for country rambles. The Yorkshire moors never seemed bleak to us, wild perhaps but not bleak, and I retain happy memories which came oddly back to me when I was reading some of the Brontë stories.

Among the plays we saw I remember J. B. Priestley's *Eden End*, Noël Coward's *The Young Idea*, also one about Nurse Edith Cavell shot by the Germans in 1915 and a dramatised version of *Wuthering Heights*. The films were usually Elisabeth Bergner's (*Ariane, Catherine the Great, Dreaming Lips*), also *M* directed by Fritz Lang and *The Wandering Jew* with Conrad Veidt. A Yiddish theatre company, in 1934, found no great interest beyond three performances. Occasionally I attended lectures at the Leeds YMCA and the World Progress Friendship Club in Bradford. In December 1934 a play was to be staged dealing with 'the Nazi persecution of the Jews', but this found no favour in the eyes of the censor and so alterations had to be made: the Brown Shirts changed their colour to Yellow and the Nazis appeared as 'Nordics'.

I spent a great deal of my free time in the Leeds public library, a recreation as it were from the strains of the day, much perhaps as A. E. Housman (*A Shropshire Lad*) did when he settled in the British Museum after duty done at HM Patent Office. But to me those hours also were a kind of evening class to teach myself general knowledge as well as especially knowledge of England, her history, her literature, those beliefs and thoughts of her great men which determined a national outlook on the world, her *Weltanschauung*.

In a series of memo books (cheaply bought at Woolworths) I kept what seemed to me characteristic extracts on such subjects as Pericles' ideal of democracy, Burke's thoughts on the English Constitution, Cardinal Newman's definition of the gentleman, Anglo-German relations before 1914, Kipling's poetry (*Recessional* and later *The Hun is at the Gate*). As I was much oppressed with the progress of Nazi propaganda, I noted these lines from Molière's *Le Misan-thrope*: 'But really people will laugh at you if they hear you speak in this fashion', to which the crushing rejoinder was: 'So much the worse for him who laughs' (*Tant pis pour lui qui rirait*) – how true it was I then thought, and still think.

I also made a note of the foolish things G. K. Chesterton and Hilaire Belloc were still saying about the Jews. I jotted down this passage from *G.K.'s Weekly* in 1936: 'The reaction of Israel against the Government of Berlin still awaits the order to mobilise. That will come. Close observers say that from the first attack to the counter-offensive there should be a delay of four years. We shall see.' We did see. Chesterton (mercifully dead by then) might have relished the spectacle of making a fool of himself.

Belloc's book *The Jews* (1922) aroused my special critical attention – which reminds me: I once wanted to acquire a copy and went to Foyle's Oriental department which was then in the charge of the somewhat eccentric Jewish nationalist Jacob Sarna. He immediately taxed me on why I wanted that book – didn't I know how bad it was? I confessed I had heard it was and that was the reason why I wanted to find out for myself. This just was not good enough for Sarna and I could not prevail on him to sell it. I don't know whether his employers were aware of the way business was (or was not) transacted in their Oriental department. But it was during the war, in the terrible year of 1942, and they might conceivably have made some allowance in this particular case, especially as it would not have been easy to replace the exceptionally qualified and knowledgeable Sarna.

Meanwhile my stipulated year in Leeds was drawing to a close. In February 1935 Capt. Davidson, one of the London Committee's chiefs, arrived, and altogether five youngsters were summoned into the very comfortable home of the Committee's Viceroy to meet him. Among those present were our bosses, the chairman of the local Zionist Society and two other worthies. The agenda was our future – not so

106

much as we saw it but as our London well-wishers had mapped it out for us. Captain Davidson informed us – a standard piece of information this – that it would be extremely difficult to obtain a renewal of our permit to stay in England. The Government had already been most generous in granting us one year and we could not expect this favour to be repeated. If any of us hoped (some did) to remain as agents of a Continental firm, they must be warned that the Home Office had no sympathy for any such plans. Applications for this kind of job had already been refused. We were advised to make our arrangements accordingly.

I am telling these facts in no spirit of recrimination. For one thing, too much has happened since, and 'time hath, my Lord, a wallet on his back wherein he puts alms for oblivion'. It is just part of the story of the Wandering Jew.

So far as I was concerned, I could honestly claim that I had not yet learnt sufficient to qualify as a competent mechanic able to earn a living that way. At the same time, there were moments when, frightened and frustrated, I felt doubts about my future in England, sometimes graver doubts too. I was taking an ominous interest in the subject of suicide, and in two (unpublished) letters to the *Yorkshire Post* I criticised the formula 'Suicide while of unsound mind'; one of them purported to be written by 'a comity of deceased souls' who felt 'stigmatised for all time' by having been dubbed 'temporarily insane', etc. As in those days the 'law and practice relating to coroners' happened to be under review, the souls wanted to say 'how deeply our feelings were hurt by those remarks and how much we still suffer from them'.

This topic was among the many that were passing through my mind as I wondered whether I should perhaps, like so many others, see the folks back home only for a visit – for reflection and something like a new perspective. I decided against it. I would not be discouraged by the Committee. I would call their bluff. When the year was up, I blandly requested an extension of my permit via the

107

London Committee and was granted one without ado – a short-term one, it is true, three or six months, which sometimes meant that when my passport came back and was shown to the police, I had to send it off immediately for another extension, and so this little ping-pong game went on until I decided to quit.

Truly my mind was not in my work, and if I thought of sewing machines it was as a subject for irrelevant reflection. I mentioned swearing before, the grey monotony of it. As I also indulged in it (if only to appear more acceptable and sound authentic), I remembered having read, in an article by an English professor of philosophy, that swearing could help you a lot – after such curses, things would behave very differently: a crooked nail would be more easily hit straight. Only of course one must not overdo it – which probably was the reason why my damned sewing machines, even after the bloodiest curses, would obstinately refuse to work.

There I was then, having just boldly attempted to study law for which I was just as ill equipped as for sewing machine repairs. Was this perhaps something the two had in common? Not really. Here there was nothing abstract, nothing dry as dust, and theory was only that a machine I had 'repaired' would actually sew. Why had I taken on sewing machines in the first place? Perhaps for sentimental reasons, remembering the lamentable fate of the man who invented those machines, that poor Parisian tailor whom none of the pretty young seamstresses now will ever think of because they fancy only rich tailors or no tailors at all. And yet when this poor devil invented his machine in 1841 it was for the eminently profitable purpose of manufacturing uniforms for the army. No wonder he was kept busy. There were soon as many as eighty machines working and it appeared that military uniforms were about to become a vogue in Paris. Alas, the gently rising Monsieur Thimonnier had not reckoned with his not so successful fellow-tailors who, copying the English Luddites, misunderstood the sewing machines as a threat to their livelihood and simply

108

smashed them to pieces as if they were parts of a new Bastille. The wretched Thimonnier was lucky not to be 'shot while trying to escape' (as the Nazis would have put it). Perhaps I now felt one should commiserate with the poor man and his sewing machines, so that it could be seen as nothing less than a duty to repair what he had bequeathed to us.

Such idle reflections with which I was feeding my mind did not, however, make me attend to the business in hand. I was lacking in the magic touch that was required, and I had reason to suspect that Mr Bellow was not amused at the sight of 'dem fellows' who, if not frequently 'hopeless', simply were 'no good'.

I would not have argued with him on that score, and I knew only too well why I never applied for a rise as I might have done through the London Committee's Viceroy. It would have been foolhardy, as well as disingenuous. I could not doubt what I was worth. Later I learnt that others, employed in the clothing trade, youngsters with much of my background, had indeed asked for a little more – and were turned down in humiliating circumstances. They were found to be 'really quite useless', 'not even worth the wage they were getting'; their 'mind was elsewhere', like the one who was 'spending most of his time at home as a musician which appeared to contribute to his living.'

I cannot claim that my mind was in the sewing machines but neither did I run away from them. Those others may well have felt like David Copperfield – 'my hopes of growing up a learned and distinguished man crushed in my bosom: the deep remembrance of the sense I had of being utterly without hope now, of the shame I felt in my position'. I had hopes of better days and they did not flag: however low they might have sunk at times, they would rise again. I was also fortunate in one particular respect. I enjoyed the good will of the man who was the outstanding figure of the Leeds Jewish community, Professor Selig Brodetsky, one time President of the Board of Deputies, who was also occupying a Chair of Mathematics at Leeds University. I was introduced to him by Dr Weizmann's private secretary, Dr Josef Cohn, whom I had met at the London Group of Young Zionists.

In his comfortable home in Headingley, far from the Jewish quarter of Chapeltown, and in the charming company of his wife (a Belgian refugee of 1914), I spent many agreeable hours, in common with other young men and women, mostly university students, who were frequently invited, the host showing himself at all times conscientiously concerned that each should have a chance of meeting appropriate specimens of the opposite sex.

The Professor often spoke to me of his own student days in Leipzig and with gentle sarcasm described his encounters then, forty years ago, with the local *Central-Verein* of German Citizens of the Jewish Faith, though as far as the Jews were concerned, he 'loved the human form' in all alike. He never tired of emphasising the essential oneness of all Jews. I remember how he once startled us by explaining that, whatever the experts of raceology and the theorists of theology might say, he thought that a Jew was simply anybody who called himself a Jew.

I often heard him when he addressed the local League of Nations Union or the Workers' Educational Association; sometimes too he would share a platform with such people as the MP for West Leeds, Major Vyvyan Adams. He was held in the very highest regard among Jews and non-Jews alike. Among my workmates in the factory he was well known as a famous Leeds Jew and respected as a gallant champion of his people. One who heard him at the Salem Brotherhood Chapel discussing the international situation, came back saying it was 'a real statesman's speech'. I often thought that once there was a Jewish State, he would (or should) be its first Foreign Secretary.

I sometimes felt it would be a fine thing if the ardent young men who were his guests might become his disciples and his home a cell of some distinctive thought. Nothing, it seemed to me then, was more important than that a great man stand forth and set the example of his active life not only before the meetings of the many but also in the stillness of the few. Yet no such thing ever happened in Leeds. I thought this was sad because only recently the Professor had deplored 'the low level of intellectual life in Anglo-Jewry' which he said was 'immeasurably below the English Gentile's'. I myself heard him say: 'If a Jew wants to be a *goy*, at least let him be an educated *goy*.'

A close friend of the Professor's was 'Monty' Burton, whose name of course was a household word in Leeds, for the city was the headquarters of 'the largest men's clothing organisation in the world'. There were few tailors who did not at one time or other work for Burton's (who at that time employed about 20,000), and every sewing machine mechanic possessed of any earthly ambition dreamt of the day when he would be so privileged as to obtain work there. I never met Sir Montague but there were many who remembered his early days when he took to the road as a humdrum commercial traveller. I was told by people of good authority he used to walk down North Street, hawking laces, braces and other useful articles, and so severely was the good man – Moshe David Osinsky – said to have felt his humble station that he hardly dared step on the pavement but moved along the gutter. When I heard the story I felt all the greater must be the respect for him and his astounding achievement. It was an early example of what the Dictionary of National Biography later described as his 'humble and self-effacing' nature which 'disliked any kind of ostentation or personal publicity'.

Nor was Sir Montague's mind content with business. He had travelled in many parts of the world and described his experiences in two volumes entitled *Globe Girdling*. He seemed to agree with his namesake, Robert Burton, author of *The Anatomy of Melancholy* (1621), that 'the most pleasant of all outward pastimes is ... to make a pretty progress, a merry journey, now and then with some good companions, to visit friends, see Cities, Castles, Towns.' He certainly took pride in the fact that he was the only industrialist elected as a member of the PEN Club. I remember I made a note of his globe-girdling confession that 'having looked at the world and its divine beauty, having met many of its peoples and found them individually generous, hospitable, and kind, I refuse to believe that mankind will turn into a shambles its heritage of loveliness.' I could not but admire his fine optimism, yet I also wondered, vaguely, how so successful a businessman could be so unsophisticated a philosopher.

But then man's mind is apt to move in peculiar ways. When I first jotted down my Leeds reminiscences which included those data on Burton, I decided (to keep on the safe side as it were) to submit that particular paragraph to him for approval. He replied that 'obviously someone has confused the issue, for the subject of your notes did not know North Street nor indeed Leeds, until he was an employer of labour in a substantial way of business, neither was he ever a vendor of laces and braces.' He sent me a reprint from the *Dewsbury Reporter* (a small local paper) of 5 June 1943 which he said gave 'a brief and correct outline' of his business, the authorised version.

This was very considerate of him but (if I may say so) he had got hold of the wrong end of the stick. I did not intend and would have been unable to describe his business. I explained that I was concerned only with 'my personal recollections of Leeds and I intend to refer to you as a part of them'. It seemed to me, I wrote, that 'the stories or legends if you like, which have settled around your name, are a real part of this experience. They were in fact, I found, inseparable from the name', and 'my recollections of Leeds would not be complete without them'; this I thought was 'a case where fiction has a claim to be considered fact.'

Sir Montague severely disagreed. My opinion seemed to him 'akin to the Hitlerite theory that, if a lie is repeated often enough and loudly enough, some people will believe it.' Not only was it a Nazi theory, the great man was also

112

reminded (though on second thought he might not have been) of an identical Yorkshire saying, 'If you throw mud long enough, some of it will stick'. After this encounter, no more letters were exchanged but I could not help comparing Mr Montague Burton with Sir Simon Marks who never objected to being reminded of his lowly beginnings which he could well be proud of as Burton could be of his.

The official standing of Jews in Leeds was indicated by the fact that in 1941 one of their leaders, Alderman Hyman Morris, became the first Jewish Lord Mayor. At the same time, antisemitism was by no means to be ignored. Jews were not popular, and any visitor would soon have discovered, as Nehru did at Harrow, that it was the proper thing to show disdain for 'the damned Jews'. I often thought it strange that although in the factory very few ever spent great care on the niceties of the King's own Yorkshire English, there was one man, an elderly devout Christian, a Sunday School teacher too, who as a matter of sacred principle would never swear – except in respect of one subject: the 'bloody Jews'. It seemed odd too that this man did not mind joining many less conscientious colleagues who, during the Palestine disturbances of 1936–37, held me responsible for the sad news that British soldiers were being killed not indeed *by* the Jews but, as they put it, *for* the Jews. At the time of the Abdication crisis (December 1936), when the King, Edward VIII, and his paramour, Mrs Simpson, were intensely unpopular among my workmates, I remember one of them coming up to me and, as a kind of impractical joke, telling me they felt like murdering the (suitably demoted) lady – and blaming the Jews.

A friend of mine had the greatest difficulty in placing his son with an engineering firm: non-Jews did not want the boy simply because he was a Jew, and as for Jewish employers, they seemed slow to expand their Jewish staff for no apparent reason other than to avoid giving offence to supposedly hyper-sensitive customers.

The fact that my fellow-refugee friend and I were

113

German Jews was well known though we were not of course on that account treated with any consideration (nor did we expect it). We did not, however, escape the contradictory impact of the news from Germany: when our colleagues were pleased by it, they would tease us by announcing 'Good ol' 'itler', but when it was not so pleasing, we would be included among those 'bloody Germans'.

The characteristic threat of Nazi policy was of course not realised. A colleague told me in 1935 he had been offered a good job in an aircraft building plant; the wage was excellent but he would have nothing to do with it: he strictly refused to help prepare for the next war.

Oswald Mosley's Fascists played no very conspicuous part. Before coming to Leeds I had read in the *Jewish Chronicle* about a man called a 'Yorkshire Hitler', a glass manufacturer at Morley, who was distributing among his work people 'Fascist leaflets' (to be obtained from the 'British Fascists' in London SW7) which quoted from the 'Protocols of Zion' and praised Hitler and Henry Ford as 'outstanding champions of humanity'. I never heard of Mr Hailwood while in Leeds. He probably was a freak, certainly when compared with Mosley's budding British Union of Fascists. They had a small out-of-the-way shop where I once went to buy some literature. I also went to Fascist meetings in front of the Town Hall and all I remember is the hostile reception they met ('lot of lunatics', 'dirty rats', 'shit on him'). I don't think they had much of a chance in Leeds; not even Mosley's visit in February 1937 made a great deal of difference. There were no sympathisers among my workmates.

They would take a more conscientious interest in the also more manageable subject of prostitution which in fact occupied a substantial part of their attention. There was frequent reference to a lady plying her trade in the centre of Leeds who was said to be sporting a pince-nez. This was thought to be an unusual mark of distinction and it was considered, at the very least, a *must* not to miss the extraordinary sight. Such fuss of course was made long before the services of prostitutes were not only publicly advertised but became the subject of extensive and appreciative comment in 'quality' newspapers. Lately, a retired prostitute, now no doubt a reformed character, actually served as Lord Mayor of a city not too far removed from Leeds, while Madonna's bottom graced the more respectable section of the Sunday press.

*　　*　　*

On conditions in Germany we were competently informed. The *Yorkshire Post*, then regarded as the mouthpiece of Sir Anthony Eden, the Foreign Secretary, not only carried sound reports but also effectively criticised Nazi policy. At the time of the British Legion's visit to Berlin, two months before the Nuremberg Laws (1935) depriving German Jews of their civil rights, an editorial regretted the approval which the 'misguided journey' had received from the Prince of Wales (later Duke of Windsor), and pointing to the persecution of the Jews, the paper remarked that it was 'utterly illogical to expect honourable conduct, moderation and tolerance, according to our standards, in foreign relations from a Government which treats whole sections of its own population in a way which violates every principle of humanity.'

It so happened that about this time Yorkshire was visited by the famous German-Jewish playwright Ernst Toller, a militant anti-Nazi, best remembered perhaps (next to his *Book of Swallows*) for the play *The Machine Wreckers* which I was now able to appreciate so much better! He was lecturing in Halifax and Huddersfield. I did not hear him, only know he spoke on such non-political topics as amateur drama (at the invitation of the British Drama League), but he apparently always managed to deliver a message condemning totalitarian oppression and demanding 'banishment of the spirit of war from schools and universities, newspapers, history books, films and plays'; he actually said (and no one could fail to understand whom he meant): 'The peace-breaker is the State which teaches its people to glorify war.' He spoke of the 'bitterness' he felt when he thought of the many German writers and actors then in exile.

He was to have lectured in Leeds too but he didn't; I can only guess the reason. We now know his activities had come to the notice of the Nazi Government which regarded them as a threat to Anglo-German relations, so much so that they actually wanted the British Government either to expel such political refugees or to threaten them with expulsion. Naturally the British tradition of free speech was upheld, but it is just possible that a discreet hint was dropped to Toller and his friends.

I of course knew nothing of these secret Anglo-German exchanges, and my ignorance was truly bliss. For I too was engaging in 'activities threatening Anglo-German relations', simply by writing (under various *noms de plume*) letters to the *Yorkshire Post* in which I tried to expose Hitler's lies by simply confronting them with his true thought as expressed in his book *Mein Kampf*. It was there that could be found, in the plainest possible terms, the spirit which was dominating German policy. Later I was pleased to read in Churchill's memoirs that in those days 'there was no book which deserved more careful study'. Precisely this was my view, and I was acting on it.

Much later I heard that, in the first few months of 1933, as part of the cunningly devised campaign of fraudulent propaganda, the German press had been forbidden to publish any 'unauthorised quotations' from *Mein Kampf*.

I had asked my parents to send me a copy and I devoted tireless attention to it, far more than to any of my sewing machines. I probably knew many of the salient passages by heart. Nazi propaganda had made sure that the full text was then barely known outside Germany – in England only in a specially licensed, severely misleading because heavily emasculated (and by no means even literally correct) 'translation'. The blatant discrepancy between the letter of Nazi foreign policy and the spirit of Nazi ideology was of course the decisive issue in those years, and in exposing it I was hitting at the very heart of the matter, though I could hardly realise just *how* vital it was (and how unavailing my efforts). It now seems to me that it was the failure in these years to grasp the character of Hitler's ambition that eventually produced the much maligned endeavours of appeasement. In fairness, Neville Chamberlain could only build on the foundations laid by Stanley Baldwin who, alas, took no interest in foreign affairs. The man who at least opened the umbrella received the blame which by rights belonged to the man whose all too genial pipe blew the clouds of delusion.

One day, thanks to an introduction by Professor Brodetsky, I was received in audience by the eminently dignified editor, Mr Arthur Mann, who seemed to be interested in my letters. He thought I was 'a good controversialist' with 'a logical mind'. We talked a little about Germany, and I shall not soon forget the slightly hesitant, almost incredulous tone as he summed up the gruelling facts, 'So you think Herr Hitler's declarations of good will are all so much moonshine?' It was for me a memorable moment – I was enlarging my vocabulary by one word: I had never known before that moonshine might have a meaning so strangely unromantic.

Nor did I then know, and only learnt later from a distinguished British journalist, Iverach McDonald, that Mann was undeterred by 'violent protests from readers and shareholders' – all pukka Conservatives – who disliked his 'attacks on the appalling weakness of the Conservative Government in facing Hitler.' I did know, because I saw the printed evidence, that in those days (1935–37) a good many gullible people were taken in by Nazi propaganda, especially after they had been on a visit to Germany.

One of them, I regret to say, was a local Anglican cleric, the Revd Yate Allen, Vicar of Moss, near Doncaster. He had swallowed all the lies about the Jews. He knew of their 'alleged persecution', but, he reported on his return, 'it has been largely brought about by the Jews themselves' as 'many of them were avowed Communists', etc. Just what the doctor (Goebbels) ordered. Others came back telling us

117

all about the 'Strength through Joy' trips for workers and parroting Hitler's soothing assurances that of course he was all for peace.

I referred them to Hitler's book which, naturally, none of them had read. I recalled the Nazi boast that 'no one who has not read *Mein Kampf* knows what National Socialism is and what it wants.' Therefore, I wrote, if Hitler now claimed (as he unblushingly did) that 'National Socialist Germany desires peace from its innermost philosophical convictions', it must be realised that *Mein Kampf* glorifies force, the 'German sword' and the 'mailed fist'. As we had just seen murder made 'a legitimate political weapon' (in the massacre on 30 June 1934 of storm trooper chief Ernst Röhm and hundreds of his associates, many alleged to be homosexuals) so too lies were 'officially recognised arguments.' I repeatedly quoted Rudyard Kipling's remarks about 'State-controlled murder and torture, open and secret, within and without the borders of the State.' I also referred to Sir Eyre Crowe's famous Foreign Office Memorandum of 1907, unaware of course that this historic document was then being used, just as ineffectually, by Sir Robert Vansittart, Permanent Under-Secretary of State for Foreign Affairs, and many stimulating parallels were found in the less well-known book by Emil Reich, *Germany's Swelled Head* (London 1914) which offered a devastating criticism of the Wilhelminian mentality.

At that time I also discovered in the central public library a book dealing with the 1914 German atrocities in Belgium, and I remember thinking: ah, this is what we were told at school was English propaganda – all lies. Now with the Nazi barbarism in mind, I had second thoughts: perhaps it had not all been 'lying propaganda'. I also noted with interest a reference to those atrocities in the *Yorkshire Post*'s column 'Twenty Years Ago', where the Mayor of Dinant was stated to have mentioned them now in a memorial speech saying 'Dinant does not forget, the children of Dinant do not forgive. Even today the butchers show no repentance and do not confess their guilt.' I was tempted to revive

118

these memories in my letters. However, I resisted the temptation and decided to concentrate on the record of infamy of which I had first-hand experience.

In February 1936 I wrote: 'Don't let us make fools of ourselves ... Was it not rather humiliating that the British Prime Minister had twice within one year to admit misjudgment and misinformation?' I quoted from a recent biography of King Albert of Belgium in which the author, M. Cammaerts, told how the king 'wisely ignored a series of German official denials that Germany had any intention of violating Belgian neutrality in case of war', and it seemed to the writer 'somewhat difficult to believe that this series of statements could have been made in sincerity'. I said that little had changed since then in this respect except that 'today we are in the happier position to know exactly the German aim beforehand. They are explained in every desirable minuteness in Hitler's book *Mein Kampf*.'

Consequently, I argued, we had 'only ourselves to blame if we are stupid enough to be deceived by the claptrap of official German declarations' (1935), and I concluded one of my 1936 letters with these words: 'As long as Hitler holds one whit of power, I emphasize and am firmly convinced that one way or the other he is bound to bring war and will bring war', for his 'words may give life but the spirit killeth'.

Alas, I did not convince people. I was told for example – an echo of Nazi propaganda, this – that quoting *Mein Kampf* was 'hardly fair, as in the dozen years since the book was written Hitler may have modified his views somewhat, as we all do, with experience and the passage of years. We are just as likely to "make fools of ourselves" by not realising this as by rigid adherence to "backnumber" statements.'

Having repeatedly documented the character of Nazi policy, I invoked John Bright speaking on partisanship in the American Civil War: 'You wish the freedom of your country. You wish it for yourselves. You strive for it in many ways. Do not then give the hand of fellowship to the worst foes of freedom the world has ever seen, and do not, I beseech you, bring down a curse upon your cause which no after-penitence can ever lift from it.'

This was the spirit that drove me. I was full of it, haunted by it, beset by the then quite unreasonable hope that I might prevail over the 'enlightened mentality of 1936' paraded for my benefit. I was crying in the wilderness. I had to resign myself to an unkind fate. I was reminded of all this later when I came upon Winston Churchill's confession in *The Gathering Storm*: 'To be so entirely convinced and vindicated in a matter of life and death to one's country, and not to be able to make Parliament and the nation heed the warning ... was an experience most painful.'

Now these letters to the *Yorkshire Post* had a postscript – many years later. I feel I should mention it here because it is, in its way, relevant to the history (and the misery) of the time. After the war, in 1952, I described this experience, as part of my Leeds memories, in an article which appeared in the journal of the Association of Jewish Refugees. It seemed to me that, in their limited way, my letters were an act of resistance. I tried after all to arouse people to an understanding of the realities with which they were confronted, pathetically hoping that if thus warned, they would act in good time. Had I and others like me succeeded, the disaster that befell all of us might well have been averted.

But the reaction, even among my fellow-refugees, was very different. I was severely taken to task by one who commented as follows; he 'apparently does not know that it is most improper for any non-British subject to meddle into any political question or write any letters on any political subject to any paper and he would indeed have been much better advised to keep his mouth shut and ... leave the country ... This type of refugee is most unwanted here.' This was said by one who himself had suffered persecution and who now enjoyed the freedom of a country whose very survival was at stake.

There is occasionally talk of anti-Nazi resistance among

120

German Jews, invariably asking, how much of it was there? If my critic's behaviour was an example, the question must rather be, how *little* of it was there? For what sort of resistance would he have approved of? Come to think of it, how deserving was he of freedom? Or had he, having escaped, not rather chosen to remain a slave?

His was a reaction not under duress, not in fear of the Gestapo, but long after the end of the war, in England where men are free and we all knew what had happened, even to Jews. Is it not legitimate to wonder how that craven mind would have reacted to any stir of Jewish protest, Jewish resistance, let alone Jewish revolt, under Nazi tyranny? I was indeed grateful for the refuge I had found here, and in writing my letters I think I may in fairness claim I was trying to repay my debt. Surely I was entitled to a modest measure of appreciation, but not of course from the likes of this wretch. I confess the recollection of this incident leaves me with a degrading nausea.

Incidentally, no one ever guessed who the anonymous correspondent might be, least of all that it might be one whose mother tongue was not English. I was intrigued when, in an argument with an admirer of Lord Halifax, I jocularly mentioned Carlyle's reference to 'the population of England consisting of 30 million people, mostly fools', and I was thought to have 'faintly echoed Carlyle's style'! I did not then know much about Carlyle – except that I remembered his famous letter to *The Times* congratulating 'noble, patient, deep, pious and solid Germany' on her victory in 1870 over 'vapouring, vainglorious, gesticulating, quarrelsome, restless and over-sensitive France'; that letter, extolling 'the hopefullest public fact that has occurred in my time', was presented by my history master as an example of the world's approval of German policies, though I would not now have thought much of the Chelsea sage's Teuton infatuation, and as for the mannerisms of his style, I would hardly have been anxious to emulate them.

I also sent to the *Yorkshire Post* letters signed 'Not Fascinated' attacking the then very vocal propaganda of

Mosley's British Union of Fascists who, believe it or not, presented Fascism as 'a movement of persuasion and conviction', seeking 'the suffrage of the nation to elect a Fascist Government in a constitutional way', etc. I recalled, as an illustration, Dr Goebbels' boast that Nazi Germany (with its concentration camps) had 'the finest form of modern democracy' in that Hitler's Government, having been called to power by the people, 'feels itself just as responsible to the people.' I extensively referred to the writings of Mosley's much admired friend Mussolini who was glorifying violence and war (just then demonstrated in the conquest of Abyssinia), and by contrast I quoted from the Letters of Junius which I mentioned before – from his letters and those of 'Philo-Junius' (printed in the same volume). This knowledge helped me much in my campaign (if I may call it so) but it also caused me some embarrassment.

I hoped to be reinforcing my argument by also writing in as a supporter of 'Not Fascinated'. I was not doing my job very professionally, though. I was promptly debunked by the Chief Assistant Editor who wrote back saying that 'on comparison of the handwritings, there arises a very strong presumption that your postcard – signed C.C. – and the letters of "Not Fascinated" were written by the same hand. In the same handwriting we have also had letters signed R.T. ... In these circumstances we regret that in the absence of any explanation from you we cannot print the postcard.'

I owned up and the reply was that 'while no newspaper favours multiple pseudonymity, especially where a writer under one name praises himself under another', in my case 'there was so complete an absence of any attempt to conceal from us what you were doing that the Editor will probably take the view that your action was merely due to your being unaware of English custom in such matters.' Oddly enough, I had assumed the precise opposite, thinking of 'Philo-Junius' whom I had always regarded as identical with Junius. Apparently I was wrong; this merely seemed to me a precedent which I considered safe to follow.

But the idea of my anti-Nazi resistance by way of writing letters to the press exposing Hitler's designs gave me some comfort and perhaps a little solace even though I never thought of the effect I might be producing. I felt I had to do it for its own sake. Of the effect I learnt later when I realised that, in however modest a manner, the biter had been bitten and that his own inhuman behaviour was recoiling on him. On this subject I wrote an article which I have here reproduced as an Appendix because I believe it carries a hopeful lesson.

*    *    *

I wrote not only letters to the *Yorkshire Post* but also, occasionally, articles for the Berlin *Israelitisches Familienblatt* which was then edited by Rabbi Joachim Prinz. One of these articles dealt with the British fascists who were then (1936) quite conspicuous, especially in the East End of London. The article was strictly factual, based on extracts from fascist literature which I had studied. Perhaps for this reason it sounded so unusual that an editorial preface presented it as a contribution to the understanding of current affairs, and the point was made that however unpalatable some of the facts, being facts they had to be faced.

It was an only too well warranted caveat, for when the article was read by a Berlin businessman recently settled in Leeds, who did not seem to have heard of British Fascists, he fancied, like the schoolboy seeing a giraffe for the first time, that 'there ain't no such animals', so he severely disapproved and complained to the Committee's Viceroy. Who was I to write such an article?, he wanted to know. What did I really know about the subject? He would meet more English people in one day than I in a month. The Jewish paper had printed the piece only because they had nothing else to fill their pages. If anybody were competent to discuss the matter, then it should be one of the notables in the Leeds refugee community, such learned academics as 'Doctors' X, Y and Z, etc.

I was promptly summoned into the Viceroy's august

presence, and on the evidence before him which he was no more able to read than to assess, he told me that being a mere factory hand I had no business to write such articles, or for that matter any articles, and in appropriately high excitement, tempered only by the careful attention with which he was winding up the precious bulging bales of newly arrived cloth, he added: 'I am going to get rid of you! I send you back to Germany!'

I don't suppose he quite knew what he was saying or if he did, meant it. I like to think that the London Committee would have stopped him from acting on his foolish threat. (It so happened at that time there was some uproar when a Polish-born Jew claimed he had been threatened by a provincial Jewish chief he would be 'deported' – it turned out (or so it was said) he was threatened with being 'reported'.)

After the German attempt to stifle the freedom of opinion in Britain, it seemed sad (though not surprising) to come up against a Jewish attempt to curb freedom among Jews. But then theory and practice do not always move in tandem as was shown on a different occasion. Anti-German feeling was organised in Leeds so far as the prevailing political conditions permitted. A Jewish Representative Council for the Boycott of German Goods had to struggle in the face of British Jewry's official indecision largely due to fear of Nazi reprisals. Some Jewish firms also were by no means in sympathy and I happened to know of some that were not averse to doing business with the enemy. The melancholy fact brought home to me the inadequacy of economic boycotts generally. However great the ideological enthusiasm (for instance among the black states fighting South African apartheid), it will rarely stand up to the lures of material interests.

*   *   *

At about this time, I happened to notice a new book entitled *Greek Ideals and Modern Life*, by Sir R. W. Livingstone. I cannot say what made me choose it in the public library. I might have been expected to be more inclined towards

Hebrew ideals and modern life, for on them I had been brought up and certainly in Leeds I had plenty to reflect on them. But perhaps it was the very contrast that attracted me as I have always tried to approach truth from opposite ends. I had learnt at school about Greek philosophy, it was part of my education but apparently it was not to be part of my life, for Jewish education taught that Greek ideas were opposed by the Maccabees as a manifestation of crass paganism. Perhaps, it occurred to me, this was true in those days but today it seemed to me that Greek ideals, like Hebrew ideals, were not dependent on space and time, they were world-encircling human ideals that bore a timeless challenge to all of us.

I was pleased to read in Livingstone's book: 'The only reasoned views of life which Europe knows come from Greece and from Palestine ... Greece starts at the human end. In building up an ethical system, Plato begins with human psychology... They work from the seen to the unseen. Palestine begins at the opposite end and works from God down to man.' This I thought was a very true remark, but the two did not seem necessarily impossible to reconcile. I was reminded of Jacob's dream about the ladder set up on earth, with its top reaching to heaven, and the angels ascending and descending on it. This was, I thought, how our ideas travel, even if we are not angels, ascending and descending, for ever changing direction. So too I understood the grand confrontation which I now encountered for the first time, never to forget it, of 'Hebraism' and 'Hellenism' as Matthew Arnold defined it: 'The uppermost idea with Hellenism is to see things as they really are, the uppermost idea with Hebraism is conduct and obedience... The governing idea of Hellenism is spontaneity of consciousness; that of Hebraism, strictness of conscience.'

The two concepts seemed to me not excluding but rather complementing each other; and I could not accept the opinion I sometimes heard of those who were deprecating 'Greek wisdom' as if it were something to be eschewed.

125

Among the famous 'Sayings of the Fathers' I was taught at an early age, I remembered the very simple one by Rabbi Ben Zoma 2,000 years ago: 'Who is wise? He who learns from all men.' I at least could not visualise wisdom bearing a sectional label; if it was true of anything it was certainly true of wisdom that there is 'neither East nor West, nor breed nor birth', and few things ever seemed to expose Nazi absurdity as much as the hankering after 'German physics' and 'Aryan mathematics'. I thought wisdom was, whatever its origins, something to be desired, to be cherished and treasured as a possession for ever.

An example was the idea of tragedy which then often occupied me, not only in connection with the theatre on which I read Coleridge's *Progress of the Drama*, but also in a very general way, and I wondered about the difference between the Greek and the Hebrew concept of tragedy. As I understood it, the essence of it, according to the Greeks, was the conflict not between Right and Wrong but between Right and Right. The conflict resolves itself in a combination of pity and terror which purges the soul of every passion and so hopes to produce that harmony of human life which I think is at the heart of the Greek ideal.

It seems to me that Jews do not recognise this sort of tragic conflict. They do not admit a clash of Right and Right but so far as they are concerned, the issue is every time clear cut between Right and Wrong. Where the Greeks aim at harmony, Jews proclaim holiness; where the Greeks behold fate, Jews struggle with destiny; where the Greeks can see both sides, Jews see only one, enjoining strict obedience to the law as interpreted by often differing authorities.

In any conflict, we seem to hold, man must be either right or wrong – all according to whether the anger of the Lord was kindled against him. Israel frequently enough was so chastised. Our exile was ordained because of our sins. One of the best known Hebrew prayers says it (rightly or wrongly): 'On account of our sins we were exiled from our land,' etc., and yet the otherwise relatively indifferent Roman who destroyed the Temple, Titus, is gratuitously dubbed 'wicked', as if that most poignant tragedy in which he, far from any personal ill will, found himself professionally involved, were a conflict not of Right versus Right but of Wrong versus Wrong. It seemed to me that if the Greek definition is accepted, tragedy is not really a Jewish conceit, and if the Jewish definition is acknowledged, it seems no wonder Jews often show so little tolerance.

But if the Jews' story in their 2,000 years of exile is not a tragedy, what is it? I cannot attempt to answer the question, any more than another, related question that has often intrigued me – the challenge of religion to logic, or vice versa. There are obvious contradictions between the two. God clearly moves in mysterious ways and human reason cannot hope to follow them. I am not a philosopher and I cannot reconcile the contradictions. All I know is that when I read Scripture, it is impossible for me to shut out my critical mind. God does not seem entirely beyond our understanding, and as Abraham argued with him and God was prepared to listen and in fact graciously conceded points sensibly made, so I also feel free to criticise. God is not infallible; according to the Bible, he often repented of what he had done (for example, Genesis 6:6, Jeremiah 26:19, Jonah 3:10), and he cannot in fairness resent being held to account as he was by the famous Victorian Thomas Hardy: 'The Supreme Power or Movers, the Prime Force or Forces, must be either limited in power, unknowing or cruel – which is obvious enough and has been for centuries.' He must put up with strictures, and while we respect tradition, we can never dismiss interpretations that will recognise an advance of man's reason and understanding. We are not in every way the people we were 3,000 years ago and God does not speak to us now as he spoke then. We do not for example believe that adulterers, any more than disobedient sons, deserve to be stoned, that a priest's daughter who 'profanes herself' shall be 'burnt with fire' (Leviticus 21:9), nor is the death penalty regarded by all of us as a deterrent. The Second Commandment tells us of a 'jealous God visiting the iniquity of the fathers upon the children unto the third and fourth generation', but Ezekiel, the Prophet among the exiles in Babylon, thought differently. 'The soul that sins, it shall die. The son shall not bear the iniquity of the father, neither shall the father bear the iniquity of the son.'

The difference between 'ancient and modern' may also be illustrated by a more lighthearted example. When an interested and knowledgeable Christian friend of ours was shown round the synagogue for the first time, he made a careful note of everything he saw but then enquired, somewhat hesitantly, where did we keep the animals? The animals? Which animals? Well, he explained, the animals required for the sacrifices as prescribed by the Law of Moses...

The teachers of the law make every effort to pass it on as a continuing, valid way of life, one that will take account of human progress in a variety of 'traditional alternatives'; in doing so they cannot get away from the fact that while the letter of the law is ancient, the spirit is ever new, blowing where it listeth, even at the risk of falling into the clutches of 'the devil', as Heine says about Faust's encounter, 'the struggle between religion and science, between authority and reason, between believing and thinking'.

I was aware of that struggle when I read some of the Bible commentators who, frankly, amazed me. I set down my reflections in a few articles which, like any odd 'undesirable alien', were firmly kept out of the Jewish press. I reproduce one of them now.

## NONSENSE COMMENTATORS

I suppose we all rather like reading nonsense at times, certainly the Nonsense Rhymes of Edward Lear's, and when it comes to prose we rarely have a choice when we look into some of our daily papers. If (as has been said) true nonsense is 'rather specially an English achievement', because 'nonsense is extravagant', then many of our Bible commentators may fairly claim to be (naturalised) Englishmen of the Hebrew persuasion.

They provide an example at the very beginning. Why does Genesis start with the creation of the world?, Rashi, one of the foremost medieval commentators, asks and he replies: it is to justify the allocation of the Holy Land to Israel, because surely the creator of the world can assign any part of it to whomsoever he desires. True, only the text does not say so, does not even suggest it, and if the land can be allocated, what about the people living in it who should be at least as worthy of consideration as the land? Actually, the only statement God is reported to have made is not 'Let there be Israel' but 'Let there be light', light to reveal that the world was created for all men – a fact that confers so much greater sense on the stature of the Hebrew Bible.

But Rashi has his own way of interpreting events, and as he shows it at the beginning of the five books, so he does at the end. There it says 'Moses was buried', but as literally the words mean 'he buried him' (which some say mean that God did it), Rashi comes up with the interpretation that 'Moses buried himself'. Unfortunately he does not linger over this intriguing phenomenon which must surely rank as one of the major miracles in both the Old and the New Testament, opening up undreamt-of vistas of life after death. Few commentators can have reached similar depths in digging for the truth.

Since the sailor's experience is notoriously fertile ground for fancy, a fair share of nonsense has been inspired by the story of Noah. While much and hackneyed comment is devoted to relatively insignificant matters (such as that Noah walked *with* God but Abraham *before* him, or Noah was 'righteous' but only 'in his generations'), surprisingly little attention is attracted by the central fact that God decided to

129

destroy mankind indiscriminately – 'both man and beast and creeping thing and fowl of the air'. Noah did not even attempt to argue with God as Abraham did at Sodom and Gomorrah, and Rashi refines the indifference by making God say: 'I have now to agree with those who urged me at his creation, What is man that thou art mindful of him?' (Psalm 8:5)

Now this strikes me as not just ordinary but quite extraordinary nonsense. Who were they who quoted the then non-existing psalm? Those dubious counsellors certainly gave it a cruelly callous twist, justifying merciless mass destruction when in fact what is conveyed by the psalmist is man's humility while beholding 'his own infinitesimal smallness against the vastness of the galaxies' (Samson R. Hirsch) – a thought which so far from suggesting, let alone justifying, destruction, ought to redound to the honour and glory of man. That man so conceived should be held indiscriminately undeserving of mercy, regardless of his action and behaviour, seems to me frankly outrageous, and no hair-splitting distinction can here make sense of a God either of 'justice' or of 'mercy', for it is neither.

It is so as little as there is logic in raising the Flood to drown man as 'corrupt' and yet hoping to create a new one while retaining the old model (Noah). Besides, if man is undeserving of mercy, why reproduce him? Any Second Chance is bound to be doomed as the proclaimed root cause of the evil, the violence, remains.

Nor are the animals getting a better deal. If they too had to be destroyed, it is because they too had 'corrupted their way', Rashi says. He does not explain how but proceeds to offer an 'alternative' reason for their wholesale destruction: they – though not all of them – had been 'created for man's use', and 'since man was to be destroyed, there was no need for them'. Is it fanciful to regard this utilitarian reasoning as specious? Surely animals, all of them, were not just

130

created to satisfy man's appetite and needs; they are entitled to a life of their own, indeed 'the righteous regards the life of his beast' (Proverbs 12:10), not for any selfish reasons, one likes to think, and therefore to suggest that since man was to perish, they too could go hang, must again seem callous nonsense. A sage of the *Jewish Chronicle* tells of a story that Noah was practising 'charity' in the Ark by staying up day and night to feed each animal – while all the time giving no charitable thought to the creatures drowned outside. They were considered dispensable, perishing pointlessly too, for if they, like man, had been 'corrupt', then those that came after them were so no less.

Inside the Ark, apart from the scouting dove, only one had a bit of an adventurous career, the raven that 'went forth to and fro': it kept returning to the Ark, says Rashi, 'because it suspected Noah of having designs upon its mate'. What sort of designs, one may wonder, and why only on the raven? We are not told. Was it because (as Rashi says) Noah had 'degraded himself' through drink?

Or was it perchance anything to do with sex? The question is not as strange as it may appear, for sex is very much on Rashi's mind and he may conceivably have made a good disciple of Freud. When we are told that 'Noah went into the Ark with his sons and his wife and his sons' wives', Rashi comments: 'The men separately and the women separately because they were forbidden intimacy when the whole world was in distress.' The text does not refer to any such injunction. It would rather seem a gratuitous surmise, possibly based on the belief that unless securely separated, men and women will insist on intimacy, anywhere. Actually if anything can be surmised (and were worth surmising), it is just as likely that there was no separation, and in view of the world-wide distress this little crumb of comfort was indeed not *verboten*.

However, the problem much exercises Rashi's mind.

The thought of it occurs to him when he reads (Genesis 41:50) that 'unto Joseph were born two sons before the years of famine came'. Quite an indifferent, innocuous piece of information, we may think, but not so Rashi. According to him, 'from this we learn that one may not cohabit in time of famine.' I do not know whether this prohibition figures among the frequently cited 613 rules and regulations, but if a link between famine and cohabitation can indeed be construed, it would seem (one hopes) more likely in favour than against.

Rashi's odd concern with sex also appears in his comment on Joseph's meeting with his brothers (Genesis 45:4): 'Seeing them hang back, he spoke gently to them and showed them that he was circumcised.' Though the Egyptians probably did not have the equivalent of our laws against 'indecent exposure', it does seem highly improbable that Joseph would have behaved in the manner indicated, even assuming that it was an effective method of establishing his identity. Surely the fact that he was speaking in Hebrew was sufficient, though admittedly Rashi's version adds pep to the occasion.

The commentary on other matters often leaves room for improvement. That 'the Lord gave Solomon wisdom', is of course well known, but when Kimchi quotes 1 Kings 5:26 as 'stressing that it was displayed in his vast building operations', the statement makes no good sense, not only because of the deplorable resort to forced labour which must have been a reminder of the bondage in Egypt, but also because we now know, with the experience of our own time, that 'vast building operations' do not necessarily demonstrate wisdom. The European dictators were not notorious for their wisdom but their building operations, meant to outlast the millennia, were certainly vast, the magnificent *Autobahnen* guiding the deadly raids of the RAF.

In his commentary on a different chapter of history,

132

'the bitter enmity of the Edomites to Israel' (as referred to by the prophet Obadiah), Hertz says it was 'particularly inexcusable because of their common descent'. But it happens to be a characteristic of bitter enmity that it rages *especially* between people of common descent, beginning with Cain and Abel. In our own time, no two nations have fought each other with greater ferocity than those two ill-starred cousins, Germany and England. Yet eventually they relented. The enmity that remained is not between peoples and men but rather between concepts of life, between good and evil, and who will say which faction will always stand for the one and which for the other?

Of course commentators will always be found to oblige with suitable interpretations since words lend themselves to a motley of meanings. What Heinrich Graetz, the historian, said in a different context, may well be understood as a timeless truth: 'The interpretation of the Scriptures was a power which was able to make the greatest nonsense acceptable and the least credible things appear necessary.'

*   *   *

On the whole I kept in good health except once when I contracted in Leeds an eczema on the left leg which a doctor mistreated, over a number of weeks, to such an extent that the leg began to swell to twice its size. Eventually I insisted on being taken to hospital where the application of one particular, olive-green ointment restored the natural size literally overnight. The gourd in the story of Jonah could not have changed its condition with greater dispatch though I needed five weeks to recover completely. I retain a most affectionate memory of one of my nurses, the appropriately named Nurse Darling, who confided to me not only that she wished she could speak English the way I did (!) but also that it was her great ambition to work in an asylum. I never knew whether she felt I would then be an ideal object of her care.

Another memorable experience was the very slight toothache which made me feel I might need a filling. As I could

133

not afford a dentist, I went to the dental department of the Victorian Royal Infirmary where you paid the flat rate of 6d ($2^1/_2$p) which covered everything. Having passed time in what was to be regarded as a waiting room, we, a gang of about twenty, were herded into another room where each sat down on a backless block to await professional review. In due course an inspector arrived, taking as it were the salute by ordering each one of us to open their mouths wide whereupon he would pronounce treatment. When my turn came he pointed decisively at three teeth, saying they would have to come out, and before I could start gasping I found myself in the equivalent of an electric chair, made unconscious by gas, and the next thing I knew was an order to go next door, lie down on the wooden couch and stop the profuse bleeding by continuously rinsing with a glass of water that was kindly supplied. I am glad to report I did not feel the worse for it and after a while managed to get up and launch myself on a twenty minutes' walk home where my landlady at once recognised my need for a cup of tea which, as the saying then went, would 'revive' me.

Meanwhile I gradually came to the conclusion that, in spite of much conscientious if fatuous effort, I could hardly hope for a future as a sewing machine mechanic. Clearly this was not the sort of work I was cut out for. The bell was beginning to toll for me. Even while I was supposed to be earning my mechanic's wage (£1.10s which never varied in three years), I was busy thinking about the subjects I would be writing on to the *Yorkshire Post*, composing my letters, scribbling them down on the empty, usually dirty cigarette packets with which my colleagues generously provided me.

These scribbles would be copied at home or, if it was too cold, in a small café nearby, then, first thing next morning, delivered by hand. Then again, after tomorrow, I would wait in the public library to look up the paper as I could not afford to buy it every day, and then somebody would be reading it – the sports page perhaps of all pages – with no hope of early withdrawal, and here was I waiting in mighty impatience: was not horse racing a calamity and football a curse! But then, at long last, I would get my chance, and with the solemnity due to the occasion, I would slowly turn the pages until I found the letter – had not been printed.

Still, enough of them had been printed to encourage me to think of my future as a journalist, and I twice plucked up courage to apply to the *Post* for a chance of some practical training. I was, however, unlucky: neither in 1936 nor in 1937 was there any vacancy (or so I was told), and none of my established knowledge, talent or experience was considered to be a likely asset. I had no choice but to seek my fortune elsewhere.

But where? I was to have been trained as a sewing machine mechanic so as to merit a Certificate for emigration to Palestine. That training had been a shambles, and had I emigrated on the strength of this Certificate, I would have been acting on utterly false pretences. Return to Germany was out of the question. I certainly was not to join the family again, as the parents devoutly wished. Little did they know of my feelings in that respect. Yet the idea of Palestine was still bestriding my mind, and in the welter of my frustration and confusion, I was at one time prepared to 'go home' – for a very specific, strictly limited time and purpose: to take advantage of the more intense preparations for life in Palestine that were available in Berlin, more especially to acquire a competent command of modern Hebrew.

My parents made enquiries. They were told by the Berlin authorities – in September 1935, the month of the Nuremberg Laws – that if I came only 'on transit' as it were, if I could prove that I was on my way to Palestine, if I could show that I had been trained in England, plus another couple of 'ifs', then there would be no objection to a limited stay. I was amazed when I heard this. I noted in my diary: 'Quite apart from the fact that where Jews are concerned a German promise is no promise, how can I be sure that they will believe me, regardless of any proof that I may be able

135

to produce?', etc. I had actually read in the *Daily Telegraph* that some German Jewish youngsters back from abroad were sent to a concentration camp; this must have been in March 1935.

So having mulled for a while over the idea of a temporary visit to Berlin, I dismissed the whole thing. I decided that my future must lie in England. I resolved to leave Leeds and return to London. Beyond all doubt I was wasting my time. Beset by frustrations everywhere and seeing no chance of progress, I was getting restive. I should have gone long since, even though I had no prospects at all in London. If it was a move into the unknown and I could only hope for 'something to turn up', I felt I must trust my stars: they would guide me.

# 5

# VIA LONDON TO AMSTERDAM

I had travelled to London twice in my holidays, to meet my
mother who wanted to hear what my plans were. I could
not tell her much but I did what I could to urge her and
through her the family to think of getting out of Germany,
remarking (much to her chagrin) that I would never return.
But she would not hear of it. Like thousands of German
Jews then she refused to believe the worst could happen.
Among the stories she told me was one about Herr Köhler,
our greengrocer; he had said that if he were a Jew and his
people were treated the way the Jews were, he would lose
all faith in God.

There were many like him, perhaps millions – but what
did, what could, they do? Mother seemed to be putting
implicit trust in these 'good people': things couldn't go on
the way they did, surely, and when I stubbornly refused to
come back – I can't, I said – she implored me why can't I?
'This is your *home*, is it not?' she wrote in one of her letters:
'It is *our* home, the home of our forefathers...', and she
would always be there whenever I needed her and happy
to help her children find their way into the future ... Yes, I
knew, and never could I have any doubt on that score, not
the slightest. But a time was when I also had to make my

137

own decision – I had been driven to leave that accursed land which Mother said was 'our home'. This is what I had done, *had* to do, and never would I, could I, turn back.

*   *   *

Once, in the summer of 1936, she came with my younger sister, then fourteen, who had a talent for drawing. It was the year of Edward VIII's kingship and in July he presented colours to three battalions of the Guards in a grand parade in Hyde Park. Flo went there to see all the pomp and circumstance, and she managed to get herself a sufficiently advantageous position to do a portrait of the king in his splendid uniform complete with the magnificent bearskin. She showed it to me and I immediately suggested she send it to Buckingham Palace. The idea electrified her, her eyes were glistening: indeed, could she really do that? Promptly the drawing was dispatched to its exalted destination.

Now a tense time of waiting began – until one day the reply arrived in a suitably large envelope with, perhaps ominously, a heavy black border: it was the time of mourning for George V. The black border might just as well have been chosen for our special benefit. The Private Secretary thanked us for the kind thought but unfortunately, etc.

Flo was crestfallen beyond words, and I thought why did they *have* to show so little regard for the child's fine effort. Why this crude red tape? They might have kept the sheet – to throw it away like many other no doubt innumerable humdrum tokens of respect for the sovereign and just acknowledged receipt in some routinely 'well-chosen words'. Such a formality would have been appreciated in measureless pride, and the budding artist would have been able to rejoice in the great feeling, however fictitious, that the King of England had deigned to receive with pleasure her loyal gift. Alas, it was not the only unhappy memory that has remained of the reign of Edward VIII.

My older sister had been in London since 1934 when she came with our mother, and she had a good position with the Central Bureau for the Settlement of German Jews (operating under the Jewish Agency for Palestine). I was thinking of a job with the *Palestine* (now *Jerusalem*) *Post*; its editor was in principle prepared to take me on once I had the necessary technical training which the Central Bureau together with the Refugees Committee tried to arrange for me. But nothing came of it, even after I had pursued my hopes at the Zionist Congress in Zurich where I met some people to whom I reckoned I might be able to make myself useful. It was a sterile attempt. The only gain I brought back was (as I noted in my diary) an impression, judging by what I had seen and heard, that Jews collectively did not seem mature for democracy, and if their State was to be a democratic experiment, then I feared this might well be a reason why it could founder. I still have that fear because there is lacking that essential element without which no society can long hope to survive – tolerance, not so much between Jew and Arab but rather between Jew and Jew, orthodox and non-orthodox.

Back in London, I, alone or through intermediaries, approached several papers which I fancied might offer some opening, however slight, either in London or overseas, but without success. I advertised, in the *Daily Telegraph* and the trade paper *World's Press News*, and I replied to adverts. Nothing doing, not even translations, proof reading, office chores or other casual labour. One editor told me they were a Union paper wherefore he could consider only members of the National Union of Journalists – and membership there was open only to those who worked for a paper. So there I was, locked up in a vicious circle. When I wrote to Wickham Steed, the one-time famous editor of *The Times*, he had no practical proposition but obliged me with this gratuitous advice: I must write my way on to the press by proving that I had something to say and could say it. That was how he himself had begun, and he quoted the advice given to him by the renowned W. T. Stead that when he had written an article he should imagine that it would be cabled to Australia at his own expense, at the rate of 5s. a word. Having thus removed everything superfluous, the article might have a chance – if anything remained of it. I thought that, however irrelevant to my present predicament, it was sound advice coming from so exalted a source, and I have tried to follow it to the best of my ability.

I did not approach Sir Albert Levy again – if only because he had died that year. But I felt so desperate that I wrote to a relative of his who had moved into the same Piccadilly mansion. I might have saved myself the trouble, for back came a note from the secretary shooing away the importunate bum by referring me (again) to the Committee: 'We have written them asking that should you call, they should please do their best to help. We ourselves are unfortunately totally unable...' etc.

As I glance through my diary of those days, I notice two entries – quotes that I had come across as fruits of my reading. They must have struck me at the time as relevant to the state of my mind. Theognis, the Greek philosopher, 500 BC, said: 'Of all things not to be born into the world is best, nor to see the beams of the keen sun; but being born, as swiftly as may be to pass the gates of Hades and be under a heavy heap of earth.' And this from Dr Johnson: 'When I survey my past life, I discover nothing but a barren waste of time, with some disorders of body and disturbances of the mind, very near to madness, which I hope He that made me will suffer to extenuate many faults and excuse many deficiencies.'

I tried to forget my troubles when I joined the refugees club which was run by the West London Synagogue near Marble Arch. Its guiding spirit was Rabbi Harold Reinhart, an artist as well as an efficient and popular leader of his congregation. I remember a grand Chanucah function for which he had written a lively children's play; afterwards he delivered a fiery address extolling the spirit of the Maccabees. The club always attracted large numbers who enjoyed the general atmosphere as well as the delicious food to which we were treated.

I sought other relief in study. I began to draw up something like a genealogy of antisemitism in England, and I

140

frequently visited the Mocatta (now 'Jewish Studies') Library at University College where I usually found myself in solitary confinement: no one appeared to take an interest in Anglo-Jewish history, apart from Cecil Roth, the historian, who would occasionally drop in for what seemed to me a quick reference, undistracted by the unusual sight of a student. I remember with gratitude the College librarian, Mr Scott, who kindly unlocked for me the gates to these treasures. Here I first came across the very excellent book by G. F. Abbott, *Israel in Europe* (1907) of which in 1971 I was able to produce a new edition. Also I made copious notes from the *Jewish Chronicle* for the war years and the 1920s. I was as it were holding my own little seminar on Jewish history in modern England.

In between I tried again a school of journalism. This time the fee was accepted without a test of my English. We were in the midst of the Spanish Civil War, and I wrote two pieces on the then highly topical subject of Fascism – one on 'Fascism in Britain' (which the tutor could understand) and one on 'Fascism among Jews' (which he couldn't).

But of course these essays in theory did not banish reality for long, though things were slowly beginning to look up. I realised that what I must do was try my luck with local papers, study conditions in a given borough and write up stories of specific interest. It was something I had never tried before and I was about to settle down to it when a gratifying windfall offered me some secretarial work for a prominent German Jewish industrialist to whom I was introduced. Salman Schocken, owner of a big German department store, had been a resident of Jerusalem since 1933 but travelled far and wide in pursuit of his interests in London, Amsterdam, Zurich and USA. He was wise to keep clear of Germany where the 'department store Jew' had just been attacked as an 'anti-German boycottmonger'. The double-dyed businessman was also head of the Schocken publishing firm, and his cultured interests were apparent when I noticed in his room at the Dorchester Hotel such books as the *Essays* of Montaigne, Plato's *Republic* and Goethe's *Faust*. He was a strict, exacting master, could be an embarrassingly candid one, but always most generous. He warned me, if I intended to go to Palestine, not to do so until I had acquired a firm command of Hebrew: even then I would find life hard going; he had recently read in the Tel Aviv Labour paper *Davar* the story of two workmen, one remarking that prices were going up all the time, the other replying it did not seem to make much difference as they could not afford to buy anything anyway.

The acquaintance with Schocken which I owed to my sister Frieda was most exhilarating, and later I came to look upon it as an omen of truly good tidings. It seemed to me like the skein of the ocean gulls which Columbus took as a sure sign that, at long last and after much frustration, doubt and almost despair, land was in sight. I was indeed about to reach my goal.

Even while working for Schocken, I met, again through Frieda's good offices, the man who was to give my life the decisive direction – Dr Alfred Wiener, founder of the Institute of Contemporary History known as the Wiener Library. Like Schocken, Dr Wiener called at the Central Bureau whose director, Dr Martin Rosenblüth, was an acquaintance of his from Berlin. As a leader of the *Central Verein* of German Citizens of the Jewish Faith, the foremost Jewish anti-Nazi organisation, Dr Wiener, a Prussian right-wing conservative, had escaped in good time to Amsterdam where he managed to set up, on the basis of his own private library, a Jewish Central Information Office. This he did with the assistance of a leader of Dutch Jewry, Professor David Cohen who occupied a Chair of Ancient History at Amsterdam University and was later one of the heads of the Nazi-appointed Jewish Council.

It was in connection with the work of his Information Office that Wiener came to London in February 1938. The purpose of the Office was 'to collect and disseminate information on the position of the Jews throughout the world, primarily in Germany'. This information was of course

142

designed to be action in the struggle against Nazism, and Wiener, having by great and never daunted effort survived the first four years, was now planning to extend his campaign by establishing something like an English department for which he required a person able to process German material in English. It was a few weeks before the *Anschluss*, Nazi Germany's first international aggression when Austria was annexed, and Wiener sensed the need for an expanded service to cater for a gradually increasing clientele in Britain, USA and other English-speaking countries. That was where I came in. He spotted me immediately in a fairly crowded hotel lounge where we were to meet, and samples of my work satisfied him. Altogether, he later confided to me, a man who had been good enough for Schocken must be good enough for him! So before long I left London for Amsterdam to begin an association which was to last for over a quarter of a century.

I was able to travel to Holland as the correspondent of a London journalist to whom Wiener had been introduced, W. G. J. Knop, foreign news editor of the *Financial News*. I was to supply him with 'essential information, especially on oil and rubber'. He later used much of the material we sent him for his book *Beware of the English!* Knop, as director of a virtually one-man Union Time Ltd, was a protégé of Sir Robert Waley Cohen, the Shell magnate, who in turn was associated with an organisation called Focus for the Defence of Freedom and Peace which counted among its well-wishers Winston Churchill, Lady Violet Bonham Carter, Sir Norman Angell.

As the correspondent of a London paper I could hope for a measure of good will from the notoriously strict *Vreemdelingen Politie* (Aliens Police) who favoured me with fortnightly extensions of my original short-termed *vergunning* (labour permit). Twice, however, their patience gave way and I had to go back to my relatively less marked insecurity in England where I continued to work for the Office until it seemed safe to resume the little cat and mouse game.

The Information Office was situated in the distinguished

south of Amsterdam, in the strictly residential Jan van Eyck Straat where few would have suspected so professional and militant an activity. There was nothing to indicate the presence of a body bearing so portentous a name and indeed an unwritten constitution required it to be as inconspicuous as possible. Heaven knows what the Nazis would have made of it had they ever heard of a Jewish Central Information Office in Amsterdam. At the very least they would have seen here the headquarters of the World Jewish Conspiracy, the veritable Sanhedrin of the 'Elders of Zion', and Holland would have had cause to fear for her neutrality long before it was violated. So everything was very much hush-hush, and strict confidentiality became the hallmark of Jewish Central Information – so much so that the Nazis never knew of it nor found out in all the years of occupation. Nor did they trace any of the Office correspondence in any of the European capitals they occupied; even when they searched Cohen's flat in May 1940 they did not discover anything.

Wiener felt that much useful information could be extracted from German publications not otherwise readily available, especially those little known outside Germany – the provincial press, trade journals, also of course books, brochures, etc., for which he as a bibliophile had a well trained eye. So I 'processed' not only the SS paper *Das Schwarze Korps* but also among others the *Hitler Jugend* paper *Der Stürmer*, dailies like *Hamburger Tageblatt*, *Westdeutscher Beobachter* (Cologne), *Hakenkreuz-Banner* (Mannheim); also *Der Deutsche im Ausland* ('Germans Abroad', dealing with Nazi activities all over the world); the Nazi 'German Christian' weekly *Deutscher Sonntag* and the ingenuously anti-Nazi *Allgemeine Evangelisch-Lutherische Kirchenzeitung*.

On this last-named paper I should like to say a special word. Few utterances have more deeply moved me than the leading article which appeared there after the nationwide pogrom of 9–10 November 1938. It was – on the surface – purely an exercise in theology, a sermon seemingly unconcerned with topical events which were barely

144

hinted at. Its title was 'Of the End of the World', with the motto from Matthew 24:14; 'And then will come the end'. The unfortunately unknown author, who must have been a kinsman of the Hebrew prophets, was thinking not only of the terrible crime that had just been committed but also of the official gloating satisfaction and rejoicing over the blow that had been delivered at 'World Jewry'. Reproving those who – after Munich and the pogrom – had been 'high with exultation', he interpreted the 'dark signs' as follows: 'People before the Flood also were high with exultation, but then the Flood came and did away with them all. Mankind is being blinded with false joy. Those who can look deeper will see the signs of death – nations wading in the blood of new wars, truth laid in chains, justice with broken limbs lying in the gutter.'

I have often quoted this article as proof not only of inspired foresight but equally of the existence of dissidents and anti-Nazis even after and in spite of Hitler's resounding triumphs in 1938. Though their burning anger could not stop the abomination of Nazism, they, greatly daring, remained captains of their soul, refusing to call evil good.

Evidence of anti-Nazi feeling could in fact be gathered even from the Nazis' own papers. The *Schwarze Korps* was then thundering against the 'scum' of 'grousers' who were 'even worse than the Jews' – and pretty widely scattered too: 'Each one of us had an opportunity during the last few days to meet some such kind-hearted representative of arch-Christian charity; in fact you simply could not escape them – they were everywhere.' They were people who could be heard saying 'this Jew business won't pay us in the long run', and six weeks after the pogrom it was found 'rather strange that one should constantly come across folk who keep pitying the "persecuted Jews"'.

This was the type of subject – man's defiance of tyranny – in which I had always taken the keenest interest, and I was now able to do the very work on which, in a way, I had trained myself in Leeds when writing to the *Yorkshire Post*. Then it was on a minimal scale, now on one so much larger, drawing on vaster resources and likely to reach a wider audience.

Of course not all the information was culled from printed material. A very important source was the 'special correspondents' and 'illegal' agents operating inside Germany whom Wiener had a knack of picking up through his far-flung connections in various countries. Especially at certain dramatic moments, for example at the time of the November 1938 pogrom, the place would hum with their reports which had to be edited and translated immediately, and there was no respite day or night; a holiday I certainly never knew anyway.

We were an interesting team in the spacious two-floor flat off Beethoven Straat. Wiener of course was very much the commander-in-chief and no one could fail to note his dictatorial presence. He knew a great many people though I suspect he also missed a good many who mattered. He regularly scanned *The Times* which he held in a reverence usually due to the Bible and, much like true-born Englishmen, regarded it as a source of information more valuable than (it has been said) the whole of Thucydides. He knew Wickham Steed, the former editor, but had no access to those who were now running the paper under the deplorable Geoffrey Dawson. He also knew the *News Chronicle* columnist (later MP) Vernon Bartlett who in 1933 had written a naive book *Nazi Germany Explained* but had since seen the light. Other notable figures I vaguely remember were the French specialists on anti-Nazi propaganda Raymond-Raoul Lambert and Maurice Vanikoff; Dr M. van Blankenstein, the prominent Dutch journalist; Torgney Segerstedt, editor of one of Sweden's foremost papers, *Göteborgs Handels-och Sjoefartstidning*.

Being a prolific letter-writer, Wiener maintained a vast correspondence, but he also was tirelessly on the move. Visiting the leaders of nearly all European Jewish communities, he would have made an admirable commercial traveller laden as he was with samples of his wares – documents of Nazi theory and practice – which were to

146

bring home the urgency of the situation but which, alas, met rarely more than varying degrees of indifference. As his occasional companion and interpreter, I once saw him literally on his knees rummaging in his crowded suitcases to find the item most likely to impress, usually the 'Protocols of Zion', *Der Stürmer* and evidence of anti-Christian propaganda. I doubt whether he ever covered the cost. Still, he was not discouraged.

The second-in-command was Dr Kurt Zielenziger, one-time deputy Press Officer of the Berlin City Council. He was a political economist, had recently (1937) published, in the journal *Population*, a much quoted article on the statistics of Jewish emigration and possessed of course a thorough knowledge of German affairs. In his angular appearance, usually escorted by the whiffs of a substantial cigar, he might in fact have been taken for a somewhat starched Prussian but mellowed by an unmistakable Jewish manner. Like Wiener he had next to no talent for languages – his Dutch occasionally was apt to recall Heine's verdict on Bellini's French: 'incestuous, suggesting the imminence of Doomsday' – but unlike Wiener, he would be content to stay at his desk, perhaps wisely so, and never ventured out to follow in the steps of the itinerant boss.

Very different was Mme Olga Bauer, the wife of Professor Ignacio Bauer, a lay leader of Spanish Jewry, now a refugee from the Civil War. She was the daughter of the St Petersburg banker Baron Günsburg, and so had an equal command of both Russian and Spanish. She also knew many other languages – I never discovered how many – and this talent of course was a capital asset. She read most of the foreign publications from which she prepared extracts, usually in French. This tall, beautiful woman, every inch an aristocrat of the *ancien régime*, always bore a strangely innocent and bewildered expression, as if unable to make any sense of the stories that passed before her melancholy eyes.

Shortly before I arrived the Office lost the services of one who must have been invaluable, Kurt Baschwitz, an expert on propaganda and journalism; his book on this subject gained him a professorship at Amsterdam University. But four weeks after me, we were joined by another young man, also from London, Louis W. Bondy, later the author of a now rare book, *Racketeers of Hatred*, based entirely on the Institute's material, about 'Julius Streicher and the Jew-baiters' International'.

We worked hard, often far into the night, though naturally, being young, we also found time for relaxation. Amsterdam was a fair city, even if sometimes, over the canals, I could see the ghost of the Flying Dutchman who seemed related to the Wandering Jew, to me. Some of the Dutch secretaries took pleasure in teaching me their language which I thoroughly enjoyed as a gratis benefit received from grace-ful tutors. Together we often moved around by Holland's national transport, the *fiets* (bicycle), and more than once we visited the splendour of the tulip groves at Haarlem.

However, inevitably, a heavy shadow lay over every-thing we did. Germany was too close for comfort, and the Dutch were as nervous as any of the Nazis' neighbours. I remember most vividly the people's determination that they were Netherlanders, not *Nederduitsers* ('Nether-Germans') as the detested *Moffe* ('Huns') would have them believe. I often thought of this sturdy spirit of independence, but often enough my thought also turned back to England.

Nor mine only. When the Nazi aggression began to darken Europe, it seemed wise to think of removing the Office to greater safety. The decision became urgent when the Dutch Government, with a worried eye on the bully next door, became aware of our potential for creating difficulties. They objected to a certain passage in Konrad Heiden's *Kristallnacht* book (*The New Inquisition*), printed in Amsterdam, which was found to have been written with material provided by the Office. Clearly further operations were bound to carry grave risks, and the first steps were taken to transfer the collections to London.

I was ordered to leave Holland by the middle of July 1939, and by then, thanks to the cooperation of the Board of

Deputies, a home had been found for the Office at Manchester Square, near Baker Street. Not all of us came over, however. Zielenziger, Mme Bauer, the accountant Bernhard Krieg, and Wiener's private secretary remained in charge of a branch. Of them Zielenziger and Krieg perished; Miss Bielschowsky survived, and the Bauers were able to return to Spain.

In London the Office was opened on 1 September 1939. It retained the original name but when the exigencies of war called for more general information, most of the work began to be produced under the seal of 'Dr Alfred Wiener's Office' which in turn became the Wiener Library.

# 6

# A WOMAN OF VALOUR

By now my parents were settled in London. Like so many others they had long hesitated to get out of Germany, and of course it was no easy matter for them, either materially or emotionally, in contrast to a young fellow like me. Fortunately, through the Central Bureau where Frieda worked, we had some contacts which helped. I was still in Holland when the parents left; they came through Amsterdam and we met though the Dutch authorities were rigorous in the extreme; they barely allowed the minimum of comfort on this temporary break of the refugees' journey. I was worried as I was not able to do much. We had not been in regular contact during the past few weeks or even months. They just knew I was in Holland but of course had no idea what I was doing. They understood when I explained to them now and they were relieved when at last I joined them six weeks before the outbreak of war.

They had come without Grandmother. She would not leave Berlin. She was eighty-two, she had torn up her roots once but would not, could not, do it again. She knew hard times were coming but, Mother reported, she thought 'at least they will let us live'. In this she was mistaken. In September 1942 she was to be deported to Theresienstadt. Clara, the older daughter who stayed with her, had already been 'evacuated' to Lodz, but she was resolved, come what may, to remain the captain of her life. In a farewell letter to Clara she wrote: 'Now I shall have to travel the same road – I prefer a voluntary death for there it will only be a slow dying.' Four days after these words, on 10 September 1942, she attempted suicide, and on the 14th she died in Berlin's Jewish hospital. A 'non-Aryan' relative sent us this Red Cross message: 'Mother peacefully passed away after short illness.'

*     *     *

I should like to interrupt my story here and say something about this remarkable woman. I mentioned her before when I said she had as it were kidnapped me and brought me up as if I were her son. I too must have felt as if I were. She kept some of the letters I wrote to her when I was eleven, and there I referred to my mother as 'Mama II', clearly implying that I regarded her as 'Mama I', although the letters were in fact addressed to 'My dear grandmother'. I am inclined to believe she loved me far beyond the love that would be expected between grandmother and grandson.

When I once thanked her for all the favours I had received from her, *she* thanked *me*: I had brought 'sunshine' into her room whenever I came to see her; she had felt 'warm and cosy' in my presence, and whenever I had been her escort I had guided her with a care she had been shown by nobody else (1934); even now, when my letters arrived her 'eyes were filled with tears of gladness', she felt 'as if in a fairy tale when heartfelt wishes come true' (1934).

At her age (she wrote in 1935) she could not expect much – only one thing and that she would not like to put off for too long: a reunion with me. Did I really as she had heard intend to go to Palestine? She did not object but she wrote, 'It cannot be your intention to leave without having seen your grandmother: you know how old I am, you know that nature has laws which all must obey, whether they like it or not, and once you are gone we could never hope to see each other in the foreseeable future. I would go with you were it not for the human laws that keep me here.' In all her thoughts, she said, I came first and foremost, I was 'the beginning and the end'.

It was (perhaps) a perfectly natural love but I cannot help reflecting on the presence of love in her life. She lost her husband when she was thirty-five and she never married again. She was in touch with Gustav in Peru and she had a very great affection for him. I can remember her talking about him as if he were a sweetheart, certainly a man greatly to be admired if not revered. Did she ever think of marrying him, of joining him in Lima or of him returning to Exin? The prospects would have been better in Peru, but she might not have liked it. Peru was still a far, far-away country: how would she adapt to the utterly alien milieu, even with Gustav at her side? He had come as a boy but she was at a mature age and so bound to find it that much harder to strike roots. She was clearly shy if not scared of leaving Germany, the land to which she was deeply attached, especially with the two young children – even if Gustav was interested in the idea (which was by no means certain).

Having achieved wealth and distinction in a famous capital city, Lima, he would hardly have cared for the petty affairs of small-town Exin and, like so many emigrants at the time, was probably glad to have got away from Prussian rule. Possibly also he was not the marrying type, much like his six-years-older brother Michael who emigrated either with or before him. Both were perhaps happiest with the family at a safe distance (in more than one respect). At all events, whatever feelings Grandma might have had for him remained practically unrequited. In Exin she apparently never found (perhaps never looked for) an eligible partner. So I became a receptacle of her unfulfilled love.

As far as I know, Gustav never showed any great tangible interest in the family. If he ever wrote any letters, they have not survived. I only have picture postcards of Lima with the very briefest greetings. What sort of letters, I wonder, did she, being apparently more articulate, write to him? Did she say she wanted to see him – as she later wanted to see me? These questions have never been asked and there is now no answer to them.

No doubt when Gustav died it was a cruel blow to her, perhaps one of the first of the sorrows which made her confess in 1934 that her life was 'not blessed with joy'; 'the bright side of life had been hidden' from her; she had 'seen little of the beauty of the world'; all her life, she claimed, had been 'saving and working, working and saving'. What money was left had, for the most part, been swallowed up by inflation, and half of the Peruvian inheritance was taken by the 'rich Americans', she grumbled, reflecting on what she thought was a sad fact of life that 'what we sow will too often be reaped by others'.

I must doubt whether things were really quite as bad as that. Her frustrations had made her bitter. She was 'old and worn out', she wrote in 1936, but in fact she had been bitter long before. She was writhing under the unkindness of a fate that had deprived her of the one thing she treasured most, her independence. In Exin she had been mistress of her life: she had her own house, her own business, she could do as she pleased. Now she felt she was dependent on her daughters for whom she still had ambivalent feelings. She thought she was now living on sufferance, eating the bread of affliction. She kept a diary under the title *Das Gnadenbrot*, the bread of mercy, or charity. I noticed it once, rummaging in one of her cupboards. The mere title gave me quite a shock: I did not unfortunately dare read it. The idea was absurd, preposterous it seems to me now. If there was any dependence it was much rather the other way round. She was definitely better off than we were. She employed my father as an investor of her money and she was able to support my mother. She merely proved the notorious fact that it is not, as a general rule, the realities that determine our lives but our reaction to things as mirrored in our imagination.

She complained of 'frequent tensions' between her and the family. To some extent she was prepared to blame herself albeit in a somewhat devious manner. She had believed, she wrote in 1936, that her daughters would show as much understanding for her as she had done for her parents, but the fact was that nobody seemed to understand her, she was not kept informed about what was going on, and if Mother had visited me three times in London (1934, 1935 and 1936), did she *have* to do that? Surely, she wrote in 1936, one can be a good mother without seeing one's children every year, nor will the children be any less loving if they don't see the mother every year? Why, instead of being with Mother, didn't I use my holiday to travel to a country I had not been to before?

Clearly she was very bitter. For she certainly would have loved to see me every year, even more than once, would have thought this quite natural too, and it was only the burden of age that prevented her. She certainly would never have allowed her criticism of Mother to be applied to herself. Gradually too her bitterness became critical of me. I did not write to her as often as she felt I ought to, especially in the late 1930s. In this complaint she was not wrong, but of course she could not know what was going on within me. I was ill.

I felt a great pain, in several ways. I suffered in mind and spirit. I lived in freedom, yes, and I had saved myself from a fate that I felt even then was unutterably worse than the slavery in Egypt, and I was grateful for the life I had been granted here. Yet the sight of evil triumphant and unchallenged arrogantly bestriding the earth often seemed enough to threaten my sanity. My mind was a running sore, bleeding from wounds that nothing could staunch.

I could not be surprised (though I resented it) when one of the *Yorkshire Post* correspondents accused me of 'hysteria', 'hysterical fears' and 'screaming pessimism'. I could not deny it: wild passions were raging within me and there was nothing to assuage them, nothing that lay within my power. I was condemned to behold the insane, increasingly,

154

revoltingly insane spectacle that the world was presenting. It was devastating me. I had some friends, but their company could do nothing to set my mind at ease. I was on my own even then, restless, close to despair, and the terror of the time was all around me.

Writing those letters to the *Yorkshire Post* provided some balm but I did not seem capable of keeping up simultaneously my correspondence with the family in which I would not be free to speak my mind – quite apart from the frustrations caused by the unloved daily routine and the absence of any prospect of progress. Since I had no news of any substance worth reporting, each letter home became a tortuous effort, struggling, exhausting and long delayed, and naturally I was treated all too often to reminders and reproaches.

Later, when I joined the Wiener Library in Amsterdam, things became even worse. Now, even before the outbreak of war (and so close to the German border), I was already engaged in warlike action. The Library was for all intents and purposes an anti-Nazi propaganda agency. If the Germans had ever known of this strictly secret work, I, like the family then still in Germany (as well as my colleagues), would have been exposed to mortal danger. Kidnapping was even then no unknown political practice and the Nazis would not have recoiled from it.

I therefore had to be most cautious in every move I made, and it seemed to me that the fewer the contacts I had, anywhere, certainly in Germany and even with the family, the better for all concerned. This was no easy decision to take but I felt neither the general situation nor my badly disturbed mind left me any other choice.

This of course Grandma could not know, and I could not quarrel with her when she wrote in March 1939 that I seemed to be 'devoting to your work your time, your strength – I nearly said your love (I am merely hinting at it).' When she was referring to this work of mine to which I was indeed devoted heart and soul (though its character was of course unknown to her), she was, she said, '(a little) jealous', and that jealousy may well have been at the core of the bitterness she felt about me. It was then not unreasonable for her to fear I was not reciprocating her love – one more frustration in an already mournfully long catalogue. She could have found out the truth by joining the parents and coming to London where we would have been at long last reunited. She decided otherwise. Was her love too grievously wounded? Was she still haunted by the fear that she would not get on with the daughter and that the old 'tensions' would become an intolerable strain? The love she felt did not conquer this fear, and so she remained to meet her doom – alone.

# 7

# PROPAGANDA IN WAR

When war broke out, the parents and I came before the Aliens' Tribunal set up to investigate especially the credentials of those who had found refuge here from Nazi persecution. I was then able to produce an effective testimonial from the Editor of the *Yorkshire Post*, and on the strength of it we were all put into the most favourable category, 'C', where we were free from all restrictions and certainly spared the terrors of internment which befell so many of our people.

The seriousness of the occasion was relieved a little when the chairman of the Tribunal seemed inclined to consider my testimonial almost too good to be true. He enquired if the Tribunal might keep the letter, and would I mind if he got in touch with the editor in order to ascertain his 'private' opinion of me. There were of course no objections as far as I was concerned, but his Honour then decided to drop the suggestion on the ground that he was 'not going to run the risk'.

My work at the Library was at once recognised as 'Auxiliary War Service', and I resumed it with buoyancy and hope, though working conditions in the spacious hall that must once have been the rendezvous of high society were as primitive and makeshift as can be imagined. Large

157

numbers of crates and chests were being unpacked, with workmen fixing the shelves and generally adapting the ancient place with its Spanish-style ornamental balcony to more matter-of-fact purposes.

I later heard it said that so important was the Jewish Central Information Office considered to be that HM Government arranged for a destroyer (no less) to bring it to England! Whoever concocted that egregious story could have had no idea of how little known, let alone appreciated, the JCIO then was, nor how humdrum was the removal operation by Messrs Schenker, International Freight Forwarders. One of HM ships, my foot – it wasn't by any chance *HMS Pinafore* under the command of Rear Admirals Gilbert and Sullivan?

We were in the period of the 'phoney war', and this may have given us a chance of settling down, taking stock quite literally and both renewing and extending our contacts in London, with the result that the Library gradually became more widely known, especially among those responsible for 'political warfare', the Ministry of Information.

Before long, however, events took a hand in our affairs. The blitzkrieg which engulfed the West claimed among its victims Dr Wiener, who suffered a severe nervous breakdown. He had had a similar experience in Berlin during the first weeks of the Nazi regime, and as he then determined to remove to Holland, so he now set his mind upon assuring his Library's future in USA.

The bulk of it would stay in London but he would go to New York to organise an uninterrupted supply of vital information. This was the intention, but the reason why Wiener went to New York was in fact that he was physically in no condition to stand the strain of life under the deepening shadow of the Nazi threat. I can understand it now, but at the time, not knowing all the details, I felt he should have stayed, and I told him so when he came back in April 1945. He appreciated my candour, however pained to listen, and I shall not now sit in judgment on him.

As for the work he did in America, it was undoubtedly of

158

considerable value to us in London, though some of the British agents in New York, conducting a more unorthodox sort of 'information', tended to misjudge the great potential of the man whom they patronisingly regarded as 'our book scout'. To be sure, Wiener could not hope to compete with some of the methods employed by these slick propagandists whose chief performer in New York was Sefton Delmer of *Daily Express* fame. In a recent survey, a US authority on Latin America, Professor Ronald C. Newton, told an interesting detail of these activities: 'In a black propaganda campaign devised by Sefton Delmer to demoralise the average German soldier or civilian, British psychological war operatives planted evidence which indicated that Nazi leaders and their henchmen, mistresses and mad scientists were fleeing the crumbling Third Reich with new identities and as much loot as they could carry. Many purportedly had turned up in South America, particularly Argentina, whence they proposed to resume their diabolical plotting against the peace of the world. What effect, if any, Delmer's tarradiddle had on the German will to resist is unknown; the Americans, however, had not been forewarned of the operation and were taken in by it.'

I am unable to pass any judgment on this opinion, though I am prepared to believe that not all of these stories were figments of Delmer's admittedly fertile imagination. All I know for certain is that such methods were not part of Wiener's arsenal. He relied on printed evidence, well documented and first-hand, that could be made to serve propagandist purposes: chapter and verse always were of paramount importance.

Much of his material, which often arrived barely dried after salvage from sea water, was used by us for two strictly documentary newsletters which we were issuing. The one was entitled *The Nazis at War*, dealing with Nazi Germany and occupied Europe generally; the other, on the same lines, was *Jewish News* which I started after consultation with the President of the Board of Deputies, Professor Brodetsky. Opinions on my work differed. The German and Austrian Employment Exchange, the job centre for refugees, not perhaps supremely qualified to judge, thought I could do 'more productive work' in a factory – an assessment on which Mr Bellow, my Leeds boss, might have obliged with an expert opinion. I am glad to report that its director, Dr von Waldheim, was open to reasoned argument when Wiener's deputy, Mr Bondy, pointed out to him, in great detail, why I was, from a variety of considerations, 'quite irreplaceable to the satisfactory functioning of our work.' Since I am now past applying for jobs, I might perhaps safely also quote the testimonial received from Professor D. Cohen in 1939 that I was 'an honest man and wholly trustworthy in every respect' who could be 'recommended to everyone whom it concerns.'

I kept up my contact with the *Yorkshire Post*. I had written many letters from Amsterdam and, as a Special Correspondent, also published a feature article on 'German Radio Propaganda: Nazi Technique of Foreign Broadcasts'. I now became particularly interested in the Hitler-Stalin pact which soon reminded me of the treaty between Napoleon and Tsar Alexander I. I pointed out the parallel in *The Nazis at War* (12 December 1940) where I quoted this striking passage from J. Holland Rose's *Life of Napoleon I* (1922):

On the surface, indeed, everything was friendship and harmony... But beneath these brilliant shows there lurked suspicion and fears... For both potentates that treaty had been at bottom nothing more than a truce. Napoleon saw in it a means of subjecting the Continent ... The Tsar hailed it as a breathing space wherein he could reorganise his army, conquer Finland and stride towards the Balkans ... Napoleon hoped that before so mighty a confederacy, England would bend the knee ... The conqueror who had shattered Prussia in a day, might well believe that the men of Downing Street, expert only in missing opportunities ... would not dare to defy the forces of united Europe ... Both Napoleon and the Tsar desired peace, so that their empires might expand and consolidate ... But the means adopted were just those that were destined to defeat the aim.

Here was a case where study of the past provided a glance into the future. Rarely can history have repeated itself in such almost identical terms.

Soon the Library began to swarm with people of many nationalities engaged in the practical business of 'psychological warfare' which required an exact knowledge of Nazi history and ideology. If Bondy had described me as 'indispensable' to the Library's work my claim to fame rested chiefly on a then rare familiarity with *Mein Kampf* acquired when I was supposed to be repairing sewing machines. I knew much of it by heart and my memory worked in respect of its page numbers as it has always worked in respect of telephone numbers. I probably was the first to write a history of the book and its translations, also of its career after 1945. The 'big lie' of which Hitler complained (p. 252) as having been spread by his enemies, was now shown to be in fact his very own. Altogether I was able to draw a self-portrait of Hitler by simply compiling all the abuse he was heaping on 'The Jews' and by illustrating it with his own actions – a perfect example of 'projection'. I made this quite clear when I prepared a special analytical Index to *Mein Kampf* which revealed to the critical reader both the psychology of the author and the characteristic features of 'National Socialism' which the book's own Index was designed to conceal. My Index drew attention to such matters as brutality (30 references), extermination (13), lies (23), might is right (12), Nazi method of advance: 'one by one' (10), Nazism as a religion (19), Nazis and Germans (8), world domination (26).

I had always given careful attention to Nazi propaganda world-wide, especially the antisemitic variety of it. I never regarded antisemitism as a matter affecting merely, or even mainly, Jews. It always seemed to me naive to look upon it as dependent on the number or even existence of Jews in any one country. If no, or only few, Jews could be found there, people wondered, why should there be antisemitism? The characteristic implication being that antisemitism must be a reaction to the presence or behaviour of Jews. Antisemitism was taken at its treacherous face value. The mechanism of modern antisemitic propaganda was not understood. It was not seen to be indifferent to the realities of Jewish life (which would reveal the nonsense of it all). It operated with the fiction of a gallery of hobgoblins – 'World Jewry', 'The Elders of Zion', 'The International Money Power' – which could be animated wherever Nazi interests needed them. Such was the great innovation that Hitler introduced, even on a worldwide scale.

I therefore concerned myself not so much with his obsessions, his crude, stale, a thousand times discredited lies which, once tackled, merely breed more lies. I rather concentrated on the cunning calculations behind them, more especially the manipulation of every form of Jew-hatred to promote his imperialist campaign. As handled by him, it became a revolutionary expedient that could use the prejudices of traditional, social, even Christian antisemitism as a spearhead of his advance towards that ultimate goal of world domination which he openly avowed in *Mein Kampf* and which, characteristically, he imputed to 'the Jews'.

It was not he who wanted to conquer the world, it was 'the Jews' (according to his propaganda), and it was not the 'Aryans' who were resisting him, it was 'the Jews' whose 'power' ('the hidden hand') in every sphere of life was using the unsuspecting Gentiles as pawns and stooges to further 'Jewish' interests which (according to him) had nothing to do with, and were in fact opposed to, those of their 'host' nations. He was going to 'liberate' the world from this 'yoke'.

What Hitler here imputes to 'the Jews' was precisely the conception of his own antisemitic propaganda. Its purpose was to induce his enemies to do without the valuable contribution that Jewish intelligence, Jewish goodwill and Jewish resources all over the world could make to their cause. Clearly the Nazis could expect to gain tremendously if their enemies had fallen for this trick. That calculation had worked in Hitler's drive for power at home – now it was to be repeated world-wide. He once actually confided the secret of his success to his then friend Hermann Rauschning: 'You will see how little time we shall need to shatter the ramparts of democracy by attacking the Jews.' He proved right in 1933 and he very nearly proved right again in 1939 when the skilful manipulation of antisemitism, combined with 'anti-Communism', had gone far to make him master of continental Europe. It was only then that the duped victims of Nazi aggression began to discover the power-political reality behind the propagandist smoke-screen of antisemitism.

So I now organised the vast material stored in the Library according to countries as well as to the several agencies engaged in the trade of treachery that was to reinforce, and/or prepare for, the advance of German arms, even though (we now know) the Nazi Fifth Column was not quite the formidable threat it was made to appear.

*     *     *

An interesting colleague during the war years was Elisabeth Jungmann who in 1956 married Sir Max Beerbohm, having been his private secretary in Rapallo for ten years. In the Library she did relatively subordinate if essential work, administering the material handed to her. But she was accustomed to very different work, having been the con-fidante of famous men, notably the German author Gerhart Hauptmann who basked in an outward resemblance to Goethe.

I often spoke to her about some of them, criticising them for what was their silent subservience to the Nazi rulers, but she would not hear of it and instead, with great warmth, defended especially Hauptmann, his humanity and the integrity of all the good people one would meet at Agnetendorf, Hauptmann's home. It was a world that was very much alive to her, and she did not seem to comprehend why it should have been allowed to disappear.

Having been separated from these great men, she was yearning to find others of like calibre who would compensate her for the loss. She seemed to me for ever hopefully inclined to see shades of greatness where none existed, and perhaps there was something of a hero-worshipper in her. I believe she considered it her vocation in life to be the servant of genius and an utterly self-denying, even self-sacrificing one she was.

It seems a pity she was not endowed with any literary skill. She might have established a plausible claim to being a minor Boswell or Eckermann, or at the very least another Malwida von Meysenbug, the intimate friend of Nietzsche and Wagner. She was, however, fortunate in striking up a happy relationship with men like Gilbert Murray, David Cecil, and of course Max Beerbohm.

# 8

# THE WIENER LIBRARY

Wiener was an intriguing mixture of extraordinary gifts. If Jews are known as the People of the Book, he was most truly one of them, however unorthodox by traditional standards. He not only knew his books and loved them; he had an occasionally almost innocent trust in the power, bordering on magic, of the printed word. That pious belief contrasted oddly with the sure realism which guided his transactions, for though preoccupied with books, of which he knew wellnigh all there is to be known (apart from the contents), he was no bookworm and quite unspoilt by cloistered virtue. His achievement bears witness to the unusual combination of talents that helped to establish and maintain it – his gifts as a scholastic connoisseur and journalist, a book lover and shrewd businessman, an intuitive psychologist and diplomatic charmer. I am indebted to him for a good many skills of practical journalism, and one of his more philosophical sayings that I remember is that when you divide the world by reason (to which he attached great importance), a lot still remains to be accounted for. I was reminded of this later when I came across Pascal's saying about the 'two extravagances' – 'to exclude reason and to admit only reason'.

Of course the end of the war profoundly affected him, his

prospects and the prospects of the Library. The struggle against Hitler had been his life's content for twenty-five years, ever since he published his first brochure, in 1919, *Vor Pogromen?* He then drew a record of German antisemitic outrages after the last war which he feared might result in pogroms. At that time Hitler was not yet sufficiently prominent and so it could not be known that he, for all his antisemitic obsessions, did not believe in pogroms which in fact he dismissed as the practice of an 'emotional anti-semitism' that treated as it were only symptoms of the 'disease' – a pogrom here, a pogrom there, while the Jews remained – whereas his was a 'rational antisemitism', doing away with the Jews root and branch, a 'Final Solution'. Well, now in 1945, that enemy had been laid low; so what next?'

Immersed as he was in the past, Wiener now canvassed the idea of an inventory of what had happened. He spoke of a Cambridge History of the Nazi Era. This was no doubt a good idea but, like many good ideas, it came before its time. Years had to pass before such an inventory could be attempted. The official documents so far as they were available had to be assessed; the dramatis personae to produce their memoirs, and the Library's own material, used up to now for 'psychological warfare', had to be marshalled for purposes of research as soon as the scholars were ready. Among the earliest seen at the Library were Norman Baynes, author of an English edition of Hitler's speeches up to 1939; Alan Bullock, author of a standard Hitler biography; Gerald Reitlinger, the first to tell the story of the Holocaust.

I was naturally, and eagerly, involved in this work, but I also tried to see the Library's relevance not merely to the past but to the events now unfolding in the new world. I took an early interest in the story of South Africa, especially after the Nationalists came to power in 1948. They had attracted my attention even during the war when (according to General Smuts' United Party) 'they made common cause with our enemies to the uttermost extent that they

166

dared and to the uttermost extent that it was physically and geographically possible for them to do.'

On the basis of the current information which we received from friends in South Africa, I wrote a great many articles which appeared in various parts of the world. One was printed in the London *Jewish Chronicle* in May 1948, shortly before the Nationalists' victory. In this article I set out the character of the party – both its antisemitism and the wider aspects of apartheid as it affected 'the politically dispossessed four-fifths of this top-heavy nation knocking persistently at the uneasy White conscience and ominously shaking the shackles of the colour bar.'

Though well documented and the result of painstaking enquiry, the article drew complaints from the leaders of South African Jewry. The editor did not tell me officially but when I met him privately he did mention the 'unfavourable comments from South Africa' which he seemed to imply might have to be taken note of. No further articles of mine about South Africa appeared in the *Jewish Chronicle*. The 'Organ of British Jewry' may well have been as unwilling to offend the racialists of apartheid as *The Times* once was to displease Nazi Germany.

I also tried to see the relevance of the Library's resources in other ways, such as the rise of the new Germany, the Arab war on Israel, international antisemitism – subjects that were regularly covered in the *Wiener Library Bulletin*. However, this is not the place to tell the story of the Wiener Library except to say that a tolerable foundation was laid. Wiener once again succeeded in drumming up private support and in doing so he was fortunate in having the good will of one who had long known him – Leonard Montefiore, OBE, the son of Claude, the famous theologian of Liberal Judaism, whose life he finely described as 'a spiritual pilgrimage'. He was, however, in no way to be compared to his father. He was something like an 18th-century country gentleman whose considerable fortune permitted him a variety of interests in charity and scholarship. He also played, though perhaps with less distinction, a part in Anglo-Jewish public life as President of the Anglo-Jewish Association and Joint Chairman of the Joint Foreign Committee of the AJA and Board of Deputies.

He knew German well, had spent some time in Wilhelminian Hanover and it pleased his fancy to display a by no means casual acquaintance with German literature, especially Heine and Goethe's *Faust*, preferably the more obscure Part 2. He had been in touch with the Information Office in Amsterdam and from this source drawn much of the documentary material which he used in popular brochures presenting facts and figures to expose the Nazi persecution of Jewry. He was doing ideally the sort of work that Wiener would have wished scores of people to do.

In London he was a regular caller at the Library, enquiring or merely browsing, discussing business or conversing with visitors, and all his efforts would be amply rewarded if we could tell him an amusing little story that had come our way. ('A jest, a jest, a kingdom for a jest!') He agreed to be Chairman of the Library's Board of Directors – on the tacit understanding that not too much routine was involved. He was all for the bright and lighter side of things, a puckish humour would relieve any dry agenda, and he loved to address Wiener as *Herr Direktor*. Wiener in turn was devotedly grateful to him, 'the father of the Wiener Library', he called him, and 'no father,' he said, 'could have felt fonder affection for a child.' The affection showed tangibly in the substantial contributions he made to our budget – on a regular basis or in between, on the flimsiest pretext. It may fairly be said that but for his liberality the Library would not have managed to tide over the worst of its financial problems.

Below his velvet surface, however, was hiding a determination that could be unyielding. It showed in one particular painful episode. Wiener had long known the Revd Dr James Parkes, the famous Christian scholar who was probably the first to tackle the Christian roots of anti-semitism. He had founded a library which was to be a research centre for 'the relations between the Jewish and non-Jewish

168

worlds'. It was similar to the Wiener Library but different in that it covered also Bible studies and the more religious aspect of Christian-Jewish relations, from the friendly to the unfriendly. As a research centre the library had the disadvantage of being situated somewhat off the beaten track, in Barley, a village between London and Cambridge, but this was probably due to necessity not choice, for Parkes' work was not well endowed.

He had gained the support of Israel Sieff, head of Marks & Spencer's, because of his Zionist sympathies reflected in his publications and appreciated especially because of their anticipated impact on Christian opinion, but that support stopped short of ensuring an independent existence. In fact it declined to such an extent that Parkes began to fear for his library's survival. After the immediate Zionist aim – the establishment of a Jewish State – had been achieved, Sieff (according to Parkes) was 'involved in too many demands to give us the minimum financial help we needed'. Several years passed before Sieff could arrange for a Parkes Library Ltd to be set up, and the result of an appeal dinner in 1956 guaranteed a 'modest security' for a number of years. Soon afterwards, another dinner was held at which, Parkes relates in his memoirs (*Voyage of Discoveries*, London, 1969), it was proposed to merge the Parkes and the Wiener Libraries. The proposal was essentially Sieff's. Parkes agreed that 'the two institutions fitted admirably into each other', but at the same time he doubted whether the project was sensible because he, getting on in years though eleven years younger than Wiener, did not feel sufficiently strong to run his own work and at the same time spend several days a week in London running the Wiener Library.

But the idea apparently appealed to the practical mind of Sieff who must have seen here an opportunity of a financial burden being fairly shared. I have reason to believe that, at this time, Sieff had lost interest in Parkes, and Parkes felt, rightly or wrongly, that for all intents and purposes, Sieff had let him down. Be that as it may, it seems strange that

169

Parkes to whom the Zionist cause must be beholden as to few other Christians, is not as much as mentioned in the memoirs of Israel Sieff.

Parkes frequently visited Wiener in London, and Wiener, so far from regarding him as a rival, took a rather condescending view of him. What prospects could this man expect to have, he asked, with a library set up out in the wilds of Hertfordshire: who would take the trouble of making that laborious journey? It seemed an absurd idea. Parkes would not have been entirely convinced had Wiener told him so, but a close cooperation was indeed his dearest wish. A somewhat delicate plant called Wiener-Parkes Association actually sprang up in the beautiful country garden of Dr Parkes, but it withered almost overnight.

I am inclined to believe that, on suitable terms, Wiener was not unwilling to consider the proposal. He was about to retire; his succession was uncertain, so was his health and the financial prospect. He might not have been enthusiastic about the arrangement but he would resign himself to it. However, Montefiore objected. According to Parkes, he held that since essentially Sieff and his friends were its supporters, the Parkes Library should have the full benefit of that support, and 'he refused to have the income divided between the two institutions'. I would broadly agree with this.

Montefiore, who did not mind regarding himself as 'a relic of a bygone age', was a predemocratic feudalist, and most likely he did not wish to share control though he was prepared to consider support from such bodies as the Wolfson Foundation, for he always made it clear that he would provide for the Wiener Library only during his lifetime; thereafter he felt it should be incorporated, like the Warburg Institute, in London University.

As for Parkes, Montefiore simply refused to take him seriously, a man who deserved – certainly among Jews – admiration, respect and every support for the unique work he was doing. I was saddened when I read in Parkes' memoirs about his relationship with Claude Montefiore –

'a friendship continued by his son Leonard'. The two differed too much to have stayed in friendship in anything like (literally) close quarters. Eventually Parkes was driven to realise the impasse. He told me, with feelings of bitter resignation, that his Christian colleagues (Anglican clergy) regarded him as a freak and a faddist, and Jews also entirely failed to appreciate the value of his researches which began as far back as 1934 with his standard work *The Conflict of the Church and the Synagogue: A Study in the Origins of Antisemitism*. He felt, with good reason, he was after all a champion of the Jews but he told me he came to suspect Jews were not keen on having a Christian champion. I did not disagree.

Parkes now hoped that by courting my favour he might improve his chances but this was quite out of the question. I was in no position to exert influence on Montefiore once he had made up his mind. I visited Parkes several times, also met his assistant who came to see me on 'special missions', but this was shadow-boxing at best. I was all in favour of the project but this was an occasion where Montefiore would not budge and listen either to Wiener or to me. In the end, Parkes tried to interest one of the great universities but when he found no takers, he had to be content with his library to be housed once again in a backwater, at the University of Southampton.

*     *     *

Whatever the advantages of a close association with Dr Parkes may have been, we received a strong boost when German restitution money arrived and the Wiener Library came to the attention of the Bonn authorities. They, no doubt for good reasons of their own, showed great interest in the collections, so much so that we were offered tempting facilities for a transfer to Germany. Of course we never seriously considered the idea though contacts were soon established with a number of German historical institutes and German money unconditionally given, apart from restitution, was not on principle refused.

Meanwhile we had been reorganised. A Director of

171

Research was appointed, Wiener's friend and colleague from his Berlin days, Dr Eva Reichmann, author of the standard work on the Weimar Republic, *Hostages of Civilisation*, and the books were in the care of a trained librarian, Mrs Ilse Wolff, later the owner of the Oswald Wolff publishing firm. I was the editor of a printed *Wiener Library Bulletin* which began to appear in 1946 (and once in my twenty years had to pay libel damages). I was also looking after the far-flung archives and press files which were gradually attracting the attention of students and scholars.

Among them were quite a number of well-known people such as Alan Bullock, H. R. Trevor-Roper, J. W. Wheeler-Bennett, David Astor, Thomas Mann (who gave a lecture), Theodor Heuss, the first German President who looked in during his state visit to Britain in 1958; and Louis de Jong, director of the Dutch State Institute for War Documentation.

I remember particularly Gerald Reitlinger, author of the first Holocaust history, *The Final Solution* (1953). He used our material and agreed to contribute occasionally to the *Bulletin*. However, endowed with what seemed to me a rigid sense of hierarchy, he would approach me only through the director, and when he once felt that an article of his had not been treated with the respect due to it, he complained to Wiener whom he wanted to reprimand me. I was of course informed and thereupon wrote to him saying, in effect, that I was not going to shield behind my superior, that I wished to explain my action and, if found to be at fault, would apologise for any inconvenience. I received no reply.

He apparently deemed it beneath his dignity to engage in argument with a 'junior'. So far as I remember, he retained a grudge. I still believe it was an ungracious, ungenerous behaviour, especially regrettable in one whom I was prepared to regard as a man of considerable intellectual stature. I did not then know of his great interest in art which would have made his behaviour, in my eyes, even more deplorable. But then of course genius and character are two very different things, and not every genius (as such I regarded Reitlinger) has the high character one might expect. Later I learnt that others had found him 'very rude indeed', and according to Anthony Powell (*Faces in my Time*), his 'strange nature, macabre humour, disconsolate appearance, might fittingly have found a place in the pages of Dostoevsky'.

A very different man was Otto Frank, the father of Anne, whom I was able to assist in some of his efforts to deal with copyright matters concerning the daughter's *Diary* and, more especially, to track down the liars alleging the book was a forgery. He much impressed me by the dignified modesty with which he bore the family's sadly acquired fame as the burden of a noble legacy.

Occasionally also an odd breed of freaks showed up. One came with this cloak and dagger story. He was planning a film dealing with the growth of a Nazi movement in Britain. For this purpose he said he had joined one of the several Nazi factions where he said he was accepted as one of them. He claimed in fact to have wangled his way on to the Committee and showed me a batch of correspondence with friends in various parts of the world. More recently, however, he had begun to wonder whether it was safe for him to carry on in a position where he had been warned he was 'playing with dynamite'. Could I name any people who would be interested in this story? Of course I declared myself entirely incompetent to deal with matters like this and as courteously as I could showed him the door.

Among other characters I remember none is more strange than the young woman who one day appeared in my office, in the summer of 1961, at the time of the Eichmann trial. Evelyn (then twenty-five) said she was greatly distressed by the trial reports which she was reading every day. This was so horrible a story that one would think nobody could ever be an antisemite again. But clearly this was not so. In Rochester where she lived and taught at Sunday school, nasty remarks could be heard about the Jews, though the Eichmann trial was making it perfectly plain that those terrible crimes were only the ultimate consequence of such antisemitic talk, and if things had taken that turn in Germany, could not the same also happen in England?

She could find no peace of mind after reading the papers every day, and she felt something ought to be done to prevent such things from happening ever again. She had talked to her husband but he had said: Forget about it; and her MP had told her she was being too emotional. But she would not take No for an answer. She had to confess she knew nothing about Jews but now she wanted to know all about the history of antisemitism. Could I help her?

Well, I did my best. We had a voluminous correspondence. I suggested some reading, she gradually built up a library of her own and, through her sheer enthusiasm, she soon made contact with quite a number of like-minded people. Unfortunately her husband was not interested and left her, but it was not long before, in the course of her tireless investigations, she met Pierre Le Chène (of Anglo-French origin), a member of the Special Operations Executive (SOE) who was captured by the Germans, 'interrogated' by Klaus Barbie and sent to Mauthausen where he survived, albeit broken in health; he died in 1979.

Pierre, whom she married, became the heart and soul of her life. She spent much time with him in France where she acquired a near-perfect command of the language, and in England she formed a lasting friendship with the late Terence Prittie, the journalistic champion of Zionism, who aroused in her a passionate interest in Israel. She in fact lived there for a time and became an English announcer on Israel radio. She also wrote a book about the country, as well as one about Mauthausen which became a standard work on this camp.

It was at that time that she thought of converting to Judaism. 'For years,' she told me, 'my life has been conducted as if I were a member of the Jewish community – theologically speaking, that is – and I have only desisted from converting because I think I can better help Israel and

174

Jews as a whole by staying where I am.' Only five years previously, she had learnt, much to her surprise, that her late father was a Jew, a fact which the mother who she said was actually antisemitic had tried hard to conceal from her.

Had the father unconsciously influenced her feeling towards Jews and Israel? Possibly, she thought, but not to the extent of identifying with him: if she followed her father, she said, she would 'become a Jewess talking in the Jewish cause' – which she definitely did not want to do.

I encouraged her in this. I do not believe that, as a general rule, Gentiles do right in converting to Judaism, in any circumstances other than marriage, and anything like a Jewish missionary effort comparable to the Christian would seem to me stillborn. In those days I was thinking about the problem and I explained my attitude in an article in *The Times* in 1972:

These are times of searching. Christian convictions are declining. Men grope for a new religion, and once more they turn towards the East. Many are attracted by Buddhism, by the Bahai, by Islam, and not a few wonder what Judaism may have to offer. As a Jew I should perhaps be pleased by this interest, and up to a point of course I am. But in fact I confess, I rather am intrigued. For so many centuries Christians have tried to convert Jews that this new interest can hardly fail to appear unusual. Not that Christians never wished to be Jews. There have been conversions to Judaism, albeit relatively few, at all times and in every land – quite apart from the special circumstances of intermarriage – and today many liberal Jews plead for an effort to spread the Hebrew gospel among those who weary of the old dispensation.

It is surely a characteristic Jewish belief that the ancestress of King David, and so eventually of the Messiah, is an Arab woman, Ruth, who chose to worship the God of Israel. Her story, like that of Jonah, is one of the finest witnesses to the universal message of

175

Judaism, giving short shrift to the facile fancy that Jews are, by nature, of a ghetto mind.

It is true that many Gentiles, however sincere, find it difficult to enter the Jewish fold and orthodox rabbis do their best to keep them away. There is however nothing racialist about it. The Chosen People are not a Master People. They were chosen not by any wanton superstition of the blood but by an answerable obligation of rational conduct, not by an exaltation of race but by a vindication of faith. Indeed they are different not because they *were* chosen but because they *have* chosen. Their choice of a life governed by the exacting and unrelenting commandments of a jealous yet compassionate God is open to all mankind.

Yet, though by no means orthodox, I would hesitate to encourage any one to 'convert to Judaism', however welcome they assuredly will be. For I believe that Judaism is not merely a religion. It is more, and of course all the tortuous debates as to 'Who is a Jew?' turn on this point. I shall not lose myself in this maze. I will only say that, as I see it, any definition of Judaism must take into account a historical and social experience which seems to me no less essential than the religious.

Those who have adopted the faith of the Jews and live in accordance with the law of Moses, still have a long way to go. They still have to enter into the fellowship of a thousand years' exile, a thousand years' sorrow and a hope upheld alike by a universal vision and a national dream. They must know that to enter into such a fellowship will be a long and baffling journey. I am not saying that it cannot be done. It can, precisely because Judaism is not exclusive. But, in all conscience, it cannot be easy, it must be daunting, at least for those without the comforting ties of intermarriage.

It must have been difficult enough in all the centuries up to the destruction of the second Temple when the Jews led a relatively normal life. Today, after the harrowing experience of Western civilisation, it must seem incomparably harder. How many can fairly be expected to identify themselves not just with an abstract faith but with the vibrant personality of a people whose story stands as an often bewildering challenge to the whole world – not least, uncompromisingly, to their own friends? How many are likely to endure this trial?

As a Jew I feel they should not be expected to, and indeed they need not. For I believe that those who seek Judaism will find it in Christianity, whose moral and ethical core, so far as conduct and action is concerned, is Jewish. I think there was great truth in Pope Pius XI's remark; 'Spiritually, we [Christians] are Semites', and I am sure another Pope will yet declare: 'Essentially, we are Hebrews'. There are differences, of course, important differences, but, from the would-be convert's point of view, I believe none can compare with the stark challenge of reconciling the loyalties that spring from identification with the Jews.

I firmly believe that all a Gentile needs to do, if he wishes to be Jewish, is to lead the good life by the best standards of the Christian tradition in which he grew up. If he did not grow up in it because it no longer seems fashionable, then I, a Jew, being the ancient stiff-necked non-conformist, earnestly beseech him to revive it, to defy the pagan cry that 'God is dead' and turn to the faith in him who came not to destroy the Law but to fulfil it.

# 9

# ZIONISM AND ISRAEL

Of course it will be said I am a Jew not only by faith but equally by race, and while faith can change race cannot. This is true but also irrelevant. For one thing I believe faith being of the spirit can overcome race which is of the body. It cannot be argued that because a person happens to be of a certain race – even a Jew – therefore he cannot adopt a certain faith, different from the one into which he or she may have been born. I changed my faith. I am today what is called a Zionist: I was not always. This is what I wrote in my diary in June 1929:

> The aims of Zionism do not seem to me worth pursuing. Does this 'modern, highly civilised people', as a Zionist leader, Max Nordau, has said, really have no higher ambition than 'to live secure and unchallenged in the land of our fathers'? Was this the idea of 2,000 years' sojourn and struggle among the nations that we should now resume a narrowly confined existence in a phantom-like home? What meaning would history have then? and what sort of an idea of Judaism is this? Israel was thinking too little of itself when it created this Zionism. Persecuted and harassed, it sought a refuge in nationalism. But this is not the destiny of

Judaism to withdraw into itself, and it has no right to do so. 'In all its essentials,' Leo Baeck says, 'Judaism is destined to spread its message among the nations.' Israel is chosen to be, through its actions and example, a witness among the nations to the eternal truth of a divine revelation, to uphold the ideals of its prophets. For the cause of Judaism is the cause of all mankind, but Zionism is the trivialisation of Judaism.

Such were the beliefs on which I had been brought up. They did not, however, long survive when I began to suffer persecution. Now it was making sense that there should be a refuge for the persecuted in a homeland of their own. Such a land was 'promised' after all, and history seemed to be wending its way towards a fulfilment of that promise. The war with all its terrors and travails seemed to be giving birth to a providential consummation – the rebirth of a Jewish State, the Land of Promise, to which the exiles were returning from the four corners of the earth.

*   *   *

These ideas were still very much alive in my mind when my wife and I visited Israel in 1963, but there I had a peculiar experience which sowed the seeds of a new idea. On a trip from Tel Aviv to Elat, the plane was flying for a short time over the Mediterranean, heading for Ashkelon, and I could see, quite distinctly, not too far to the West, a shore of brown desert sand, and standing on it the silhouette of a town also of brown sand colour, with something like a medieval castle and tall tower, all built in brown sand. There was of course no coastline anywhere near, the nearest land was Cyprus, 200 miles away to the north-west. What I had seen was a mirage, a *fata morgana*, an optical delusion not unusual in this region. Oddly enough, or so it seemed to me, I alone had seen it – my wife to whom I pointed it out, hadn't, nor had the stewardess whom I naively asked whether we were perhaps over the Dead Sea; she understandably did not know what I was talking about.

179

I have never forgotten the experience. It kept coming back to me, and gradually I began to see significance in it. Was perhaps the whole of the 'Promised Land' a mirage? After all, the Promised Land stands for an ideal as do other concepts such as the City on the Hill, the Kingdom of God, the Messianic Age. But if the establishment of the Jewish State is to be regarded as the flourish of the trumpet heralding the approach of the Messiah, would this not be essentially comparable to the Christian belief that the Messiah has indeed come in the person of Jesus? Yet such belief has always been rejected by Jews. I look upon the Messiah as the image of an ideal that we see only from afar, that is to guide us on our trek through the wilderness of life but which we can never hope to achieve. The Second Coming, like the first, is merely a figure of speech. It is very different from the destination of the Wandering Greek, the resourceful Odysseus, who roamed the wide world, saw the cities of many peoples, learnt their ways and endured many hardships until eventually he did reach Ithaca, his ancestral home.

Few episodes in the Bible are so pregnant with meaning as the fact that Moses was not allowed to enter the Promised Land – not I think because of any wrong he had done that would have denied him this fulfilment of his mission, but because of the allegorical truth that the moment he (like any of us) enters, the Promise would not be fulfilled; the Land would prove to be like any other as indeed it was – and can be seen today. It is simply the reality in which men, all of us, must play the game of the world, where good is what seems expedient, evil only what others do, and truth is held identical with propaganda. The rules of that game lay down that while a 'peculiar people', we nevertheless do precisely as everybody else does. It is, alas, not given to man to see the fulfilment of his ideal; it is like the messenger of good tidings scampering over the mountain ridge and we must be content to hear the message that should be a light unto the nations.

But in this again I find reflected the image of the Wandering Jew which I have mentioned before when I left one home and then another. It appears in my mind every time I see or hear the *Flying Dutchman* who sails the seas without ever casting anchor – until he may be redeemed through a woman's love. This motif of course is absent in the Jew's story as is the Christian-invented idea of a curse, unless it be the curse of homelessness which Zionism seeks to banish.

It is perhaps significant that Richard Wagner, the anti-semite, was attracted by this theme for he himself was much tossed about in tempestuous seas and spent the most important of his years outside his homeland. He must have felt, like the Dutchman and the Jew, that (as Ernest Newman puts it) 'life maltreats him and death rejects him', that many lands have harboured him but the land he longs for escapes him. While the Dutchman is to be redeemed through the love of a faithful woman, the Jew can only hope for redemption through the love and faith that an enlightened humanity will show him, for even if his 'ship is without anchor', his 'heart' certainly is not 'without hope'.

If Wagner was attracted by the Flying Dutchman as a symbol of the homeless, even the homeless Jew, it seems also significant that Theodor Herzl, who endeavoured to find a home for the Jews, was attracted and indeed inspired by Wagner's music – 'only on the nights when no Wagner was performed', he wrote, 'did I have doubts about the correctness of my idea', and the second Zionist Congress in 1898 was opened with the overture to *Tannhäuser*.

Mention of Herzl leads me to wonder what do I think of him? No longer what I did when the struggle for a Jewish State was on. He then seemed to me the man who had realistically tackled the 'Jewish Question' as an inter-national issue and presented a 'modern solution'. He had shown himself possessed of amazing vision. At the first Zionist Congress in 1897 he boldly foretold that in fifty years the Jewish State would be born, as indeed it was, almost to the day. I could not help seeing in Herzl as others had seen in Napoleon something like the 'World Spirit' in action, at least as far as the Jews were concerned.

I still see him as a Man of Destiny but I also see the blemishes. When he demanded a Jewish State, it was because he recognised the Jews were a nation differing from others, so far as he was concerned, in that they had no national home; being homeless they were entitled to a home. Without it they were like a ghost among the nations, leading an abnormal life, and he wanted them to lead a 'normal' one. But what if a number of them return to a normality lost 2,000 years ago, while most of them remain in the lands of their dispersion, simply because they feel safe there, at ease and 'at home'?

Herzl realised that they, the majority, would not move until they had suffered the *Judennot*, militant antisemitism, as the Russian Jews had in his time. But does this mean that therefore Zionism must be interested in the survival of antisemitism? Surely not, it would be absurd. He seriously believed that when the Jews begin to leave for Palestine, they will 'put an end to antisemitism' – 'at once and for ever'. In the preface to his booklet *Der Judenstaat*, he explains: 'Everybody is familiar with the phenomenon of steam power, generated by boiling water, lifting the kettle lid. Such tea kettle phenomena are the attempts of Zionists and of kindred associations to check antisemitism. Now I believe that this power, if rightly employed, is powerful enough to propel a large engine and to despatch passengers and goods'.

Inasmuch as he expected the Jews' departure for Palestine to check antisemitism which he clearly perceived to be a scourge not only of the Jews but of society at large, he, still a 19th-century optimist, was certain 'the Governments of all countries ... will serve their own interests in assisting us to obtain the sovereignty we want.'

In this he proved himself trebly mistaken: firstly, with all his searching analysis of antisemitism, he clearly failed to understand its nature, since antisemites are not appeased by the absence of Jews from any one country but will pursue real or imagined Jewish influence wherever they may fancy to see it (as Hitler has shown). Secondly he failed to appreciate the Arab presence in Palestine. He broadly accepted the formula popular among Zionists about 'The land without a people for the people without a land'; and thirdly he assumed that in a 'land without a people', the Jews would, almost automatically, be assisted by the Governments of all countries to obtain control of that land.

This was in fact a disastrous miscalculation, for the Governments of all countries would certainly have to consider not only their own immediate interests if in favour of a departure of the Jews but also the interests of any country expected to admit them and not necessarily prepared to do so, for this exodus would differ in that it would not lead into land delivered into the hand of Israel as it was under Joshua.

Of course there were countries that would still welcome immigrants, among them the USA and Argentina, but others definitely would not – England for example whose plans to restrict immigration were well known to Herzl – but if one assumed that there was such a thing as 'a land without a people', then obviously the temptation was strong to believe that the Jews would be assisted to settle there.

Herzl tried his best by soliciting the interest of the great powers – Britain, imperial Germany, the Sultan of Turkey (who might 'give us Palestine if we in return pledge ourselves to regulate the whole of his finances'). Animated by the visionary power of his dreams, he wanted the Jews, installed by the Asian Turks, to 'form part of the rampart of Europe against Asia, an outpost of civilisation against barbarism'. That kind of terminology was more fitting for a 12th-century Crusader, and only a romantic mind could hit on the bizarre suggestion, made for the benefit of the Pope, that the Jews 'should form a guard of honour about the sanctuaries of Christendom' – even if the agreement of the Pope and other Christian leaders had been obtained.

183

But apart from my view of Herzl, am I still a Zionist? Am I back to where I was in 1929? Not quite. I do believe that Jews are a national as well as a religious community and that as such they are entitled to have a state of their own if only as a refuge in the event of those persecutions of which the centuries hold ample proof. Those who live in that state must be allowed secure, internationally recognised borders. If the state is in Palestine, as for historical reasons I think is must be, proper regard must be had to the Palestinians when they claim their own state: unless they agree to be settled in other countries and those countries agree to accept them – a by no means certain prospect.

I was saddened and dismayed by reports that Palestinians were killing fellow-Palestinians on wanton charges of being 'collaborators' with the Israelis. The same has happened (and may well happen again) among Jews. A striking proof was provided by the Israeli assassin who claimed divine authority when he killed the Israeli Prime Minister Yitzhak Rabin who had concluded a peace deal with the leader of the PLO, Yasser Arafat.

Jewish dissidents outside Israel will be accused by fellow-Jews of 'putting their own interests before the rest of the community', showing 'no interest in Judaism or Zionism'. An Anglo-Jewish academic (!) abused the non- and/or anti-Zionist fellow Jews at the time of the 1917 Balfour Declaration as veritable 'traitors', and while a Jewish Zionist MP, Greville Janner, warned against the tendency of 'branding as traitors' all those Jews who 'do not support current Israeli Government policy', a President of the Board of Deputies of British Jews demanded total solidarity with the State of Israel – 'even when it is in the wrong'.

Such views carry dangerous implications, and Jewish history offers sombre examples and grave warnings. I drew attention to them on the occasion of the Fast of Gedalia, the anniversary of the assassination of a man who, at the time of Judah's defeat by the Babylonians in 586 BC agreed to

184

serve as Governor of the conquered cities (Jeremiah, chapters 40–41). In an article on 'The Lesson of Gedalia', I wrote in the London *Zionist Review* (October 1948):

It is true Gedalia was anxious to bind up the country's wounds and gather the remnant from Egypt and beyond the Jordan. But this anxiety seemed so obviously displayed on behalf of the foreign conqueror: 'Fear not to serve the Chaldeans', ran his writ to the fugitives abroad: 'Dwell in the land and serve the King of Babylon, and it shall be well with you.' And indeed 'all the Jews returned out of all places whither they were driven'.

To the champions of Judah's freedom Gedalia must have seemed Babel's all too willing tool ... In these circumstances it was plainly in accord with time-dishonoured custom that men should band themselves together ... to remove by violence an authority which they alone would judge in the wisdom of their savage passions, traitorous.

'Yet by the Fast of Gedalia, the history of Israel has signally and severely condemned those lawless men whose crime struck not at one human life but at the Sixth Commandment. The Fast of Gedalia is the stringent vindication of the moral law over and against the wild fury of outraged patriotism. However invidious Gedalia's position may have been, however distasteful and offensive his policy, this was not and never could be the way to put it right.'

Talking of Israel, I should like to relate a very different experience which may not be easily matched in any other country. When my wife and I were there in 1963, we booked two tours – one to the South, which passed off without incident, and one to Galilee which was badly marred by two mishaps. I then wrote to Egged, the tour operators, explaining the circumstances. They replied that they were sorry to learn of our troubles but they hoped that

185

when visiting Israel again, we would give them the opportunity to compensate us with any other tour. This was in 1963. I carefully kept the letter, always hoping, however uncertain the prospect, that one day, like the people of Israel generally, we would return.

Well, we did, even if perhaps a little late. It was twenty-two years later, in 1985. So I contacted Egged by letter referring to 'previous correspondence' and saying how pleased I was we would now provide the opportunity they had wished – we were coming. I admit when I told our friends about this plan they thought we were, not to put too fine a point on it, bonkers. Those tour operators, being in business not in charity, would think we must be joking: fancy staking a claim like this after twenty-two years. I disagreed. Twenty-two years? What of it? The Israelis had been waiting 2,000 years when they claimed their Promised Land. Anyway, I happen to be a believer in trying, and we left for Israel even before we had received a reply.

When we called at the company's Tel Aviv office, they were, understandably, surprised, not so much at our letter – greater miracles are known to have happened in the Holy Land – but at the fact that we actually had not been there for so long. They had never heard of any such case. However, the long delay notwithstanding, and overwhelmed by the incontrovertible evidence, they stood by their word. There was no argument; if anything, there appeared to be a feeling we actually deserved a reward for our tenacity and our trust in the company's good faith. Care was taken to ascertain we had not used that letter before, and so as to make discreetly sure we would not use it again, the manager asked for permission to keep the time-honoured document – as a 'souvenir'! Thereafter we were ceremoniously invited to choose a tour from their prospectus, and two complimentary tickets were handed to us to make up for the loss in the far-off past. No summit conference could have produced more winning smiles, and needless to say we now doubly enjoyed the tour.

If there was a joke in the story, as our friends had

suggested, it came later, at home when we found the company's reply to my original letter. Here they said it was not their usual practice to compensate beyond one year, but in our case they would make an exception in view of 'this nice manner of keeping a letter for 22 years': they would allow us a reduction by 50 per cent. Clearly, our personal appearance made such an impression that we were in fact granted 100 per cent! A little patience, combined with a good memory, had gone, literally, a long way to pay off.

I was so delighted I told the story to the *Jerusalem Post* which printed it, and as a result the manager of Egged was interviewed on Radio Israel. He was asked what he had said to this British tourist: 'I told him not to wait another twenty-two years before he came back to Israel'; and what did he (I) reply to that? Well, I do not remember what I said but according to a listener who heard me quoted in Hebrew, it was this: 'In another twenty-two years I hope to be viewing the world from a very different angle.' I may well have said it – it certainly would have been true, though I am surprised to find I am still around to tell the tale.

While in Israel in 1963, I had an opportunity of acting the part of an (unsuccessful) marriage broker, at the very least a liaison broker, or perhaps an Arab-Jewish friendship broker. When on that unfortunate Galilean trip our Egged coach conked out in what seemed to be the middle of nowhere but actually was near the Arab village of Nahif, about fifteen miles east of Akko, I, realising that we would not soon move on, walked with a South African friend in the direction of the village, off the main road. We noticed a small farm yard with chickens, some brown, a colour familiar to us, some a most unfamiliar pink. We saw the elderly Arab owner, resting on a wooden bench in the shade of his hut, and we walked towards him to enquire about this peculiar colour. He, in his flowing wide robes, got up to meet us, possibly regarding us as potential buyers. Unfortunately he did not understand English, but while we were hanging around there, two young Arab fellows came up behind us, students it turned out of the Haifa Technical College. The one, a bright and lively boy, at once asked what was going on; we told him and he elicited this explanation: some of the chickens were in the habit of straying on to a neighbour's yard, and in order to identify them the owner had painted them pink.

Having so obliged us, Abdul wondered whether we would care to drop in at their home, a few yards further up the dusty lane. We accepted the kind invitation and were led into the 'sitting room' where we met a tall figure, so rigid and apparently immobile that at first we thought it was a statue, but Abdul introduced us: his father. There were a table and chairs, cushioned wooden benches along the walls, and in one corner a flat heating plate. Abdul enquired whether we would like hot and sweet coffee or cold and unsweetened, and while he prepared it (or arranged for it to be prepared), we tried to start a conversation with the father who had sat down on a high-backed chair. It took some time to get things going but after we had complimented him on his 'well-bred', 'intelligent' son, he volunteered quite a bit of information: they were a family of (I believe) eight; we had met the three males, the rest did not appear. He was the headmaster of the village school with 437 children, he said, counting all the children from neighbouring villages who were attending.

He would have told us more but was cut short by Abdul who now took over. He did not waste much time but, almost like the Flying Dutchman, came straight to the point: did we have any daughters? The South African could not oblige but I could, so he said would she care to write to him, he wanted a penfriend. I replied I could not of course speak for her (which seemed to surprise him) but I would forward his request.

From the window we could keep an eye on our coach, and it seemed to us that we had better go back. So I turned to the old man, thanking him for his hospitality and enquiring if he had any wish. Yes, he said, drawing himself up in his magnificent chair and with all the dignity of a patriarch:

yes, his wish was for our happiness; he was glad to have received us, and should we at any time be in this neighbourhood again, we were welcome to regard this as our home.

When we got back, the trouble had not yet been repaired but a message had been sent to Egged headquarters in Haifa, asking for a relief coach. In the meantime, a coach of the rival Union company was passing, and it was stopped by our driver who asked them to take us on. When my friend and I arrived this was what was going on, and we all set off on our journey home. Halfway to Akko, we met the relief coach; our driver told his colleague he needn't bother, those stranded people were all aboard. But obviously he was not fully familiar with Israeli trade union practice: that driver replied he had orders to go to Nahif and to Nahif he was going – orders was orders. So in Akko we had to wait for this Egged relief coach's return.

Back home, I discharged my duty but Esther declined at once. She suggested her friend Margaret who was indeed more enterprising. She wrote to Abdul and back came almost at once a nice letter stating all relevant details – age, height, weight, father's monthly salary, plus a photo and a small parcel of presents: a tablet of soap, a comb and other items made fragrant with all the sweetest perfumes of the East that even King Solomon in all his glory could not have selected with greater consideration for the Queen of Sheba. Margaret was a little surprised and thanked him for his generous attention. Promptly another letter arrived saying now that *he* had sent his gifts, what about *hers*, and in order to save trouble he would suggest the Oxford English Dictionary and a good English camera (apart from any other item she might think of). Now Margaret decided to refer the matter back to me as after all the begetter of the scheme, and it seemed to me that, the idea of penfriendship clearly differing between East and West, it might be wiser to call it a day. No more was heard of Abdul, the bright boy of Nahif.

# 10

# MIDDLESEX HOSPITAL

I tried to make myself useful to society by becoming a blood donor and over a number of years I gave many a pint until it was discovered that I was suffering from, yes, anaemia, and instead of *giving* blood should have *received* some. Things came to such a pass that I found it a strain to walk, especially uphill, and when I saw a specialist at Middlesex Hospital in London I was immediately detained. After five weeks I was back to normal and finished this part of my career with a Donor Award Badge in respect of my twenty donations.

Life in hospital was of course a good opportunity for reflection. I received few of those cheering get well messages which some committees are reputed to pass by 6-to-4 majorities, but I had many visitors, and though they would claim to give no more than a token proof of friendship, it was heart-warming to have the comfort of their presence. Nor were visitors alone in helping to keep the spirit up. If ever I was tempted to feel bored, I would begin to count my blessings. There seemed no end of them. I hope I am not being sentimental: however accomplished the masters of medicine, they were little compared with the blessing of a good wife, 'doing her husband good and not evil all the days of her life'.

There were more of my blessings I became aware of when I saw the sufferings of others who had hardly a hope of returning to normal life but bore their fate in gallant endurance. I thought how odd (albeit rationally accountable) that suffering – our own or watching that of others – rarely makes us better. In one of his plays, Strindberg actually says suffering creates 'a sort of noble dignity' while 'happiness only makes everything commonplace'. Happiness may do that, I agree, but suffering, oddly enough, may well do exactly the same (and worse), or am I out-Strindberging the master? When we suffer we are inclined to think it is undeserved; why us?, we seem to ask. The world must owe us a reparation. We have a claim that is denied us and therefore feel entitled to take it out on others. Thus, instead of generating compassion, suffering as likely as not will often make us bitter, callous, unforgiving. We are constantly enjoined to remember that we were slaves in Egypt. How many of us do – or care? And what precisely does it mean to them?

Every care was taken for our comfort, occasionally I thought to a remarkable extent. I never knew patients in a hospital ward were allowed to smoke in bed – day or night – and I spent some time critically examining all the exits from the second floor, by lift, stairs and, more especially, by rope. I remember once seeing in a hotel room the considerate notice: 'Will smokers in bed please leave the names and addresses of next of kin'. But no similar discreet precaution was taken here.

I remember with pleasure a pitch-dark Trinidadian lass who always, at 11 a.m., punctually and cheerfully drove the coffee trolley into the ward, offering black or white. It was perhaps not only respect for the Race Relations Board that stopped me from specifying white, and I hope I pleased her by making it black.

I confess, however, I often lived in terror of meal times – far more than of my operation, for then at least I was unconscious, and I sometimes wondered whether hospital patients should not be eligible for an anaesthetising

191

injection before sitting down for their repast. Quite apart from compassion, it would be almost in the national interest, for it would save many generous portions from being ruthlessly consigned to the swill.

Mind you, there always was a choice of three to four main courses, but fancy names tended to conceal the substance, and only when the lid was off the lukewarm plates did the moment of truth arrive. I remember one impishly recurrent item called 'Russian fish' which I steadfastly shunned, suspecting it to be little more than a Red Herring. However, there is no arguing about taste, and it would be quite wrong for me to grumble, especially as I was for some time kept on drip feed which cut out the main c(o)urse and left me with 'Fluids Only', in other words soup and jelly: a great mercy I was most thankful for.

The things you mull over in a busy ward, especially after dusk – often enough to the accompaniment of a neighbour's vigorous variations on a snoring theme, or a Frenchman's howling tantrums when he misunderstood the innocent remark 'We must have your co-operation' as 'We must have an operation', or another foreigner's desperate wrestling with the enigmatic query 'Did you have your bowels open?' until eventually intense sign language managed to pinpoint the relevant locality.

I still chuckle a little over the more sedate fellow patient who was intrigued by my continuous wanderings up and down the high and by-ways of the place. I said to him I supposed he had heard of the Wandering Jew; now, I said, he had actually seen him. I am glad to report my friend was duly awestruck; among all the weird visions overhanging a hospital ward, he had never dreamt of setting eyes on this one – outside, yes, especially in the showrooms of the nearby rag trade, but up here, hardly.

A peculiar specimen of the Wandering Jew happens to be prominently associated with Middlesex Hospital. In fact I could see his name emblazoned on a huge block facing my ward – The Meyerstein Wing. Actually there are, or were,

192

two Meyersteins, father and son. Edward William, a successful member of the London stock exchange, gave the Middlesex £350,000 when it was rebuilt in the 1930s. Despite his surname, he was English, born in England of English-born Jewish parents (with German ancestors). In 1938, then High Sheriff of Kent, he was duly knighted for his benefactions to health services.

More remarkable, however, is the son, Edward Harry William, who inherited the wealth though not the interest. He was brought up as a Christian but discovered much to his chagrin that if you are called Meyerstein then you are or should be a German Jew. He did not mind that, only, he remarked pathetically, he 'happened to be an English poet', which he was (albeit in a minor key), and the *Encyclopaedia Judaica* (though not the *Britannica*) faithfully records his not inconsiderable output, both verse and prose.

He suffered much from the Anglo-German–Christian-Jewish dichotomy, especially at Harrow School where the boys made a cruel sport of him. 'I think,' he later confessed, 'a Jew who keeps his religion is proud of it and generally says "I'm as good as you anyway". But a person of Jewish (or partly Jewish) antecedents who has been baptised, especially if he has a German name, was due for hell.'

The melancholy story often kept me busy when I lay awake long after the lights had gone out. Meyerstein senior has deserved well of his fellow-men by supporting this hospital which takes care of our bodies: what about the ailing minds of which Meyerstein junior had so sad an experience? However, this is perhaps another story, and I would rather declare my gratitude to the Meyersteins and to all who have made, and continue to make, Middlesex Hospital an outstanding place for the relief of human suffering.

Incidentally, when I came home, one of the first letters I opened in the accumulated mail was from my synagogue reminding me that my increased contribution to the Funeral Expenses Scheme was now due.

As I mentioned the Meyersteins and their share in building the Middlesex Hospital, I might add that they interested me particularly as figures in a story to which I had long given attention – the history of the German Jews who came to England during the 19th century (up to the First World War), the generation of the Edwardian Court Jews like Sir Ernest Cassel, the banker; also Ludwig Mond, the research chemist, whose sons, Sir Alfred (the first Lord Melchott) and Sir Robert, founded the Imperial Chemical Industries (ICI); Hugo Hirst, founder of the General Electric Company; Marcus and Hermann Adler, the Chief Rabbis, etc. They were, in a manner of speaking, my forerunners, and I found them in all walks of life, in the provinces as well as in London. In fact I came across two natives of Exin who had arrived in Britain as early as 1863, precisely seventy years before me – Alexander Joseph, a jeweller's factor, who settled in Birmingham and was naturalised in 1873, and his brother Moritz, a watch manufacturer and also a jeweller's factor, who likewise settled in Birmingham, after three years in Glasgow, and was naturalised in 1878.

The story of these early Jewish immigrants from Germany appeared to be largely unknown. I managed to collect sufficient material for about twenty-five articles which were all printed, for the most part in the monthly journal of the Association of Jewish Refugees, but no publisher cared to make a book of them.

The history of German immigration into England generally had been studied and published, but no special attention was ever given to the Jews amongst them, at least not in England. A distinction was drawn by German antisemites who would cast aspersions on these Jews' British patriotism – while, especially during the Kaiser war, English antisemites would suspect them of secret German sympathies. An interesting feature of my research was the evidence of German antisemitism as a cause of Jewish emigration as early as the first half of the 19th century. I frequently lectured on the subject and a talk was broadcast by the BBC's German section.

*    *    *

Here I may perhaps digress a little to relate an encounter I once had with Enoch Powell because it concerned a German Jewish refugee. In October 1968 Lord St Oswald, in a letter to *The Times*, happened to mention that 'some of Enoch Powell's closest friends were German Jews in whose rescue from Germany he played a part'. I was intrigued by this piece of information. I wrote first to Lord St Oswald and when I did not hear from him because (as he wrote me later) he was abroad, I approached Powell direct. In the course of a letter dated 10 November 1968 I wrote:

> Do you think you could tell me a little about your experiences of German Jewish refugees? If it were possible and you could spare the time, I would be happy to meet you for a short interview in which I could take notes. My intention is to incorporate your story in an article which would appear in the monthly journal published by the Association of Jewish Refugees in Great Britain.

Powell replied immediately: would I fix an appointment with his secretary? I did and we met on 29 November at his Belgravia flat where I was graciously received and we had a most informative conversation which yielded many (to me) unknown data on his interest not in Jewish refugees generally but in one particular scholar, Paul Maas, an authority on Byzantine Greek learning.

I made careful notes which I used for an article that appeared in a paper different from the one I had mentioned in my letter though also published by German Jewish refugees. It was a few months after he had delivered his now notorious 'rivers of blood' speech, and I briefly if critically referred to what *The Times* had called his 'doctrine of the new tribalism' in connection with the recent immigrants.

I sent him a copy of the article to which I received this reply on 7 May 1969:

This is to acknowledge your letter and enclosure of 3rd May. I gave you the interview on which your article is based because you told me you were engaged in a serious study of the Jewish emigration to this country during the 1930s. I would not have done so, had you told me that your intention was to base upon it an article in a Journal. I will say no more than the article is vilely tendentious.

I was not surprised he did not like the article. In my reply of 11 May I said I perfectly understood that he considered it tendentious, though 'vilely tendentious' seemed a little hard. But I was surprised at the suggestion implied in his letter that I had obtained the interview under false pretences. I said so, quoting from my letter, and I added:

I did not tell you, because it would not be correct and you must have misunderstood, that I was 'engaged in a serious study of the Jewish emigration to this country during the 1930s'. The study in which I am engaged is not of those who came to this country 30-odd years ago, but of those who came during the 19th century. I probably did not make myself sufficiently clear.

I went on: 'I feel I ought to say again how much I regret your reaction. I retain a pleasant recollection of the interview. It is my honest opinion that – in your general view on immigration which I found impossible to ignore – you are honestly mistaken, and I have been trying to express in my article sorrow rather than anger.'

Powell never replied. He might have acknowledged his error: I believe it would have been fair and in accordance with the virtues of a gentleman which I am sure he must cherish. As it was, he revealed, to my mind, a sorry fall from grace. I thought it was a great pity.

In fairness I ought to mention that I no longer hold the view expressed in my reply to Powell. I am inclined to believe that the development during the past thirty years is tending to lend force to his forecast.

# 11

# SPANISH HOLIDAYS

Next to the German Jews of the past, I turned my interest to the Spanish Jews – not those of the Middle Ages who were expelled in 1492 but those who had begun to return. My little book on them which appeared in New York was entitled *The Ghosts of 1492*; it dealt not so much with a modern history of those Jews, of which there was very little since they had only recently begun to settle, but rather with what I called *Jewish aspects of the struggle for religious freedom in Spain*. The German Jews seemed to be kindred to the Spanish Jews – having attained lofty heights and fallen to pitiful depths. I knew what had happened in Germany, I now wondered how Spain was behaving, and Spain's emergence from the Middle Ages seemed to me a fascinating spectacle: we are still witnessing it. The booklet was well received in the Spanish press.

We frequently went to Spain for a holiday – not among the madding crowds of the Costa Brava but down in the history-laden South, in Cordoba, Granada, Seville. Some of our friends took a dim view of our going to Spain as in those days Franco was still alive and Spain was judged to be a Fascist country. I may claim to have some experience of Fascism. I wish all of it had been of the then Spanish brand, and while nobody is perfect – Spain wasn't, we weren't – only some of the stories we heard about Spain proved to be perfect nonsense.

I once spoke about Spain to the Jewish Blind Society, and the first questioner took me up on Spanish Fascism – how could I go there?, etc. Now, you cannot always tell how blind a man is when you see him, but this one obviously was totally blind.

I was reading the newspapers in Spain (1975) and found an open public debate about the need for what was called 'social change'. Ministers, ex-Ministers and other pundits (as well as leading articles) were demanding more liberty – in some such terms as 'wider horizons', 'necessary reforms', 'political evolution' and 'not simply formulae devoid of content'. The official 'Fascist' paper actually gave prominence to the statement 'The dignity of man requires a society that is free and democratically organised.' Some 'Fascism', this.

Traces of the Jews' Marrano existence can still be found, though. When I looked for the synagogue in Malaga, I discovered it, after a determined search, at the back of the Palace of Justice, in a tall modern building which housed, among other distinguished tenants, the British Consulate. But whereas this one was clearly marked outside, no sign betrayed the presence of the Jews, and only the friendly caretaker, forgoing the delights of his transistor, directed me up to the third floor where a copper plate announced the *Comunidad Israelita de Málaga*.

After a few persistent knocks (because the bell was out of order), a slightly anaemic, not over-expectant young lady opened the door. She had a touch of the sadness which painters often lend to Oriental Jewish eyes, but she may just as well have been bored, and certainly she looked at me (in G. K. Chesterton's words) 'as a tired man looks at the flies'. However, she kindly let me in when I explained that I had written to the wrong address for an interview with Rabbi Isaac Azoulay.

Well, it was not my lucky day. The rabbi was at some conference in Tel Aviv, and here I was with *La Secretaria* who seemed somewhat panicky at the thought of having to take me on. The office was pitifully bare, on the small table just the telephone, the appointmeant book (I think), and a French Magazine *Confidences*, of the *Woman's Realm* type, in which she was reading 'How to eat well and still keep your figure'. This did not strike me as required reading in her case, but I have no doubt she had reason to expect many more 'confidences' with which my presence could hardly compete.

I thought it rather clever of her to read French, and after a few exchanges in Spanish, I discovered that she was actually French – the daughter of a French father and a Moroccan mother. She did not pretend to know much about Jews in Malaga and seemed to care even less. So, with her permission, I had a look round.

There were about a hundred wooden seats for the men and forty-eight leather-covered chairs for the ladies. Worshippers could help themselves from a large variety of books printed in Jerusalem, Tel Aviv, New York, Vienna, even Malaga (1972), Casablanca and Livorno (with the Hebrew stamp of the congregation of nearby Gibraltar). I would have loved to stay a little longer and browse in the books, but it was nearly one o'clock, the hour when the Siesta begins, and Mlle. *La Secretaria* was getting understandably restive.

So I took my leave and settled down to a *café solo* under the gorgeous palm trees of the *Avenida del Generalísimo*. Palm trees do something to me – they make me feel the desert-dweller that in truth I think I am. I thought of the lovely story of the Moorish poet who came to Cordoba a thousand-odd years ago, bringing his own palm which he planted in his patio, and he sang to it, wistfully: 'Oh palm, thou art as I am an alien in the West, far from thine fatherland'. How much like the Hebrew Spanish poet Yehuda Halevi who, about the same time, sighed: 'My heart is in the East and I am at the end of the West'.

Some believe Jews have a spiritual kinship with Spain. Talmudic authority was actually claimed for the charming

200

legend displayed in Fuengirola's little paperback shop Julius, owned by an English Jew: 'Man sleeps and in his dreams he sees Spain'. Unfortunately we did not meet 'Julius' when we were there. (I would have loved to introduce myself to him as 'Caesar'.) He happened to be away on business up North. So we were told by the matron-like lady who seemed to be the second in command, seated at the entrance where she was dealing with enquiries and presiding over the revenue. It appeared that customers had been referring to her as the boss' wife – quite a gratuitous assumption of course, but it clearly accounted for the striking announcement conspicuously displayed on one of the walls, 'We are not married'.

A good deal of attention was paid to the numerous English tourists in Fuengirola. There was a place called The Pub, a feeble, anaemic reproduction of the real thing. There was also, in several places, the bold notice 'Tea like mother makes it', even 'Lyons Tea like mother makes it'. We fell for it once but never again after we had discovered it is not the tea that matters, however English, it is the water that makes all the difference, and had we known we would have brought our own English water with us. But the most charming thing we came upon in Fuengirola was the little coffee room (if it can be so described); its name was 'In this little corner I'm waiting for you'.

In Torremolinos we had the good fortune of being invited by a gentleman, a native of Casablanca, who was the ritual supervisor at the local kosher butcher's. He and his gentle young wife treated us most royally to an astonishing variety of foods with which we were only imperfectly acquainted. While she was spending almost all her time in the kitchen, the equivalent of *purdah* I guessed, he readily provided a running commentary on each dish. Only one item was to remain unexplained until we had tasted and thoroughly digested it. All he would say was that like Guinness it was good for you, sure to give us strength and a cheerful outlook on life, and indeed I could feel my muscles bulging and my usual pessimism

201

shrinking as I got ready to brave the revelation: we had just consumed the testicles of an animal – I don't know which, in the confusion I forgot to enquire (not that it would have mattered) – and we were assured that this, expertly prepared, was one of the choicest delicacies any mortal could wish for. Later, having come to, I was dimly reminded of the passage in the Odyssey where a man is made to face the prospect of having not only his nose and ears cut off but also his privy parts unceremoniously removed as raw meat for the discriminating dogs which would relish the exquisite treat. Anyway, we were grateful for our friend's considerate timing of the information: testicles certainly make a notable change from *gefilte fish* or roast beef and two veg.

One of our most entertaining experiences though, was in San Sebastian, up North in the Basque province. I had spotted the only local Jew in a population of 135,000, Señor Martin Othaiz, to whom we had announced ourselves, by letter, as visitors from England, wishing to pay him our respects since his fame had spread as far as the British Isles, etc. He was duly flattered to hear this and jovially welcomed us into his little health food shop. The sturdy, stocky man, with his cloth cap and mariner's sweater, would have made an appropriate figure down in the picturesque harbour. Pleased as he was to see us, he (no doubt taught by experience) first made sure of our credentials, for it appeared that I at least did not strike him as the typical John Bull. So he lost no time in asking a number of searching questions: first, was I really a Jew? My general appearance might have mitigated any lingering doubt, but though in England I would pass for a fine old Hebrew gentleman, in Spain I am easily liable to be mistaken for a genuine native type – a muleteer or a bullring attendant, if not (at that time) a Government spy.

Well, if I was a Jew, where exactly did I come from? Were we born in England? What did our name really mean? Did we belong to a synagogue? Did I go there regularly? Did I know any Hebrew? How good was it? (Better, he appeared to hope, than my Spanish.) He did not, curiously enough, enquire about my business and how much money I made – which is usually of interest to Americans. But there were a number of other questions

– which I forget
And some I need not mention yet.

When I tried to reciprocate the capital interest by venturing a general enquiry concerning the state of the country, he in traditional Jewish fashion countered with another question, this time addressed, in broken but intelligible English, to my wife: was it a habit of mine to institute Gestapo-like investigations? There was 'laughter', as the Parliamentary reports would put it.

However, he was now set to unfurl his colours in style. For a start, his name was not Martin but Moshe, and Othaiz was the Spanish version of some sort of more Ashkenasi designation. He hailed from SW France, not very far away, and he was still travelling regularly on business to Bayonne. He archly confided to us that he possessed what he called an 'international passport', and to make good this astonishing claim, he pulled out – his prayer shawl.

He was pleased to see that this little joke went down well, and he now produced from under his sweater further tokens of his identity – a gold chain with two Stars of David and one mini-Scroll of the Law. With the same magic touch he produced a similar chain from under the pullover of his rather meek-looking elderly assistant who was presented to us as a Hebrew Basque.

This, with its quite anachronistic suggestion of a Marrano atmosphere, would have been sufficient to reveal both master and servant as genuine if unusual members of the House of Israel, but Señor Othaiz would not yet rest content. He hurried into the back room and emerged with a huge batch of assorted Jewish magazines mainly in French (which appeared to be his staple – health – diet), also odd Israeli and New York ones, together with Spanish-language specimens from Latin America. Not all appeared to have been thoroughly perused but the whole performance, as a demonstration of cultural interest, was truly overwhelming. He legitimately wondered whether I had ever seen anything like this before; he certainly had every reason to feel confident that no Jewish health food store in England (if any) could compete with him in this respect.

I now thought it safe to come back to my original question about conditions in the country; he brusquely retorted: didn't I know they had a Nazi Government? Frankly, I did not, or I would hardly have come in the first place. It was 1971, when Franco was still in power, but Fascism was on the decline. Besides what sort of 'Nazi' Fascism was it that would allow a Jew to conduct his business unmolested, crossing the border back and forth at will? It turned out that he was a Basque nationalist who strongly resented the 'Nazi' Government in Madrid, so I thought I had better not pursue the explosive matter any further.

It was now time for us to go, and in true Biblical manner he would not let his guests depart without showering upon them some of his choicest merchandise which I am certain did much to keep us in excellent health.

I had learned Spanish at school where it was an optional subject. I kept it up through the years, and it proved quite a help on our visits to Spain. I shall never forget the success I scored when on our first visit I addressed the customs official in his own language: how impressed and overjoyed he was, with the result that he did not bother even to look at our luggage.

But sometimes the success was less obvious. Once, in San Sebastian, my wife showed some interest in a pretty little necklace in a jeweller's shop window, somewhere off the beaten track. As we entered, announced by the old-fashioned bell, not a soul was to be seen on the spacious but rather murky, almost ghost-like premises, and only after a while a gentleman emerged from the mist in the background, making his way, hesitantly and without great expectations,

204

towards the counter where he seemed to enquire what it was we wanted.

Now I tried, to the best of my vocabulary, to explain, but no effect was visible on his bored face. He seemed to be thinking, fitfully, on what he had heard, mulling it over in his mind but apparently unable to come to a likely conclusion. I was a little taken aback and thought it advisable to repeat my message but without so improving the situation. Suddenly something seemed to strike him; he did not say a word but disappeared into the background – ominously, I thought, because I expected him to move in the opposite direction, towards the shop window. After a while he returned, carrying a heavy two-handled outsize silver fish. He carefully set it down in front of us and enquired: was this perhaps what we wanted? I did not like to spoil his quaint expectation, especially as so great an effort had been made to satisfy a customer. I merely marvelled at the magic which had turned a nimble necklace into this huge silver fish, and we pointed out the object of our interest in the window.

Still, such knowledge of Spanish as I had and have never neglected has helped to open for me not only Spain but also parts of Latin America, even Peru where Uncle Gustavo emigrated in 1865. I tried to reconstruct his life story but made little progress beyond a rudimentary article which appeared in Lima and (revised) in New York. I sought to obtain information about him by writing a letter to the editor of Lima's leading daily, *El Comercio*. The letter was published – with, perhaps inevitably, limited success, for how many of that generation or those likely to remember Gustavo Badt, could have been left? However, I managed to piece together a somewhat potted story of his life and I will tell it, as I feel it might be of some more than passing and personal interest.

# 12

# PERUVIAN INTERLUDE

Gustav Badt was sixteen when he left his native hamlet Exin, in the Prussian province of Posen, for Lima, the 'city of kings', in the land of the Incas, at the other end of the world. He was not entirely on his own: his six-years-older brother Michael went with him, and presumably the family knew somebody who had gone there before and the reports had been tempting. There were indeed many who were then leaving their ancient homes. As early as 1854, the Jewish paper *Allgemeine Zeitung des Judenthums* reported from Bremen 'not an emigration but a veritable "migration of the peoples"', and the reporter added wistfully: 'We cannot honestly say we are sorry to see them go. Unfair discrimination, humiliation, and the denial of solemnly granted civil rights can be given no better answer than – emigration.' This was eighty years before the Nuremberg Laws.

I don't know what precisely the family's expectations were when they sent the boys to Peru. It appears that, with the end of Spanish rule, the various South American republics including Peru were believed to be offering attractive opportunities in trade and commerce, and suitable youngsters were recruited by agents of enterprising planners. Some of those youngsters may have seen bright visions, conjured up by news of the gold mines not far from Lima, and some probably saw not much more. The family no doubt hoped the boys would do well in business and in a country clearly in need of European efficiency and drive. Indeed in Peru, as late as the early 1900s, the main handicap of industry was seen not only in the absence of skilled workmen but also in a 'general disinclination of working people to work regular hours', etc. The 19th century, therefore, was the time when European immigrants were welcome and much appreciated; as late as 1873 a Peruvian law provided for each arrival of this type to be assisted with a fair sum of money and a free grant of land.

There were drawbacks of course. If Prussia was unenlightened in some ways, so was Peru in others. There was liberty, yes, and no personal humiliation, but as likely as not there was licence degenerating into lawlessness, violence erupting in revolution, rebellion and *coups d'état*, assassination and the rule of the gun, to say nothing of a corruption which was accepted as a fact of public life. Judges were virtually expecting to be bribed, and Henry Meiggs, the famous North American railway constructor, found 'the only way to get on with successive Governments of Peru was to let each sell itself for its own price'.

A hideously characteristic example of the gangsterism practised in high quarters happened in 1872 when the Minister of War, supported by his three brothers, all army colonels, seized the President and declared himself dictator. He failed however to gauge the strength of popular feeling at that moment. An angry mob lynched and murdered one of the brothers, whereupon the dictator ordered the imprisoned President to be shot, holding him responsible. Armed civilians now stormed the barracks in which the dictator was hiding. He and his brothers were killed and their mutilated bodies exhibited, for all to see, high up from the towers of Lima's venerable cathedral.

Things were particularly bad after Peru had lost its five-year war with Chile (1879–84). The country was, quite literally, in ruins; Lima, the capital, once the proud residence

207

of Spanish Viceroys, suffered the supreme humiliation of being occupied by the enemy for several years. No one then could be safe from a looting and marauding mob – Chileans as the Peruvians claimed, or Peruvians as the Chileans did. A historian adds this pathetic if picturesque detail: 'It was rare to see people wearing new and elegant dresses, and when they were spotted, they were thought to be foreigners.'

I often wondered how the Prussian small-town boy made his way in this savage society. Oddly enough he soon did. He was helped by the general Peruvian attitude in those days towards trade and commerce which (according to a modern Peruvian writer) was 'reserved for members of the lower classes and acceptable only among foreigners', and the foreigners, immigrants like Badt himself, could offer a wide field. There were scores of Britons, North Americans, Italians, Frenchmen, also a colony of Chinese, and there were about 300 Germans, among them a number of Jews. Badt naturally sought their company, especially as the Germans were on good terms with the Jews. A 'Club Germania' had been opened in 1863, and its leading light, its founder in fact, was a fellow-Jew, Max Bromberg. When in 1875 the foundation stone was laid for the Jewish cemetery, the local German choral society Teutonia took part in the ceremony, and according to a Jewish reporter, their 'splendid chaunting added much to the solemnity of the occasion'.

Germany in those days enjoyed the very highest reputation – in Peru as well as in the rest of South America – particularly after Bismarck had made her the foremost power on the continent of Europe. German technology, German education and especially Krupp's big guns were regarded as symbols of perfection and prestige. So if German-Jewish immigrants in Lima preferred the German Club to exclusively Jewish society, they had sound reasons, sentimental ones but also material ones. In his study of the foreigners' stake in Peru's trade, a Peruvian economist remarks (1908): 'The Germans today control the greater

208

part of our import trade, having largely succeeded in supplanting the English. The progress of the German trade is due to the fact that they carefully study the tastes and likings of the clients. Their merchants and commission agents, backed by the talent of their manufacturers for the production of cheap articles for the mass of the people, are gradually gaining the commercial predominance in Peru.'

An association with these fellow countrymen was bound to be profitable. Badt almost certainly began his career with a German, or German-Jewish, firm. An important position was held by the brothers Jacoby who were jewellers, pawn-brokers, dealers in antiques, as well as bankers represent-ing the Rothschilds in Lima. They nearly went bankrupt in the war with Chile because, in their patriotic enthusiasm, they lent the Government money far beyond the credit it deserved. Many Jews also followed other trades such as the cigar trade which yielded substantial profits, especially from the ladies. A romantically impressionable visitor, with an eye on essentials, noted: 'The smoke of the cigars rises between rosy lips, behind which can be seen the prettiest teeth.'

Then of course Jews were involved in the clothing trade in which they soon prospered, and it was this trade in which Badt was apprenticed. He soon developed a par-ticular fancy for the manufacture of silk, which was a shrewd choice. Silk, like satin, was much in vogue among the ladies of Lima. The two fabrics, said a French expert then visiting the city, were 'the only ones the ladies don't disdain for their celebrated dresses, the petticoat and the large *mantilla*' (headscarf and veil combined). About that time too Charles Darwin happened to be in Peru and in his diary he not only mentions the attractive young ladies who wear a 'black veil made of silk,' but his scientifically penetrating eye also discovered the 'very white silk stock-ings' over their 'very pretty feet'.

So there was obviously a big demand for silk, and this was, to some extent, supplied by the numerous Chinese importers, but no industry existed that might have profitably manufactured silk, like many other commodities, at home. Here Badt had the idea of attending to the demand directly.

He started his enterprise by acquiring some land which was cheap (as the immigration law of 1873 had shown). The estate, the *Chacra Colorada*, was then outside Lima though now it is a densely populated part of the city. Here he planted some 14,000 mulberry trees which, with the help of another import from China, the silk worm, were to supply the raw material for his operations.

He had also begun to employ a fair number of native labourers when work was interrupted by the war with Chile. In the defence of Lima (1881) he organised the work force as well as his personal friends in a special Home Guard named after the Inca chief Huascar, with himself in the titular rank as Captain. He does not seem to have excelled in his military career though, which was brief anyway. The Peruvian army (according to a Peruvian historian) was altogether largely 'an army on paper', the navy 'a naval museum', and so the Home Guard might easily have illustrated the Duke of Wellington's observation: 'I don't know whether our captains will frighten the enemy but, by God, they frighten me'. Nor would the patriotic Badt have claimed to be a military genius. His qualifications shone elsewhere.

It was the time when the era of Peru's political revolutions was overtaken by something like an industrial revolution. Around the turn of the century the economy was beginning to overcome its stagnation. Industrial ventures were started which managed to raise capital locally as well as abroad. This was when Badt saw his chance in an expanding silk trade, offering opportunities for sound investment. Having practised in this field over many years, he now entered into partnership with a more technologically minded native Peruvian, Julio T. Chocano, whom he enabled to import some of the most modern machinery from Europe. Chocano built his silk factory on Badt's estate, and he showed his gratitude by calling it, the first of

210

its kind in Peru, La Germánica. It was opened in February 1908 in the presence of Government and high society representatives, also under the patronage of the German Minister whose friendship Badt had taken care to cultivate. The occasion was indeed a Peruvian-German event as the flags of both nations were flown and an Artillery band struck up the national anthem, at least Peru's: they did not seem too sure of *Deutschland über alles*.

Badt was by then securely established in Lima society. He was, and remained, technically a foreigner. In his association with Chocano, for example, at the opening of the factory, he emphasized his German nationality (which added to his standing), and the hoisting of the German flag side by side with the Peruvian must have seemed to him perfectly natural. He never applied for naturalisation (which would have been readily granted) nor did he or any of the immigrants from Germany care to change his name. He just added an 'o' to Gustav.

I was thinking of Uncle Gustavo when I later heard the little ditty (adapted from Gilbert and Sullivan) which was as true of him as it was of many (though not all) of his countrymen in Lima:

> He might have been a Prussian,
> A Scot, or Turk, or Russian,
> Or a native of Peru
> Or a native of Peru.
>
> But in spite of all temptations
> To belong to other nations
> He firmly remained a Jew.

From time to time Badt would send the family references to himself in some of Lima's glossy society magazines which in those days kept appearing and disappearing at more to less regular intervals, all according to the unsteady finance available to keep them going. There he was presented as a 'well-known German gentleman' who not only 'by hard

211

and honourable work' had acquired a 'considerable fortune' but also was 'the first amongst us to start the latest industry, that of silk manufacture, sparing neither cost nor effort in the development of an enterprise called to such high destiny in Peru', etc. In September 1907 the growth of his estate was featured as a tribute to one who 'forms part of that great-hearted band of foreigners who have come to our country not only to make their fortune but in order to contribute, solidly and efficiently, to its material and moral progress'.

I have a feeling that Badt, quite legitimately, served as a kind of midwife in the birth of these reports. The art of publicity as a science had just been discovered in Peru to be part of 'the modern spirit of enterprise', and Badt was not slow to take advantage of it in the promotion of his interests. He got himself interviewed and generously paid for the publication of these suitably embroidered stories. These magazines would print anything so long as it was handsomely paid for. In one of them I found a photo of my parents taken at the time of their wedding. This had of course been paid for by Uncle Gustavo as if it were an ordinary advert, but the relationship between him and the couple was explained, and so Badt got publicity as well as the folks back home who must have been greatly pleased to find themselves presented to Lima society.

However, Badt's interests were not only in business. He also showed himself concerned for the health and housing of the poor for whom he built, at his own expense, a whole street of one-floor houses, such houses being chosen for safety reasons because of the frequent earthquakes that were afflicting Lima. He especially took up the cause of juvenile welfare. He assisted in the building of schools for the children of the poor, and he financed the construction of a whole block intended to be a remand home. I have been assured by people who are entitled to be trusted that because of these social interests, 'Don Gustavo' (as he came to be widely known) was 'well liked by the people who thought of him as charitable and generous'.

212

He never married. Apparently there were relatively few women among the early immigrants. As late as 1876, the 6,500 Europeans and North Americans in Lima included no more than 1,500 females. There was of course no lack of native ladies. They in fact, at least those of the eligible upper classes, have been credited with quite an extraordinary charm – not only, as might be expected, by impressionable gentlemen. Their 'graceful appearance', 'defying the most seductive French woman, with their spiritual eyes, their gay manner and the very refinement of their coquetry', were noted by a Paris-born Peruvian lady, Flora Tristán, the grandmother of Paul Gauguin, the French impressionist painter, who spent part of his childhood in Lima. Knowing all about the chic Parisiennes, Mme Tristán thought 'the ladies of Lima might well be proclaimed the queens of the earth', and if they ruled the men (as apparently, according to Mme Tristán, they did) it was 'because they are much superior to them in intelligence and moral strength'.

Other visitors, with possibly unfortunate experiences, referred to 'an evil influence of a subtle kind' in the way the ladies were dressing, 'decently covering' bust and hips without 'hiding the shapely body underneath', while 'a shawl conceals all the head like a hood, leaving an opening through which one beautiful eye sparkles out on the world'. That 'one beautiful eye' incidentally – 'so black and brilliant', with 'such a power of motion and expression' – also left its mark on the keenly observant mind of Darwin whose visit to Lima I previously mentioned.

No wonder there was a great deal of intermarriage, and all the more remarkable that Uncle Gustavo preferred (and managed) to stay single. He stressed this in his Testament where he described himself as 'unmarried', adding that he had no children, and, he went on, 'even less have I recognised any child as mine'. He was much exercised by this thought and actually went to the trouble of reiterating the statement in a codicil, two days later, a week before his death, explaining that he was doing this because he feared a child might be foisted on him; an attempt had actually been made, he said, when a child's name was to be entered into the Register of Births as being his. If any such attempt were made again, he now declared, it should be recognised at once as a fraud, and the executor was instructed to take legal action.

The stress he laid on these personal matters may well be due to the fact that he had lived or was living with a Peruvian lady, a *chola* (of mixed European and native Indian stock). They were indeed never married. The embarrassment that seemed to surround the story came to the family's notice in Europe some time after his death, and they took the news in the charitably resigned spirit that nothing but good must be thought of the dead.

While thus emphatically disowning any family ties in Peru, Badt left all his property to his sisters in Germany but made provision for three 'godchildren' in Lima including the daughter of an army colonel and the executor's daughter (whose son was to be a Roman Catholic bishop who, in reply to my published enquiry, kindly supplied me with some of my information).

Nothing is known of any attempt to foist a child on Badt. On the other hand, his fears were proved to be well founded at the time of his death. Three days later, on 31 July 1914 the following 'personal' notice appeared in *El Comercio*: 'The daughters, Maria Isabel Badt and Marina Badt, also the grand-daughter, the son-in-law and other relations of the late Gustavo Badt, wish to express their most profound thanks to those who kindly attended the funeral.'

It was a weird procession, like a scene from another Beggars' Opera that might have appealed to Bert Brecht – a *schnorrers'* dance behind seven veils, performed in dead man's shoes. Badt had expressly declared and repeatedly insisted that he had no children nor recognised any, and therefore the two 'daughters' had no right to assume the name of Badt. None of these 'family' members are as much as mentioned in the Testament. It is worth noting too that

214

the one person who would be the principal mourner, the 'widow' (who must still have been alive), is conspicuous by her absence, and if there was a son-in-law, why is he unnamed and which of the two 'daughters', both bearing the 'father's' name, had he married? Who the 'other relations' might be is equally mysterious. I don't know what action if any the executor took to expose the obvious swindle.

# 13

# GROUP RELATIONS AND PREJUDICE

Life was not blessed for us when Helga and I married in 1945. We first had the upstairs flat in my parents' house, then moved to a flat of our own in a district that had seen better days. There were no burglaries round here, I heard it said, because this is where the burglars live: they work elsewhere. It was a ramshackle place, not far from being a slum and only by determined efforts did we manage to get away, soon after our daughter Esther was born.

We now moved to a more genteel area, to Harrow on the border of Wembley, and here I became more practically involved in the Jewish-Christian relations that have always interested me. Perhaps it was religion as such that interested me, in all its varieties as manifestations of the human spirit. I had strong roots in my own, and the older I get the more conscious I become of them – and probably would do even if I had not passed through the trials of my experience. I have never thought of changing my religion (if only because such a change would have involved more than a change of religious faith), and precisely because I was securely anchored in my own belief I have always sought the company of others holding different beliefs so as to exchange ideas and learn from them as they might possibly

216

learn from me, often perhaps merely by hearing me talk about the Wandering Jew, myself.

Also I have always been interested in group relations generally – Jewish-German, Jewish-Polish, German-Polish, English-German, Jewish-Gentile. After all, we live in a society which is not an island nor a ghetto, we must know and try to understand each other, and while it certainly is good to live in the heart of a society it seems vital to consider the line marking off one constituent from the other. On my visits to Spain I was much struck by the frequency of the places called *de la frontera* – in the borderland of Christian and Moorish civilisation, the sort of land where I often feel I belong, being really a frontiersman, living on the border where you can never be one but must be divided, not necessarily between Christian and Muslim but between East and West, between race and religion, home and exile, between our national and our universal vocation. I am a Jew, I am also a Briton, and I must not forget (even if I could) that my roots are in Germany where I grew up. I am a citizen of one country and I have an allegiance to a greater citizenship. All these strands of my experience go to make up the tensions of my life in which I must struggle, as best I can, to combine different, even conflicting loyalties into some kind of harmony.

Together with a Christian friend who played an active part in her Anglican church, I founded the Wembley branch of the Council of Christians and Jews (CCJ). We met six times a year, and though we rarely drew a large crowd, we were soon a small community, particularly when some of us would join in a special discussion circle meeting in members' houses.

Elizabeth Irwin-Hunt, my Christian colleague, was deeply dedicated to the work. She took a most conscientious interest in Judaism which in fact she studied for some ten years, so much so that she frequently attended Jewish services and could claim with justice to 'feel completely at home in a synagogue'. Indeed I sometimes suspected that

217

the thought of a conversion was not far from her mind. We occasionally discussed this prospect and I urged upon her the ideas expressed in my *Times* article reproduced in Chapter 8. I don't think I convinced her, and eventually she confessed she had found rulings in the Torah that worried her just as much as some of the Church's doctrine, and that wisdom was found only when we discover that God is love and see that love in all our fellow-men.

Between us we maintained the group for thirteen years. There is a considerable Jewish population in the area, there are also many churches. I was beating the drum to the best of my ability, but if we managed to get an audience of fifty we would count ourselves lucky. Eventually I had the feeling the branch was making no progress, if only because it failed to attract young people and the elderly moved away or withdrew. As there was no growth, inevitably there was decline, and I have often been thinking about the causes which would apply not only to one local group but more generally. I came to the conclusion that, putting it bluntly, Christian-Jewish relations substantially interest neither Christians nor Jews, not the generality of them and always excepting those dedicated spirits that are few and far between.

As a German-born Jew, I am reminded of what Gershom Scholem, the German-Jewish philosopher, wrote about the 19th-century 'dialogue' between Jews and Germans. It was a 'myth', he thought. In terms of 'historical reality', it was 'fiction rather than fact'. In 'assuming to be speaking to the Germans', he said, the Jews were actually speaking to themselves, 'fancying that the echo of their own voice was taking on the sound of the voice of the others' – it was 'a hopeless cry into a void'.

If the comparison is legitimate, the lack of interest (as I see it) in the Christian-Jewish dialogue now has of course different reasons. I will state them broadly, perhaps crudely, and put in this way, they may seem a caricature. I am advisedly drawing, perhaps overdrawing, a caricature to make my point. It seems to me that Christians feel: What can we do with the Jews except not to understand but possibly try to convert them; and that is hopeless, while Jews feel: What can we do with the Christians, they are all, basically, antisemites, it is hopeless. It is in the feeling of hopelessness that the two seem to meet – the hopelessness observed long ago by Scholem. I could not detect any degrees of lack of interest among Christians; in Wembley it seemed to be evenly spread among the various denominations. Among Jews, by contrast, there was a clear distinction: only liberals ('progressives') seemed to be involved, virtually no members of an orthodox synagogue, and though the (orthodox) Chief Rabbi appeared on the official CCJ letterheads, he, like his Christian colleagues, was a general without an army.

Even liberal Jews are occasionally heard to argue that Christians in general will, perhaps are bound to, feel a lack of sympathy for Jews which, in the last resort, is seen rooted in the Gospels and therefore (it is believed) very drastic doctrinal reforms are required. They will quote not only some of the Church fathers but also passages from Acts and more especially the terrible passage in Matthew (27:25) where 'all the people' are made to shout: 'His blood be on us and on our children'. No less objectionable – because demonstrably wrong – are the words attributed to Jesus in the Sermon on the Mount (Matthew 5:43) 'Ye have heard that it has been said "Thou shalt love thy neighbour and hate thine enemy"'. The reference given for this statement is Leviticus 19:18 where in fact it is said: 'Thou shalt love thy neighbour as thyself: I am the lord'. Nothing whatever about the enemy, let alone hating him. ⊗ Finally those hideous words which John (8:44) attributes to Jesus: 'You are children of your father the Devil ... a liar and the father of lying' – words which were the favourite quotation of Julius Streicher, the Nazi arch-Jewbaiter (next to Hitler), and no wonder, for hate in whichever garb, even according to New Testament teaching, is the forerunner of murder.

But then Jews must likewise remember passages in the

But preceding section of the verse : Thou shalt not avenge nor bear any grudge against the children of thy people, but ....

Talmud which are bound to offend Christians, for example, 'A Gentile who occupies himself with the study of Torah is deserving of death', or 'Kill the best of the Gentiles! Crush the head of the best of snakes!' Such rabbinical utterances (quoted by the Revd Dr A. Cohen in his compilation *Everyman's Talmud*, London, 1971) which cannot be condoned are not of course typical of the Talmud, any more than John 8:44 is typical of the New Testament, and if we quote them without at once drawing attention to the very different, overriding spirit of both the Talmud and the New Testament, we shall be little more than self-righteous hypocrites. After all even the devil is known to have 'cited Scripture for his purposes'.

Generally speaking, as a Jew, I don't think I can claim to be educated if I don't know the New Testament simply as literature, seeing that it is as much part of our civilisation as is the Hebrew Bible. But the fact is – and certainly this was the spirit in which I was brought up – that the New Testament is regarded as the gospel of antisemitism. Jesus was admittedly a Jew but his sayings, however inspired and indeed a 'tree of life', were not deemed worthy of ranking next to the Talmudical 'Ethics of the Fathers'. Neither did I ever hear of that fine passage about Hope, Faith and Love (or Charity) in the first Letter to the Corinthians even though it is, in essence, eloquently and poetically expressed, no more than the Hebrew commandment 'Love your neighbour as yourself'.

I sometimes have a feeling that the Council of Christians and Jews tends to regard itself as a Society for the Enlightenment of Christians about Jews. This of course is legitimate and necessary, but it seems to me no less legitimate and necessary to enlighten Jews about Christians, and who will say one section is more in need of enlightenment than the other? But the fact is any suggestion that for example Jews get to know the contents of the New Testament is resented by them. When the *Jewish Chronicle* carried an advertisement by the Bible Society announcing the appearance of a new and modern translation, by a Jew, which was recommended by a number of scholars, readers promptly protested because the New Testament was said to have been 'responsible for the persecution and martyrdom of the Jewish people throughout much of their history'. The editor printed the protest and, instead of attempting a reasoned defence, at once apologised to readers who had been 'offended by publication of this particular advertisement'.

I was saddened (though not surprised) by the mentality revealed in this incident. Admittedly the New Testament contains passages that are objectionable and lend themselves to gross abuse, which, as I explained, is true of other religious texts, including the Koran. I like to think we judge great writings not by their shortcomings nor by the evil use made of them but by the merits they possess. If Jews may legitimately refuse to read the New Testament and be enlightened about it, I cannot help wondering what the future of Jewish-Christian relations will be.

There was another point that, to my mind, was likely, if not liable, to cause disharmony in Christian-Jewish relations. Jewish leaders often will insist that Christians must 'understand Jews as they understand themselves'. This, frankly, seems to me a proposition not beyond argument. For it would appear to deny to Christians any standard of their own; they are implicitly expected to adopt Jewish standards. But if the proposition is to be considered, then obviously it should also apply the other way round – Jews must understand Christians as they understand themselves. Sauce for the goose and sauce for the gander. If we are to have a dialogue, surely each partner must accept the other as he sees himself. I have, however, rarely come across this broadminded approach.

It may be asked why, if I hold these views, do I take part in CCJ work? The reason is that I believe it is work worth doing for its own sake, without hope of reward. I often think of Chesterton's quip: 'If a thing is worth doing, it is worth doing badly.'

My broadly discouraging experience in Wembley was reinforced when I edited the quarterly journal *Christian-Jewish Relations* for the Institute of Jewish Affairs. It had a circulation of about 1,500 and of course I made it my business to promote it. I advertised in a number of Christian papers but am sorry to say I invariably drew a blank – not a single response or enquiry, let alone request for a subscription. Christian-Jewish relations are not a priority among Christians, any more than among Jews. If that journal, the only one of its kind so far as I know, had to exist on paying subscribers, it would not long survive.

Much the same was my experience when I associated with the English Roman Catholic Bishops' Secretariat for Catholic-Jewish Relations which was set up in 1977. I was co-opted on to it, the only Jew, and I should like to pay my tribute to its chairman, Bishop Geoffrey Burke, who treated me with the most exquisite courtesy and went out of his way to show me respect. But the fact was both this good man himself and most of the members were not, and in fairness would not have claimed to be, sufficiently specialised to shoulder the burdens of the work involved. This is in no way any personal criticism: the difficulties were built-in since the Catholic Church at large was halting between two opinions, the traditional and the progressive, and thus much good will and kind words produced no action. I soon resigned, so did others who felt frustrated at the sight of apparent indecision and indifference to make the avowed effort a success.

Among them was one whom I count one of the most remarkable characters I met: Dr Charlotte Lea Klein, a nun of German-Jewish origin. While adopting the basic belief of Christianity, she retained the deepest respect for the orthodox Judaism in which she was brought up, and one of the notable achievements for which she will be remembered is her conscientious effort to maintain the separate identity of Jew and Christian, which ruled out any missionary design, and to make Judaism so conceived known among Christians. It was for this purpose that she set up a Study Centre for

Christian-Jewish Relations. Here she built on foundations which had been laid, as early as the 1950s, by a devoted French nun, Marie-Thérèse Hoch, and before I move on, I should like to say a word about this unusual woman.

She – then Sister Alphonsa – was my first Catholic contact in England. Early in 1955 I had read about a Catholic library of Jewish interest in a West London convent. I wrote, then from the Wiener Library, enquiring whether I would be allowed to see the collection. After several weeks, I received what seemed to me a guarded, duly authorised reply saying that, on a given day, at a certain time, I would be welcome at the Convent. I then met Sister Alphonsa, obviously the librarian, who showed me into a large, remarkably bare room where a monk was to keep us company. I noticed very few books, odd copies of journals: everything seemed in the most rudimentary state. The only decoration was a crucifix on the long table.

Sister asked me what my work was and when I told her about our research into the Nazi crimes she seemed disturbed, almost terrified, certainly taken aback, and was wondering (ten years after the end of the war) how one could bear doing such work. She said something to the effect that it must be depressing to work day after day on reminiscences of cruelty and suffering. I explained as best I could, but I was thinking to myself: was it not like looking at the crucifix – is it only the killing that fills our minds? Is there no sensation other than depression?

Later, much later, when we had become close friends, she told me that in looking at the body on the cross, 'we take part in the suffering of the poor, the sick and afflicted'; it was not a desperate look but one of hope and promise, etc. Well, I might have replied that the sight of those, the people of Israel, who were 'crucified' in our time should inspire in a Christian much the same feeling – apart from much other feeling...

Sister Alphonsa, then still in her traditional black habit, often visited the Wiener Library, and after she had returned to France I stayed in touch with her, writing occasionally for a magazine she was editing (in English) on behalf of the Sisters of Sion, first entitled *The Jews and Ourselves*, then (after Vatican II) *Encounter Today*.

She in many ways clearly differed from Charlotte Klein, the German-Jewish nun, who had arrived from Israel and now eagerly and dynamically set about expanding the work begun by Marie-Thérèse as she dedicated herself to what she considered by far the most essential aspect of Christian-Jewish relations – a painstaking scrutiny of Christian textbooks, not only those for the use of pupils but, more especially and more importantly, those for the use of teachers. On this subject she published, both in English and in German, a book, *Anti-Judaism in Christian Theology*, which aroused great attention. She was a devout protagonist of the message proclaimed by the Second Vatican Council in presenting a radically new image of the Jew. She saw in her own Order – Our Lady of Sion – a symbol of the new spirit, for while that Order was founded 150 years ago for the purpose of converting Jews, she lived to see the day when that purpose became, not least through her exertions, the enlightenment of Catholics about Jews.

Before I move on, I should like to record my visit to Rome where I attended a Wednesday morning audience of Pope Paul VI. Through the good offices of a most helpful Monsignor, I was able to join a party led by a professional guide, Signorina G., whom I was to meet at a quarter past ten sharp at a certain spot under the colonnades of St Peter's Square. I was there at a quarter to ten and with keen interest watched large parties arriving, all obviously set for the same purpose. Time was passing quickly, though unfortunately without a sign of Signorina G. showing up anywhere, and as more and more coaches were disgorging what soon seemed to me an alarming multitude of rival 'pilgrims', I gradually, perhaps inevitably, began to wonder what my prospects were: would I perchance be crowded out and so miss my great opportunity, a thought almost too awful to entertain for long. I decided to try and trace my guide.

224

I approached some likely-looking ladies with persistently and dispiritingly negative results. I am sure this sort of thing, amounting to what might easily be regarded as accosting, is not normally done in the shadow of St Peter's, and I must have looked, as I certainly felt, most odd. Finally, I had just one more go, and this time the Miss proved to be a hit. No, she was not Signorina G., she said, but she was also waiting for her. This was grand news. She spoke good English but was in fact Dutch. Between us we now spotted the Signorina who was in charge of an American party, and so, for the purpose of my enterprise, I became a devout student of the Lutheran St Olaf's College, Minnesota, USA. I am not sure whether I would have chosen this particular company, remembering what a nasty antisemite Luther was, but then this was a long time ago and besides, even in Rome beggars cannot be choosers.

Having passed the smart and picturesque Swiss Guards, we were comfortably seated in a very modern hall with two large fish-shaped windows in gorgeous mosaics on either side; on the vast platform the Papal throne, and at the back of it a huge tapestry of Rembrandt's etching of the resurrected Christ. I sat in the eighth row close to the barrier of the centre gangway, and here, at the head of a party of Cardinals and other officials, His Holiness entered at the stroke of eleven, walking slowly the whole length up to the platform, acknowledging all the time the tumultuous applause that now broke the intense expectancy. In spite of the vastness of the crowd which, oddly enough, was hardly felt, it was a most dignified occasion, not least because of the dignified appearance and bearing of the Pope himself, dressed as he was all in white with a wide crimson mantle which he presently took off.

Seated on the throne, he first addressed himself to the various Italian groups, including army officers and chaplains, and then he made what was the main speech in Italian. To those unfamiliar with the language it must have seemed a little long, and unfortunately there was no simultaneous translation that might have been heard through

225

earphones. Even so I did pick up one or two remarks that must rejoice the heart of every orthodox believer. The Catholic Church, we were told, insists on the 'rigorous preservation of the authentic revelation', because 'orthodoxy is its foremost preoccupation', refusing to 'conform to the tastes of the changing mentality of the times'.

When I heard this last remark, I wondered where do I stand? 'Orthodoxy' is all very well, tradition is important, but what about change? A question which I must tackle as a progressive Jew facing orthodox Judaism. In general terms, a striking answer was given at this very audience. For here were Lutherans received by the Pope, their one-time arch-enemy, who now bestowed upon them, as on all other groups present, his Apostolic Blessing – upon their persons, their dear ones and their possessions, even upon the one fluke amongst them whose presence he showed no signs of suspecting.

Come to think of it, what would Luther have said at the sight of his followers paying homage to the one whom they had for centuries regarded as the veritable 'Anti-Christ'? Martin Luther, thou shouldst be living at this hour! But that's how the world changes, and it seems pathetic that, in this respect, so many of us still fancy the earth is flat. How true is Samuel Butler's observation (in *The Way of All Flesh*) that the life of man is 'nothing else than a process of accommodation: when we fail in it a little, we are stupid; when we fail flagrantly, we are mad; when we suspend it temporarily, we sleep; when we give up the attempt altogether, we die.'

But I was speaking of the journal *Christian-Jewish Relations*. I was editing it for the London Institute of Jewish Affairs (IJA) which I joined in 1966 when it was established by the World Jewish Congress. I then left the Wiener Library. Dr Wiener had died in 1964, and I never claimed to be the man able to succeed him. I was his assistant, I was Assistant Director, but all the time an assistant, not a principal and never felt I could be. As I thought of it, it occurred to me that though I was the oldest of four children, I was not the first. There had been a child before me, stillborn. I was 'second', apparently destined to be (at school too) from the very start. I have often thought of the pity of it. I have reason to believe that Wiener wanted me to take over and would have been glad if I had agreed, but I felt strongly I must know my limitations. I remember I dreamt at the time I was climbing a ladder which led to a door, and when I reached the top I found the door was locked. I did feel the Library had to have a head of a stature greater than mine. A learned if remarkably impersonal Director was eventually appointed, in circumstances which did not encourage me to feel that I could usefully add to my services here, and since twenty-eight and a half years seemed more than an adequate period to spend at any one place, I decided it was time for me to move.

I also felt I was becoming increasingly and unduly burdened with administrative duties for which I was in no way qualified, especially with the duties of a 'fund raiser'. There was a Board of Directors who I suppose did what they could (in their spare time) to secure the Library's foundation but enough of the groundwork was left for me. Incidentally, in May 1962 I learnt that one Robert Maxwell, said to be a Czech publisher, might be approached as a likely supporter. I mentioned his name to one of the directors, himself a publisher, who immediately and vigorously dismissed the idea, saying this man was known to him (and no doubt not only to him) as virtually a dishonest character, and we must have nothing to do with him. No more was heard of Maxwell in connection with the Wiener Library.

As I prepared for my departure, I realised this was a hazardous move. I was fifty-six and I had gained something like a prominent position in my field of interest. I had become known among a great many people, both on account of my association with the Library and through my articles here and especially in the USA – how would I fare, within my limitations, in new surroundings?

I took the plunge – even though the Directors of the

Library did not think my 28$^{1}/_{2}$ years' service sufficient to merit a pension. The Director of the IJA who was just engaged in the necessary organisation was pleased when I told him about my decision; he seemed to regard it as quite a scoop. No ten advertisements in *The Times* would have secured him a man of such qualifications, he said in a hyperbole which fell pleasantly on my ears though I took in fact as little notice of it as I did when some of my friends expressed surprise at my move.

At the IJA I bore the sonorous title of Senior Research Officer which equally meant little to me. I thought rather more of my practical assignment which was to edit, apart from *Christian-Jewish Relations*, the likewise quarterly *Patterns of Prejudice* presenting itself as 'a journal devoted to the study of causes and manifestations of racial, religious and ethnic discrimination and prejudice with particular reference to antisemitism'. It tracked down prejudice in every country under the sun, among all kinds and conditions of men – with one exception: no attention was directed to 'anti-goy' prejudice among Jews – apart from Rabbi Meir Kahane's racialist *Kach* Party in Israel. This was so not because the editor was unaware of it. No great efforts were required to deal with a subject so rich in raw material as the most casual reader of any one issue of the *Jewish Chronicle* could notice. But officially it was assumed that if Jews are a Chosen People, then one of the reasons must be that they hold no prejudices, and any that might be encountered must be classified as reasoned opinions.

Sincere criticism of Jewish affairs was not encouraged. There seemed to be an agreement with popular opinion that if the critics are Gentiles, they must be antisemites; if Jews, 'self-haters', 'psychopaths', virtually madmen in fact fit for an asylum like the dissidents in pre-glasnost Russia. I thought it was another facet of the intolerance I had come across in my younger years. This is the mentality that will reveal itself every time the State of Israel is found open to criticism. The Hebrew prophets were sufficiently outspoken to qualify for the label 'self-haters', and Jewish critics today

228

will be fortunate if nothing worse happens to them than to be told, as Amos was by the Chief Rabbi, 'Flee thee away into the land of Judah and prophesy there but not again any more at Beth-el', the home of Jewish majority opinion.

An American Jewish scholar once offered me an article dealing with Jewish prejudice. It seemed to him, he said in a covering letter, that 'we Jews have some reticence (to put it mildly) about enquiring into our own sense of history.' A 'mystical memory' which we call 'history', he wrote, was 'selectively interpreting and distorting in order to make "reality" endurable'. Having been rejected by several leading American Jewish journals, he thought we were 'more committed to our projections than to the introspection which we so highly value'. These observations were borne out by my own experience. I had often noticed that Jews – like other people – live by myths which idealise history, and while in theory we believe in introspection which would mean sitting in judgment on ourselves, in fact we practise projection which enables us to sit in judgment on others.

Though in agreement with the article and prepared to publish it, I took the precaution of showing it to the Director who, with untypical equanimity, remarked that such an article was likely to make for antisemitism and therefore did not seem a desirable 'pattern'. (If any investigation into other people's prejudices made for unfriendly feeling towards them, this was not considered sufficiently relevant to militate against publication.) The Director personally might have taken a broad view but he had to look over his shoulders and consider those directing him, a commendable procedure of which he always showed himself very conscious. I conveyed to my correspondent our great regret, with the result that the poor devil, frustrated by his experience on the Jewish market, eventually submitted the fruits of his research to the 'revisionist' *Journal of Historical Review* where they were gladly accepted.

The incident left me unhappy. It seemed to me a pity that we should not be able to endure balanced, rational criticism of ourselves, even by one of our own. After all even Moses and Aaron were candid in their by no means always flattering estimate of our people, and it has often been said that the Bible could well qualify as an antisemitic book. Would antisemites have been served by an article in *Patterns of Prejudice*? But they do not need Jews to supply them with grist. Their lies are distilled in that murky underworld where the 'Protocols of Zion' were concocted. Jews will gain little by asking what will the antisemites say, but in doing so they will lose much of their spiritual freedom and even more of their self-respect. I could not help wondering whether this was an institute of Jewish affairs or of Jewish propaganda? And if propaganda, was it likely to be sensible and effective propaganda?

I noticed that Jewish scholars could be quite merciless in their analysis and criticism of Gentile shortcomings but would admit no strictures on collective Jewish shortcomings. Jewish collective behaviour was invariably presented as above reproach, when in fact it often enough was neither better nor worse than other people's. Jewish criticism of Gentile society was assessed by objective standards but Jewish criticism of Jewish society was dismissed as 'self-hatred'. Jews would be given the benefit of the doubt and goyim the odium of it; Jews would be judged by their ideals, never by their realities, goyim by their realities, never by their ideals. This tendency, frankly, troubled me.

Clearly Jews, even Zionists, had not yet received the liberating message of Zionism which was not just concerned with the establishment of a Jewish state. The 'return to Zion' in terms of a state was merely a symbol, an outward appearance, and Gentile-conditioned at that: the substance was the moral resurrection of the Jew from bondage to freedom. Indeed the return to the land would mean little, Herzl said, unless there was a revival of the spirit, not merely the martial spirit and the spirit of playing at politics, but above everything else the spirit of a new man who was part of a people seen to be chosen through its history.

230

This new Jew was not to live in a world purged of antisemitism anymore than of any other felony or mental aberration. But he was to live in freedom from the terror of antisemitism; he was vigorously to resist it but not to be depraved by it. If he was free, it was because he had overcome the sorrowful past. He had learnt to despise the superstitions, the petty, unclean rancours of antisemitism. He had begun to respect himself and so to respect others too, refusing to wallow in the sort of antisemitism which sneers at *goyim* as white presumption sneers at the 'nigger'. The *goy* after all is the same sort of scapegoat for our permanent frustrations as 'The Jew' was, in France after her defeat in 1870, in Germany after 1918 and would have been in Britain had she lost the 1939 war. But the truly liberated Jew was to have risen above the degrading obsessions which are the offspring of fear and insecurity within ourselves.

Later, in my retirement, I wrote to my friends at the Institute, the new director and the new editor of *Patterns of Prejudice*, taxing them on the obviously awkward question of *Jewish* prejudice. I never received a reply. The idea may have seemed to them so novel and unheard of, it left them speechless. Incidentally I was by no means the only one feeling such scruples. The Secretary of the Israeli Society of Human Rights once told us that by ignoring Jewish prejudices we were in fact 'encouraging' them, and inasmuch as we were attacking antisemitism only, we were 'hypocrites'.

231

# 14

# FOREIGN TRAVEL

It was not long before I left the IJA. My time was up. I had reached retirement age, and I confess I was glad to go. I did not feel happy though in some ways I had every reason to be so. In my editorship I had a more or less free hand – thanks, in part perhaps, to the reputation I had won at the Wiener Library. I was able to travel a little, always equipped with my Berlitz phrase book as I never want to rely on English (which is to be the last resort). I much enjoyed browsing in it and was impressed by the amount of useful information provided, all well classified according to the occasions most likely encountered. There was hotel service, eating out, shopping, and most important, 'making friends' which I was studying with particular attention. This section was again split up into various sub-sections including 'Weather Conversation' (though this was perhaps more popular inside England than outside) and last and truly not least, 'Dating', starting with the non-committal 'Would you like a cigarette?' and ending, softly, softly, first 'What time is your last train?' and then 'Do you *have* to go home tonight?' (Oddly enough, this last enquiry, the very punch-line of the section, was missing from other editions, for example the Polish and Hebrew one.)

Travelling on World Jewish Congress business, I visited

Geneva (the European headquarters), Milan, Vienna, Berlin, Brussels, The Hague, Strasbourg, Copenhagen, New York, and of course several times Paris where I had a little encounter that seems worth recording.

Strolling along one of the narrow, picturesque back streets, I suddenly noticed a tiny shop actually called The Silk Shop (in English) and the words 'French scarves' written boldly across the window. There was hardly need for any French translation, for natives could easily see what was cooking (without necessarily being interested), and the obviously shrewd owner had his eyes on the Anglo-Saxon tourist who would delight in exploring these parts and almost certainly love the fine patterns displayed.

Anyway I did. I was intrigued, first of all, by the unexpected sight of an 'English' shop, and then I fancied the glorious colours – what a crimson, what a turquoise! – and the pretty designs of *Monuments de Paris*. I thought of the folks back home who would perchance fancy them even more, so I made a quick check of my French vocabulary as well as my cash, and entered the shop.

It was, curiously enough (because of the contrast with the goods), a somewhat sombre, romantically dingy place. Behind the short, secondhand counter sat an elderly, not undignified gent, who received me with appropriate, almost English, reserve, at least without visible enthusiasm. With him was a rather un-Parisian-looking young saleslady who seemed to have seen better days.

I said I would like some of the scarves to take home, as I was from abroad. This of course was hardly necessary to add (if only because of my linguistic imperfection) but calculated to make the transaction less strictly commercial. It did. 'From abroad?', said the old gent, now rising as if in the presence of a VIP. 'Where are you from, then?', he enquired. I stalled: 'Would you care to guess?' He now mustered me critically: 'You are – er,' in a tone of somewhat deflated estimation, '– either a Spaniard or an Italian.' Which, come to think of it, was not bad for (quite literally) a shot in the dark.

233

When I confessed that I was in fact from England, he seemed pleasantly surprised. 'From England?', he made sure: 'Do you know that I once had a shop in London, in Shaftesbury Avenue? And I used to live in Cricklewood!' I was duly impressed and managed to observe that perhaps he would be interested to learn that I once lived not very far from Cricklewood. But he was not a bit interested: '...and from Cricklewood I moved to Golders Green,' he concluded, as if suggesting that NW11 (and not necessarily the Crematorium there) must be regarded as the final residence of anyone at all possessed of earthly ambition.

Now I thought a certain suspicion was as good as confirmed, and I remarked: 'Lots of Jews live in Golders Green.' Whereupon his face lit up brightly, and he eagerly replied: 'Yes – are you yourself then a Jew?' Now he opened up: 'In that case you may like to know that I am a regular reader of the *Jewish Chronicle*,' and from under the counter he pulled, like a conjuror the rabbit, a copy of that week's issue. My French vocabulary was barely sufficient to convey my amazement.

By now we had of course forgotten all about the scarves, but it seemed to me that his French was not, shall we say, the President's. So I said, casually: 'Of course you were born in Paris.' 'Oh no,' he replied, 'as a matter of fact I am a Spanish-speaking Jew from Smyrna in Turkey,' a descendant of those who were once driven from Spain, I had probably heard about it. I had, and I cautiously smiled, saying that actually I had often read and enjoyed the Ladino paper of Istanbul, *La Boz de Türkiye*. Promptly we discovered that we both knew, directly or indirectly, the Cohen family who owned that paper, and as Spanish happens to be my hobby, I said, glad to have found something in the nature of a guinea-pig: 'Let's have a word in Spanish, then.'

We did, nattering away for a while, but now the young lady seemed distinctly uneasy (Cricklewood and Golders Green had been quite enough of a strain). I turned to her and said; 'But you, Mademoiselle, are French.' Before she had a chance to utter the refined French equivalent of 'Mind your own business,' Monsieur brashly butted in 'No, no, she's a refugee from Egypt!'

But the fact was we were getting a bit on her nerves, and she courteously though unmistakably indicated that it was now about time for business. We agreed, and animated by the pleasant conversation, I chose what I believed were the most splendid colours of them all (though I regret to say none of the talk helped to gain a discount). The choice proved a resounding success. I wrote back, in suitably flattering terms, ordering some more. Monsieur apparently only signed a letter that was written by Mademoiselle in strictly if impeccably businesslike terms that they would be happy to oblige as soon as I had remitted the necessary cash.

I also once visited, privately, Dublin. I greatly enjoyed the beauty of the Georgian squares and admired that jewel in Trinity College, the Book of Kells. I also chuckled a little when I noticed Henry Street close to Moore Street yet could find no Henry Moore Street. Or was this intended as a sample of Irish humour?

As I walked up Grafton Street towards St Stephen's Green, I was attracted by a large newsagent's. I entered and among the several Gaelic journals I noticed a front page article mentioning Israel. I would have loved to know what it said, and looking round where I could ask I thought a priest nearby might help (in Dublin a priest never is, or was, far away). I approached him with my request, and he held the paper as a rabbi might hold a Hebrew paper, not quite sure what to make of it. So I explained that I was a Jew. He had been rather indifferent and/or uncommunicative, but now I seemed to him not quite uninteresting, so he asked off-hand: 'Are you from Israel then?' For clearly in his mind Jew and Israel go together. When I replied that as a matter of fact I was from London, he had to think a little before making his next move, though here I no longer know for certain, did he say 'Are there *many* Jews in London?', or 'Are there *any* Jews in London?' I am inclined

235

to believe (and I hope he will forgive me) he was, in this respect, completely ignorant. Anyway I said 'Quite a number.' This information also needed some time to sink in but now he was getting aroused (within reason, up to a point), and he said: 'You know, we have a great respect for you people, because you have done what we have been trying to do all the time – you revived your ancient language, Hebrew, whereas we've not got very far with Gaelic: officially, yes, you see it at Government departments, at the Post Office, street names, but people really don't go in for it' – which, frankly, struck me as open to doubt, for surely the many Gaelic papers displayed in this shop must have their readers, and come to think of it, how many Jews go in for Hebrew? But I did not want to pursue the delicate subject broached with so much eloquence by the reverend gentleman.

While mentioning Ireland, I feel tempted to step from the sublime to the ridiculous and tell a little story which I approach with some diffidence because I must suspect myself of being prudish. Travelling around the island, I noticed what seemed to me a novelty in men's lavatories ('loos'). While you stand in front of the basin attending to your business, you are offered an extra 'convenience' of making at once even more constructive use of the occasion. You are facing a nicely framed page of the day's paper, apparently always a quality paper, which provides you with all the news that is fit for perusal in a loo, and since each basin is headed by a different page you will have no excuse for not being up to scratch. I confess I was greatly impressed by this fine example of truly Irish ingenuity, and I will at last be able to vary the all too hackneyed announcement that I am about to 'spend a penny' or 'wash my hands'. I will now simply state that I must keep up with the news.

I take the liberty of telling this tale because lavatories have become a frequent and perfectly respectable topic of discussion in such quality newspapers as the *Daily Telegraph* where the fine points of loo rolls, 'virtuous' and 'scratchy', have been set out in remarkable detail by a lady lecturer of philosophy, and 'Loos of the Year' competitions are, perhaps deservedly, deemed worthy of praise in glossy Society magazines. A garrulous columnist will inform us that 'in the lavatories I ask the man at the next urinal if he agrees with the Prime Minister...', and then he is surprised to discover 'everyone has treated me as a lunatic bore'. Nor does the subject emerge – academically or otherwise – only in the press. In his review of a new performance of Brecht's *Threepenny Opera*, an art critic remarked it was 'a little distressing to watch the Captain using the loo in front of his two wives'. I was glad he found himself at least distressed – if only a little.

# 15

# THE LONER

I met a number of interesting people, not too many as I am unfortunately no socialite. Parties hold little attraction for me, and if I could choose my way of communication it would be by way of writing rather than speaking. I rarely attended the meetings of the IJA held at the Royal Institute of International Affairs. My absence sometimes embarrassed me as I must have seemed aloof. The reason partly was that my hearing was beginning to deteriorate. Partly also, and essentially, it was different and I feel I should explain.

I lived as Hazlitt says of himself, 'in the world, as *in* it not *of* it'. I found myself as he did 'in a world of contemplation and not of action'. I was far away, even at work. Everything to me seemed far off, and I myself was withdrawn, seeing it all at a distance, often intrigued and stimulated, sometimes bewildered and frustrated. Many things present seemed blurred until they gained the perspective of distance, and vice versa.

I seemed to be a stranger in the world which I watch as through a glass screen. I make an effort to stretch out my hand but do not touch life. Was it because of this that I looked with so much personal feeling at Michelangelo's painting of Creation? No contact is made with God. Many of the good things in life do not seem to have been made for me. Not that I feel barred from them. I do not even seem to desire them. They leave me generally indifferent – now more than ever, for now I have lost much of my hearing and find the hearing aid is by no means always a hearing help. I often think of the sympathetic friend who hoped to 'introduce' me to life because he said, with great truth, 'You don't know how to live'. He was right, by his standards – for much depends on what you call living – and yet there are others by which life may hope to be fulfilled. He would hardly have made much of the confession by Heine in one of his essays: 'Who can say for certain whether the strange appearances really exist? Come to think of it, we often cannot distinguish reality from mere visions in dreams!'

As I often, naturally, sometimes obsessively, thought on these things, I wondered – was I detached from life because of that early experience when Grandma 'kidnapped' me and so denied me the natural upbringing by mother and father? Was she perhaps gently mocking when she taught me Burns' line 'My heart's in the Highlands, my heart is not here'? Was the detachment from the parents a pointer to the later, larger detachment? In fairness, I must doubt it. For the cause of the trouble could be not only in my experience but equally and perhaps more convincingly in my inheritance.

I began to remember Uncle Philipp again who was a stranger in the world albeit by his own will and action. I did not want to follow his example which I criticised, and certainly the manner of his existence; living at the expense of others, which he did not have to, seemed to me utterly reprehensible. Yet the more I was reflecting on his life, the more it seemed to be touching a raw nerve in me. Long after his death he was beginning to haunt me. Was I perhaps taking after him? Was I perhaps as much attracted by him as repelled? Was I perhaps, albeit in a far unhappier state, destined to cry, as Catherine does in *Wuthering Heights*, 'I am Heathcliffe'? Of course I was different. I was not locking myself up in my room and waiting for charity.

Even if I had wanted to, without a sense of the intolerable immorality, it would have been practically impossible. Yet, in all essentials, the identity (up to a point) was undeniable. Like Catherine, I might say, however sadly different the circumstances, 'he is always, always in my mind; not as a pleasure, anymore than I am always a pleasure to myself, but as my own being'. Not as a pleasure, indeed not, but as a terror and a haunting nightmare.

There was an ominous streak in the family. I suddenly remembered that my father, Philipp's brother, never joined the family on its holidays; he never came with Mother when she visited me in London. And now here I was with my burden. Or was it a burden always? I like to think that once, at a most crucial moment, it proved to be a boon and a blessing – when I was the first to separate myself from home and family to leave for England. In doing so I was to save my life and, in due course, the life of most of my family. Perhaps, inasmuch as I could see and read at least some of the writing on the wall, this was a freakish paradox. For generally speaking, my separation from life made it difficult for me to distinguish it from dreams which I might interpret in various ways except such as would bring me nearer to reality.

Readily though I might realise the importance of company, I am usually happiest on my own, not one of the crowd and never too tightly tied up in a team. The mere sight of crowds is apt to make me feel giddy, and whenever I telewatch one of those commercialised football matches where players have become merchandise available to the highest bidder, I seem to be having a daytime nightmare caused by a spectacle of mass hysteria. The intoxicated crowd, seething as it is already, seems to be having its wild frenzy fed as if it were served pint after pint of hard stuff – by none more so than those howling dervishes who perform under the name of 'sports commentators'. Their punch-drunk gibberish is bound to confirm the maddened and maddening crowds in their mood of befuddled violence which the police often find hard to contain. Fortunately, as

240

yet the frenzy is constant with sport: I dare not think what it might be like if manipulated by a demagogue (the Nuremberg Party rallies, the nation-wide pogrom in 1938). The occasional looting and rioting in British cities is bad enough.

Characteristically, one of the few Latin lines I remember from school is Horace's 'I hate the crowds and keep away from them'. Which reminds me again of some of the friends I did make at school, most of them hoping to profit from my ability to help with Greek and Latin translations. No doubt many thought me odd, when for example they saw me walking on my own in the school grounds during the break, and indeed there was one symptom that would have confirmed it: I had a preference for the peculiarities and mannerisms of language. Fortunately I dropped this habit and learnt (I hope) to write simply, without pretence. I did however retain a desire for that 'utter objectivity' which Karl Menninger describes as 'a correct and fruitful but inhuman attitude and typically schizoid'.

I must assume I can be classified under what the American psychologist calls Isolation Types, schizoid personalities which are '"temperamentally" unsocial and really prefer to be left out of it, although they may possess graceful social technique'. Menninger cites several examples of features to which I could feel related. Samuel Coleridge for instance 'was a misfit among boys of his own age, taking little pleasure in their sports. He said of himself that he was "a playless day dreamer"'. Isaac Newton 'was constantly with his books, avoiding and ignoring those who might have been his friends'. Jeremy Bentham 'from his earliest childhood was sensitive and retiring, felt inferior, hated social pleasures and spent much time in reading and in gloomy meditation'.

Menninger sums up: 'The common tendency of the members of this group is an inability to get along well with other people ... This lack of social adaptability is of a very special kind. These people sometimes appear to want to

241

mix with the herd. More often they obviously do not want to and they never do – successfully at any rate. They may make gestures, go through the motions … but "the pane of glass is always there". They never really make lasting contacts.' There is, Menninger says, a break or split in the internal harmony of the personality so that an external disharmony also results and the schizoid person is noticeably out of tune with the rest of the world.' A 'break or split', 'out of tune': This would also seem to be a characteristic of the Jewish existence in the world, and I personally was perhaps reflecting the divisions that rent the German-Jewish-Polish society of the place of my birth, Exin.

But allied to my strands of disharmony are also, as Menninger notes, moods of depression when a person will 'see the dark side of things. Life seems to him more or less of a burden. Each task seems gigantic. He bears with conscientious self-denial obligations of life without any of the pleasures of living… He is prone to have physical complaints and anxieties.'

My complaints were, so far as I know, purely nervous and apparently beyond the arts of the general practitioner. At one time it was eye trouble and more recently throat trouble: food used to get stuck in the throat and I had the greatest, often agonising difficulty in ridding myself of the spasm. A doctor once made the very tersest diagnosis: 'You cannot swallow your troubles' – though, oddly enough, after a while, apparently, I could.

Menninger seemed to be offering a more plausible explanation when he referred to 'the disappointment of love that the patient has suffered as a young child'. Did I perhaps suffer such a disappointment when, for all intents and purposes and however justifiably, my parents agreed to hand me over to my grandmother and so of necessity withheld from me much of the parental love to which I was entitled? Possibly grandmother's affection, however devoted, did not make up for the deficiency and later this disappointment might have been aggravated by my troubled relationship with Ruth.

Could nothing be done to cure me of this affliction? I thought it was much like a mutilation of the body – as if I had lost an arm or been born handicapped, physically or mentally. I just had to accept it and make the best of it.

I once mentioned it to my six-years-younger brother Abraham. He confessed he himself had been smitten with this 'family inheritance', but he did not agree that it was something we had to put up with. Being an orthodox Jew, he rejected my diagnosis of it – 'a work of nature, beyond good and evil as it were': this he thought was 'a pagan way of looking at it'. He insisted that the evil which was here manifesting itself had to be fought – 'no surrender to the demons of the powers of nature'. While the evil was present in the very best of men, he wrote to me while in the army in 1945, life was 'an opportunity of overcoming it and perfecting us'. Physical mutilation might be incurable, he thought, but emotional mutilation was not. We had been commanded to love God which meant that the world rested not only on the rationalism of strict law but also on 'the grace that springs from profound love'.

As I am reading this letter again, I am reminded not so much of orthodox Judaism but of standard Christian teaching – Dostoyevsky's, in *The Brothers Karamasov*: 'Love all God's creation, the whole of it: every grain of sand . . . Love everything. If you love everything, you will perceive the divine mystery of things . . . and you will at last come to love the whole world with an abiding, universal love.' Would my brother go that far? Even now? I must doubt it for he is also an ardent Israeli nationalist, and nationalism, any nationalism, surely is far removed from universal love. Dostoyevsky himself proves it: he was a nationalist, and how did he reconcile his teaching 'Love everything' with his antisemitism?

So there we are: we all have our problems. However such separation from life as I was endowed with went further. I not only avoided crowds, I also sought to keep clear of the crowd's opinions, views held by the majority. I began to regard such views as suspect and in need of careful scrutiny. The fact that most people shared them seemed to me no proof of their truth. A majority vote in a democracy was, and had to be, a useful expedient to settle controversial matters but it could not necessarily proclaim a truth. It seemed to me I would not be a Jew if I were to think otherwise, living as I do in a world in which Jews are a permanent minority. Suspicion of the majority must apply equally to mass produced opinions held among Jews. I must not run with the multitude, I must be free to dissent.

Few teachings, even early in life, have so impressed me as this passage in Rabbi Leo Baeck's book *The Essence of Judaism* (1926): 'Judaism bears witness to the power of thought over against the might of mere numbers ... upholding what is peculiar to human nature and at issue with the world ... Through its very existence, Judaism is a demurrer which nothing can silence, to the claim of the multitude to crowd out the law ... a demurrer proclaiming that in the battle between Spirit and Expediency, the last word shall never rest with the practical advantage.'

This, it now seems to me, is true in theory and of Judaism among the nations. It is not quite so true when we consider the condition of Jewish life within, as demonstrated, for example, at the time of the Hebrew prophets. Justice Haim Cohn, the German-born Israeli judge, makes some pertinent observations on this point as he reflects on the true and the false prophets in ancient Israel. 'The true prophets,' he writes in his book *Human Rights in Jewish Law* (1984), 'were highly unpopular, whereas the "false" prophets commanded huge and enthusiastic audiences. The mostly gruesome forebodings of the true prophets fell on unwilling ears, and their uncompromising exposures and rigorous accusations aroused general resentment. Small wonder that they soon became a small minority of dissenters, whereas the great majority of prophets pleased and catered for the masses and accommodated the authorities with their optimistic prophecies and palatable comments.'

Perhaps, holding the views I did of the majority, I was bound to feel isolated and in exile, and since I could not take part of life directly I laboured to enter it by proxy as it were, through literature, but even this would not work. Standing in front of my library, I often feel like the passenger in *The Ship of Fools* who had plenty of books 'but fewe I rede and fewer understande'. If anything, I was worse off. I was altogether unable to read consistently. I would begin and read on for a while, but then I would tire, lose the thread, check by running back over the pages covered. The mind would slump, as if damaged, like a car engine stalling. I would know, like Dr Wiener, *about* books, the story of their career, their authors, the reviews, any affairs attaching to them, etc., but hardly ever the books themselves – from the outside as it were, yes, but not from within.

There were exceptions, apart from the Bible stories on which I was of course brought up. I did enjoy reading some of Goethe's, Schiller's and Lessing's works, more especially, later, Heine's essay on 'The history of religion and philosophy in Germany'. On history altogether I read a great deal, notably on German history, German-French relations and the origins of the Kaiser war. I took an early interest in Ibsen's plays and their criticism of society; I had received his collected works as a Bar Mitzvah present. Detective stories also would hold my attention, none more so than the adventures of Sherlock Holmes: *The Hound of the Baskervilles* positively fascinated me.

But altogether I don't think my reading amounted to very much. I remember, as a young fellow, when still at school, I had a book containing substantial summaries of novels and plays, much like Margaret Drabble's *Oxford Companion to English Literature*, and in this I was reading profusely – until I lost it, unaccountably but perhaps significantly, as a warning that this was not the way to do justice to literature. But the fact was I was trying to take improper advantage of the writer's craft. It was simply the only way in which I could hope to benefit from it.

245

I was struggling to understand and take in as much as I possibly could, and this, as I never ceased to regret, was comparatively little, except essays which I found I could manage. Books all too often would serve me for a purpose: when I had an idea which I wanted to enlarge on in an article; my memory would then help me to trace any relevant reference I might have come across.

But it was not only the mind that seemed damaged, being unable to concentrate on reading. The brain also seemed in need of repair. It was 'leaking', I thought. As soon as an idea occurred to me I would have to jot it down or I would lose, forget it. On the relatively rare occasions when I spoke in public I would have to have brief notes on me, but almost invariably (unless I 'read' a paper) I would 'forget' a number of points I meant to make. It was another example of my separation from the world: the contact was missing, or badly tattered, and only a conscious effort could hope to secure something like an approach to the land of the living. Such was my marginal existence, perched uneasily on the fringes. My only – tenuous – communication with the centre was by way of (usually unsuccessful) writing for publication.

I often wondered whether I was a victim of heredity. Were there any ghosts as there were those besetting Osvald Alving in Ibsen's play? Like him I am 'not really ill – not what is commonly called ill', but, brooding on my disability, I feel like him 'broken in mind' at the thought of 'never again being able to work', that is to read, never to enjoy the fruits of reading, to grow by the ideas of great minds, being barred from all the treasures in prose and poetry, left stunted, wasted by the wayside.

Yet my 'disease' is not Osvald's, my mind is not 'worm-eaten', I like to think, and no one could say the sins of the fathers are being visited upon the children – what sins? None of the physical or ethical ones which Michael Meyer indicates in his book on Ibsen. I am rather thinking of one of the other debilities he mentions as Ibsen's target – 'the narrow and inhibiting effect of small-town life.'

246

This may have come upon me – though it is by no means certain. What about the countless well-known people born in the most obscure of hamlets and yet shining brilliantly among the brightest of city lights? Of them it could never be said, as a teacher once told my mother about me, 'he doesn't come out of his shell,' and medical diagnosis might detect other symptoms of a basic disability.

Uncle Philipp was clearly abnormal, having turned himself into a most odd recluse. He provided an almost textbook illustration of the 'premorbid personality' which shies away from the environment and tends to live in a world of fancy – a relatively rare case, I like to think, of ordinary abnormality combined with moral insanity. Now clearly I was not a replay of this uncle though some traits were no doubt inherited: the brain did not seem to function normally; had I consulted a specialist perhaps he too would have diagnosed it as, in one way or another, *vermoulu* (worm-eaten).

All things considered, it seemed to me quite natural that I was interested in history, because only in the past can I see the present, and I am as removed from the present in time as my late sister Frieda was removed from it in space since she took a keen interest in astronomy, the science of the world away from the earth.

Frieda actually had a telescope with which she could look up to the stars and perhaps beyond the stars, into a world in which she would find the fulfilment that was not within herself. For she had an unhappy life, an unhappy marriage and an unhappy, stunted relationship with family and friends. She tried to hide it all behind a sarcasm with which she was 'unhappily blessed'. People would appear to her all too frequently as a motley cast in a show calling for a 'dramatic criticism' laced with an occasionally mordant wit. She had, for example, heard of those who suffer without complaining, but (she would say) she had met only those who complain without suffering – and within her experience they seemed by far the majority.

247

Such characters were also the targets of some of her verse which could rise to modest heights of poetry. But she could also convey a very different mood of which I have kept this sample:

EARTHBOUND

Roar, raging sea, and leap to heaven.
Beneath your foaming fury lies
The agony of captive spirits,
Tormented souls in earthly ties.

Forever yearning in the dungeons
Of fear and lust and mortal pain,
Bound to the deep and yet defying
The drag of the relentless chain.

Rebellious waves surge to the surface,
Tear at the clutches and soar high,
Drawn by the dazzling crown of freedom
That beckons from the sovereign sky.

Enriched with golden rays they triumph
And carry in a shimmering glow
Eternal hope and deathless courage
Back to the groaning dark below.

These lines often faintly remind me of Emily Brontë, and in some ways, other than genius, Frieda had, I like to think, something of Emily's nature as Charlotte saw it: 'She had no worldly wisdom, her powers were unadapted to the practical business of life... An interpreter ought always to have stood between her and the world.' As Frieda endeavoured to understand life she came up against the masks of human experience:

What is Life? You may well ask:
If you lift its mocking mask
To detect what lies concealed,
Is the mystery revealed?

248

No, my friend, there is no trace,
You will see no hidden face,
For the mask is but a blind,
There is another mask behind.

And that mask hides many more.
You're no wiser than before.
You will still be in the dark,
Life remains a question mark.

It's a party game for fools
Who know nothing of the rules.
They play on as in a trance,
And the referee is Chance.

She was relieved of this unnerving party game by a relatively early (and merciful) death.

I share of course a sad heritage with Frieda – it is after all
a family streak. I have already remarked on the unease
caused me by crowds, also queues and crowded trains:
probably one of those more or less harmless phobias well
known to psychologists. I do not doubt the truth in Martin
Buber's saying: 'All life is meeting', and I am sure that
society and solitude must counterbalance each other. Where
had I read that 'solitude is as needful to the imagination as
society is wholesome for the character'? But I also understand, only too well, Edith Sitwell's confession (in *Who's
Who*) that her recreation was – silence. It really is an irony –
a split in reality – that I should be a journalist (of sorts), one
supposed to be in pursuit of the events of the day.
Characteristically, as a journalist I am drawn towards
foreign affairs rather than domestic, towards topics of the
past as they affect the present, towards far away countries –
the further away (like Peru) the more interesting and
alluring they would appear. I can see in the distance better
than nearby – medically I am long-sighted, not short-
sighted.

\*     \*     \*

The remoteness produced, unbeknown to myself, a sad

249

effect on our daughter. She actually remarked on it when she was no older than eight, telling us that it sometimes seemed to her as if people and things she was seeing did not really exist. I was taken aback, remembering the almost identical confession that I quoted from Heine on a previous page. I made a note of her words, wondering whether she would later have to make a conscious, possibly painful, nerve-straining effort to gain contact with reality. She passed through difficult times but I like to think that, on balance, she seems to have adjusted herself.

For she was, I thought, a cheerful child, lively and enjoying company. Like many children, she had a keen sense of observation and was quick to apply it at more or less appropriate occasions. She could, at three, offer this advice at table: 'Don't put the knife into your mouth, Auntie: Good Lord!', or 'I won't talk to you, Daddy, you've been too too terribly naughty.' On the other hand, she was concerned: 'Do you mind if I see Daddy,' she once asked, 'I think he needs me,' and Mummy was told: 'Sit by me, let's hold hands: it's *such* a pleasure.' But she also could be self-critical: 'I must not do it. It's only babies who do it – they don't know any better.'

The earliest advice I can remember having received was, 'Don't, Daddy, it's too expensive, we can't afford it.' (She, alas, had heard it all too often.) She paid her mummy a handsome compliment when, for the first time, she saw snow in all its immaculate beauty: 'Look,' she cried, pressing her excited hands against the window pane: 'Hankies!'

She also could be cute, tampering with cause and effect. Having overturned a chair, she exclaimed, 'Chair fell', and when during a session on the potty a discreet subdued sound was heard, she announced: 'Potty making a noise.'

She did not confine her comments to the home. When, in a bus, she saw a lady wearing a striped costume, she wanted to know, in everybody's hearing, 'Is auntie wearing pyjamas?' On another occasion she wondered, again for everybody's benefit, 'Why is auntie standing?', with the result that a gentleman offered his seat.

250

A cute comment was also that of a nephew of hers who, not quite three, showed himself already reasonably familiar with the facts of life. When told of an impending addition to the family, he enquired: 'Will I then have to go back to your tummy?' – though it was not quite clear whether he welcomed the prospect. (He previously had been interested to know whether the baby would come out in a pram.)

I regularly took Esther to a nearby park where she loved the playground and especially the swings. Could I give her just one more push, one more, she pleaded, and when I did she would cry 'And now you mustn't stop'. Often enough R. L. Stevenson's lines came into my mind:

> How do you like to go up on a swing,
> Up to the air so blue?
> Oh I think it is the pleasantest thing
> Ever a child to do.

Anyway I gladly obliged – to keep the dearly loved child happy. Or should I have been stern, insisting it was now time to go home? 'Loving a child,' says Anthony Storr in *The Integrity of the Personality*, 'does not mean always giving in to it' because 'children need to fight with their parents, and for the parents to refuse ever to fight back is to treat the child as less than a person and to fail to maintain a relationship with it.'

I did not muse much on the problem at the time. I did what came naturally. We realised of course that being an only child Esther had special needs and we made it our business to provide company for her whenever possible. She mixed with the children of friends, we sent her to ballet lessons, and a kindergarden proved a great success.

But all this at best touched the surface of the problem as I realised many years later when Esther (then forty) confronted me with it, talking to me as she had never done before. She had in fact largely withdrawn from the family ever since she had left school. At first she still had her little room in our small flat but soon she separated completely. I knew she was struggling hard to establish herself. She seemed a wayward youngster, refusing to stay the course at one school, then at another, so that she seemed to be setting out on life without any of the usual qualifications.

Come to think of it, what sort of qualifications did I have when I left home? I had finished school, yes, and then dabbled in law (which I never meant to practise). I certainly learnt no trade which would have meant contact with life. I acquired something like a secondhand contact by following my interests and using my natural talents for which I managed to find, within limits, the right kind of opportunity.

Esther now confessed that while growing up she had been 'overwhelmed' by me. She had always felt she could not be up to my standards and was disappointing our expectations. Storr mentions a similar case, that of a boy who 'had failed to realise his potentialities partly because of his father's attitude of anxious expectation had induced in him the conviction that nothing he did was worthwhile or ever likely to be.' But our attitude was very different. I never had (certainly never showed) any such expectation, and I now told her so: she must have noticed, I said, that in whatever she did we were, so far from stopping or obstructing, actually encouraging her and always trying to look at things through her eyes. If she wanted to change schools, well and good, however much we might have regretted it, for after all we believed this was, even then, her life and she was entitled to lead it in her way.

I like to think that I now, up to a point, made her realise her error, for she went on to say she always felt, certainly when she thought of going to university, that she was not up to it, and the same applied to company in general. She admitted she kept away from us as well as from others who she felt might find her out for 'the little' she thought she was. I made no impression when I recalled how good she had been for example as the main character in a school performance of *Quality Street*.

She had other reasons for keeping away from us. She

said she could not come to terms with Helga's fate in having lost her parents at the hands of the Nazis, and she thought she had to make up for this terrible loss – which she felt she was unable to do. Also I seemed unapproachable because of my Holocaust studies in which I seemed for ever engaged. I never seemed to be taking sufficient notice of her. So there she was, left to herself, withdrawing into herself, brooding, shutting herself up in her room, hating her parents.

She put down her unhappy childhood to the fact that she was a late child, and this was also, she said, a reason why she would not want a child that might have a similarly unhappy early life. I did not agree with this point which I thought must assume a mechanical repetition for which there seemed no reasonable grounds, much like the argument of those who refused to marry because so many marriages proved a failure. But she thought I was being too rational, as I often seemed to her.

I tried to bring up the happy memories she surely must have when we did show great interest and should have been seen trying to make her feel wanted and at ease. I recalled the jolly birthday parties, the ballet lessons where she performed so gracefully, *Peter Pan* which we saw together and Ernest Read's Children's Concerts we went to, also Miss Snow's kindergarden which she enjoyed as much as she did our annual holidays by the sea. But these positive memories only seemed to be freaks in a generally joyless picture.

Now, she said, things had changed. She was being successful (as a management consultant); she had achieved something, and this was setting her free. She no longer felt the hatred that had been within her before; having set herself free, she had as it were returned. I was of course happy to hear this though I could not help wondering: if it was her present success that had brought about the change, what had this to do with our relationship?

In one respect Esther perhaps had a point. It was probably unfortunate for me to be immersed in Holocaust studies – as indeed in the whole of the Nazi story which I was condemned to live through, first in fact and now in research.

Perhaps I should have had a different vocation, like the banker in T. S. Eliot's play *The Confidential Clerk* who always wanted to be a potter, living in 'a world where the form is the reality, of which the substantial is only a shadow'. Yes, that was it: style and presentation rather than the subject matter, and even while I am jotting this down I suddenly remember that one of the earliest little books I bought at a street corner cart (in 1927) was a profusely annotated edition of Buffon's *Discours sur le style*. It immediately attracted my notice with its reflections on *l'ordre et le mouvement qu'on met dans ses pensées*.

The idea came back to me in a different form when I later took an interest in poster-designing (which I actually did for the CCJ), also and especially in window dressing. On my frequent forays of window shopping, I often thought about the ways the goods were displayed. There seemed to be no rhyme nor reason in the arrangement, no attempt to attract attention by means of some sort of artistic endeavour. Every available item was thrown in to show it was there. I remembered how different it was on the Continent where this kind of commercial art had been developed, and it was often a treat to merely look at the shop window, almost as if exhibits in a picture gallery, especially at the big department stores. But here, as in so many other ways, this art was introduced fairly late – in striking contrast to commercial advertising which seemed to me far superior to the Continent, not only in design but also in the wit of presentation. Even now I think much could be done to refine the style of window dressing. I would have loved to pursue these things as a profession.

The IJA of course could offer no scope for any such artistic endeavour. What I missed there was in particular the sort of academic atmosphere which I had enjoyed (and to some extent helped to create) at the Wiener Library. In the ambience of the World Jewish Congress it would be frowned upon as characteristic of an ivory tower. The Congress was after all a political organisation and the Institute, its 'research arm', was expected to buttress any policy that the leaders chose to pursue. Politics in fact, legitimately in the circumstances, seemed to be infesting the place, high-falutin ambitions and inflated self-importance were noticeable, and one could almost sense the bile of in-fighting. I was not made for this kind of atmosphere, and so I was happy to retire. I had a variety of projects to which I would now be able to devote undivided attention. Certainly retirement was not something I dreaded but rather looked forward to.

# 16

# ANTISEMITISM

When I retired in May 1985, and the change in the editorship of *Patterns of Prejudice* was announced, the Director of
the IJA kindly credited me with a 'unique knowledge of
antisemitism past and present', etc. I had just published,
under the title *The Text of the Holocaust*, a thoroughly
documented account of 'Nazi extermination propaganda
1919–1945'. Though the publishers, a small-town American
firm, were no experts in handling the matter effectively, the
booklet had good reviews both in the USA and in England.
I stressed here Hitler's very own conception of antisemitism
which as I explained in Chapter 7 differed fundamentally
from any other hitherto practised – what he termed the
'rational' one as opposed to what he called the traditional
'emotional' one which, he said, would content itself with
'occasional pogroms' but shrink from what he regarded as
the only effective way of dealing with the 'Jewish question',
its 'Final Solution'.

However, on the strength of such knowledge and experience as I had been able to acquire, I also feel I should warn
that while antisemitism is indeed a dangerously destructive prejudice that can easily be manipulated – to the
undoing of many more than merely Jews – it is often
alleged (by Jews) to exist where in fact it does not. It is so

alleged simply from fear or folly but also from ulterior motives – much in the way that modern antisemites manipulate antisemitism when confronted with situations they disapprove of. Government declarations found to be unwelcome will then be accused of 'having antisemitic overtones' or being due to 'antisemitic pressures'. When US President Bush threatened to refuse an Israeli request for a $10 billion loan he was promptly accused of being an antisemite. The wanton charge was expected to secure the loan by simply discrediting him.

But antisemitism can be made to play yet a different role. It can be regarded, as Herzl explains in his book *The Jewish State*, as the power to move Jews to Israel. I was reminded of this when the then Prime Minister of Israel, Yitzhak Shamir, stated in 1989 that US criticism of Israeli policy 'won't deter us'. It seemed a strange statement to make. After all, the attitude of the United States should carry weight and it must appear wise to consider it. While its support will naturally be welcomed, its opposition might be expected to cause second thoughts (if not more). Why, then, does it not?

It seems to me fair to assume that criticism of and opposition to Israeli policies – in the USA and elsewhere – must impair the image of Israel. Perhaps wrongly so, but such are I think the facts of power politics, and they must be taken into realistic consideration. An impaired image of Israel in turn may well result in a growth of antisemitism. Greater antisemitism again may reasonably be expected to create greater interest in emigration to Israel, which is precisely what Mr Shamir wanted to achieve. 'We need a large *aliyah* (immigration),' he declared: 'We have to increase our population in all parts of our land.'

If this is a logical sequence of thought, it would be taking into account the fact that no single force has so encouraged substantial *aliyah* as antisemitism – to which indeed the whole of modern political Zionism owes its impetus and success. Consequently, those who feel the need for a large *aliyah* will be tempted, consciously or unconsciously, to consider the relevance of what has proved to be the most effective 'propelling force', antisemitism. I am not suggesting that they must seek to promote antisemitism – of course not – but I do believe that a prospect of increased antisemitism will not deter them from any course of political action that they may consider expedient.

Such a reflection may well be regarded as Machiavellian, but, alas, Machiavellian thought, *Realpolitik*, is part of the power politics in which we are cooped up. We may think the idea to be both incredible and discreditable, but we must be familiar with the world we live in.

Part of the experience also is that those who 'combat' antisemitism by asserting it where none exists, may well be causing more antisemitism than they combat. Anti-Zionism for example is not necessarily a pattern of antisemitic prejudice; critics of Israel are not all neo-Nazis, and the Vatican's one time refusal to recognise the Jewish state had little to do with the theology that was preached by Leo XIII to Theodor Herzl. The Vatican could legitimately claim the same sort of interests on behalf of Roman Catholics in Arab countries that Israel may claim on behalf of Jews in any one country. Criticism of the Vatican on this score would have been quite wrong – especially after Pope John Paul II, on a visit to his native Poland, had described the creation of the Jewish state as 'an act of historical justice'.

This view resting on rational reflection will not commend itself to those guided mainly by emotion, especially when they appear as amateur students of history. It is perfectly true, for example, that powerful forces within the Catholic Church during the Middle Ages were aiding and abetting, if not instigating, persecutions of Jews. But we are (in this respect) no longer living in the Middle Ages, and the power of the Catholic Church has been reduced. It is also true that the Gospels can still be manipulated by bigoted interpreters and calculating demagogues but their power too has been diminished, and if we look for danger it can be found lurking in very different quarters. The antisemitism which is the theory and practice of mass

258

murder is after all only one extreme form of that still rampant prejudice, totalitarian intolerance, which is the cancer of all human society. We don't have to go back to the New Testament to learn that 'he who hates his brother is a murderer' and that 'he who claims to love God but hates his brother is a liar'. I was put in mind of this simple truth when recently, 700 years after the expulsion of the Jews from England, the antisemitic 'blood libel' was spread by an organised body of British Nazis presuming to honour the memory of 'Little St William of Norwich' who was (still) said to have been the victim of Jewish 'ritual murder' in 1144 – a crime, according to a medieval Christian chronicler, 'the Jews were never said to have practised but at such times as the king was manifestly in want of money.'

This virtual incitement to murder was almost ominous, and no eyebrow was raised when the Crown Prosecution Service declined to take any action, arguing that this medieval libel did 'not appear to be threatening, abusive or insulting' nor 'likely to stir up racial hatred'. The only rational explanation that comes to mind may have been a thought that prosecution would present the villains with much coveted publicity.

Inasmuch as the crux of the matter was not merely the crime but rather the failure of the law to deal with it, the blood libel was not the only bad omen. The barefaced incitement to murder proclaimed by the fundamentalist fanatics of Iran was echoed by the Muslim community in Britain when they called for the killing of Salman Rushdie, author of *The Satanic Verses*, and if we did not agree to this sort of procedure, then, said one of the Mullahs, 'I put Islamic law first and British law second'. One of the worst firebrands, a director of the London Muslim Institute, in close touch with the Iranian fundamentalists who decreed the death sentence, was condemned by a Home Office Minister while others called for action against a man who demanded 'the murder of a United Kingdom citizen'. However, nothing was done, and assured of immunity, the incitement continued.

Even a newspaper supporting the Government found it 'acutely dismaying to see Muslims making threats in a fashion which would have caused them to be prosecuted for incitement were they members of the more extreme white groups, such as the National Front.' But, the *Daily Telegraph* said, 'if Muslim fundamentalism and its bloodier manifestations gain any hold in this country, they will have to be suppressed, employing the full vigour of the laws which were introduced to protect minority communities from racial harassment.'

Alas, remarked a lawyer's article in *The Times*, there seemed to be 'so many cowards in the ranks of those who should be defending free speech and the rule of law that the Muslim fundamentalists can trample over both without difficulty.' In fairness, some Muslim moderates were heard, but that is almost beside the point. The point is: what is the use of the law if it is not enforced? Again, I hate to say it, I am reminded of Weimar Germany: the laws were adequate, the trouble was the will was lacking to apply them. This may be as true now of the Muslim law-breakers as it is of the antisemitic subversives. The motives may be different – in the case of the Muslims it may be consideration for our Arab friends, in the case of the antisemites it may just be (shall we say) absence of sympathy. But if this is so, it must seem strange that the Jewish authorities call for more and better laws as a remedy of the malaise. Clearly the German Weimar experience is not regarded as capable of teaching any lesson. But then, how can history ever teach?

My dissident ideas found no favour in the eyes of the general Jewish press. Nobody wanted to hear that Jews not only left Egypt (to escape from slavery) but also returned (to live in freedom there), as indeed they have returned to all the lands in which they once were persecuted, including England, Spain and – Germany. For Spain a special myth was invented: Jews, it was put about, had sworn never to settle there again and a solemn ban had been pronounced on that impious country. Nothing of the kind: it was a fine story designed to flatter a collective ego which had as it were squared accounts with Spain.

No such ban (*cherem*) was ever imposed, any more than on Germany which committed crimes incomparably worse. In fact, Jews have always cherished the memory of the happy days they spent in Spain and would have settled there again had they been allowed to, as indeed quite a number did, once free to do so (precisely as in Germany).

By strange contrast, the former Chief Rabbi Lord Jakobovits, on the one hand, firmly refuses to visit not only Germany but even Spain, 500 years after the expulsion, yet, on the other hand, he has no qualms at staying and being honoured in England which drove her Jews out only 200 years earlier, almost simultaneously in the perspective of the millennia of Jewish history.

Having discovered that the *cherem* on Spain is a myth, I wondered how many more such myths there might be, parading as history. There are quite a few (not only in Jewish history). It is a fond belief, for instance, that Arabs (or Muslims) have always been friends of the Jews until the harmony was spoilt by the advent of Zionism. The truth is that the *galut* (exile) among Arabs (or Muslims) was not essentially different from the *galut* among Christians. Identifiable nonconformists live at risk everywhere.

The Koran was, or is or can be, an agent of antisemitism as much as the New (or Old) Testament. Mohammed reacted to the Jews' refusal to follow him in precisely the way that Luther did, and again Jews found friends among Christians in the so-called Dark Ages as much as anywhere else. The Dark Ages incidentally (another myth) are by no means as dark as we traditionally imagine – certainly not when compared with the Nazi or the Gulag age.

Nor are we ourselves exempt from medieval darkness. We think of our history as a martyrology, a story of suffering through persecution and other people's bigotry. But we ourselves are by no means immune to these evils. The treatment our own authorities accorded to Maimonides and Spinoza has no claim to admiration, and it makes no best sellers. I once tried to take up the matter in an article comparing the treatment meted out to Jesus by the Jerusalem Jewish establishment to the treatment inflicted on Spinoza by the Amsterdam Jewish establishment; the article was lucky enough to find space in a less committed correspondence column. The Americans, welcoming glasnost, threw it out of court immediately. I must be content to rely on the authority of the well-known French Jewish historian Léon Poliakov, who considers it 'by no means unlikely' that 'the Jews of the diaspora occasionally denounced to the authorities those whom they regarded as dangerous dissidents.'

# 17

# TOLERANCE:
# JESUS AND SPINOZA

I should like to enlarge a little on this matter. If I compared the treatment of Jesus to that of Spinoza, it was because of the two kinds of responsibility involved – that of the religious and that of the secular authorities. It is the sort of responsibility that was established in our time by the Israeli Government's Commission of Enquiry investigating the massacre of Palestinians in the Sabra and Chatila refugee camps. The Commission found both a direct and an indirect responsibility: while the crime was clearly committed by the Christian Phalangists who bore the *direct* responsibility, there also was an *indirect* responsibility on the part of the Israeli authorities who controlled the Phalangists.

On this important point, the Commission made the following statement: 'If it indeed becomes clear that those who decided on the entry of the Phalangists into the camps should have foreseen ... that there was danger of a massacre, and no steps were taken which might have prevented this danger or at least greatly reduced the possibility that deeds of this type might be done, then those who made the decisions and those who implemented them are indirectly responsible for what ultimately occurred.'

This finding drew the following comment from a recognised legal authority, Dr S. J. Roth, one time chairman of the British Zionist Federation: 'The concept of "indirect responsibility" is adduced by the Commission in answer to the objection that "if Israel's direct responsibility for the atrocities is negated – i.e., if it is determined that the blood of those killed was not shed by IDF soldiers..." (and that was indeed what the Commission found), "then there is no place for further discussion of the problem of indirect responsibility". The Commission rejected this position.'

I took up this point in a letter to the *Jewish Chronicle*, mentioning in particular the Commission's statement that 'responsibility falls not only on those who committed the atrocities but also on those (i.e. Israeli authorities) who were responsible for safety and public order, who could have prevented the disturbances and did not fulfil their obligations in this respect.'

It seems to me that these considerations of direct and indirect responsibility are essentially applicable to the treatment of dissenters such as Spinoza and Jesus. The banishment of Spinoza was directly the responsibility of the Dutch, as the death of Jesus was directly the responsibility of the Romans. But in both cases an indirect responsibility was borne by the Jewish authorities: they passed a judgment which they had no power to enforce. Their action is, in this respect, comparable to that of the medieval Church. The Holy Inquisition never removed heretics except for imprisonment. When found guilty on a capital charge, the heretic was turned over to the secular power which would then execute him or her as a traitor. The state bore a direct responsibility, but an indirect one was borne by the Church.

I believe that both Spinoza and Jesus were dissidents who aroused the displeasure of the religious establishment. Spinoza was deemed to be indulging in 'execrable blasphemies', and when the Jewish authorities denounced him to the Magistrates as a dangerous heretic, he was banished from Amsterdam as a subversive. I believe that this was essentially the treatment accorded to Jesus when he aroused the displeasure of the religious establishment and then attracted the attention of the secular power.

I do not believe that Jesus was, as has been argued, a 'freedom fighter', a zealot preaching war against Rome. To think of him in such terms is part of what Israel Zangwill, the Anglo-Jewish writer, has called the 'gross if popular error that the God of the Old Testament was a tribal deity with a pet people.' That kind of a God was the Kaiser's (Zangwill explained during the First World War), but 'the God of Abraham could no more be kept tribal than electricity could be kept English because Faraday was.' Curiously enough, the view of Jesus as a freedom fighter was shared, in a characteristically corrupted version, by Hitler who regarded 'the Galilean' as bent upon 'liberating his country from Jewish oppression', 'setting himself against Jewish capitalism, and that is why the Jews liquidated him' (*Table Talk*, 21 October 1941). This of course is utter and ludicrous nonsense.

Jesus was a Hebrew freedom fighter no more than Goethe was a German patriot. The German poet was in fact an ardent admirer of Napoleon, the conqueror of Germany. 'What does it mean to be a patriot?' he asked, and he replied: 'If a poet all his life endeavoured to fight noxious prejudice, to remove narrowminded views, to enlighten the spirit of his people, to purge its taste and ennoble its thoughts – what higher patriotism can he practise?'

Goethe hated the French no more than Jesus hated the Romans though Goethe was glad to be rid of them when Germany was liberated. As one who only cared for the difference between civilisation and barbarism, he said he could never hate a nation which he regarded – rightly or wrongly – as one of the most civilised, and altogether he kept clear of all national hatred which he had found was 'strongest and most intense on the lowest levels of civilisation'. According to him, it was possible for us to reach a

265

stage where it disappeared entirely and we as it were would stand above the nations. This, in my opinion, is a *Weltanschauung* Goethe shared with Jesus.

I should like to state here my own personal view of Jesus. I see him as one among the Hebrew prophets, and in this I am in fact not quite as original as perhaps I imagine. At least one well-known Jewish author, Ludwig Lewisohn, has visualised 'the Jew of the future' when he wrote of 'Elijah and Amos, Jeremiah and Jesus' and insisted that 'men must return to the ideals which Jesus derived from the prophets and the teachers of his people'. Other prominent Jews, among them Rabbi Stephen Wise, expressed similar views at the time (1925) when Professor Joseph Klausner's book *The Life of Jesus* appeared.

I am thinking of a 'Book of Jesus' which would carry the message that there is suffering, death and resurrection, not of one man but of the whole House of Israel. As told of one man, it is a story, a noble story, a solemn simile; but as told of the Jews, it is the living, even vibrant truth, a matter not of belief but of recorded historical fact, stretching back to the dimmest beginnings and, in body and in spirit, present here today. There is no such story anywhere, and if ever history is, as Francis Bacon says, 'philosophy teaching by example', here is the most striking case in point.

The 'Book of Jesus' which I visualise would illustrate the life, death and resurrection of the Jews, just as the Book of Jonah illustrates the nature of God, long suffering and full of compassion. In this vision, the resurrection of Jesus is no more a stumbling-block than is the whale of Jonah. It is not as fancifully irrelevant as the whale, but it is the sublimest, the most powerful of allegories.

But the story of Jesus among his own people must also give rise to another reflection. I believe little would have been heard of him had he been treated differently. If the Synhedrion had taken a broad view, if they had regarded him as a legitimate non-conformist, a freak perhaps, one that deserved to be treated with a sense of our common

266

humanity, rather than a felon to be hunted down by the full force of the law, if in other words tolerance, disguised as psychological insight, had been shown to a teacher of Judaism holding that a religion need not be uniform but had room for many varieties – in modern terms, both 'progressive' and 'orthodox' – then I think it more than likely that his sect would have shared the fate of such other sects as the Essenes of whom comparatively little is heard in Jewish history where they nevertheless hold an honoured place.

I am inclined to believe that the Synhedrion, the 'orthodox' establishment, would have done themselves (and us today) a notable service had they refrained from yielding to their offended, fear-ridden emotions and instead followed balanced reason and a sense of perspective rather than the Grand Inquisitorial fundamentalism which is the creed of the modern fanatic. In our time, and in a different sphere, the Government of Israel showed itself aware of the challenge when, during the Gulf war, it refrained from replying to the Iraqi rockets in kind and rather, in obedience to realistic reason, suffered without hitting back. It was a behaviour that might well be described as a power-political equivalent of tolerance; it certainly avoided the havoc that any 'text book' reaction would have wrought.

But I was speaking of the absence of tolerance amongst ourselves. We do not have to look far. The behaviour of the Orthodox establishment towards non-conformist fellow-Jews – either here or in Israel – is no model of the religious freedom which we expect from others, and the proud boast of enlightened progress becomes sheer mockery when Jewish fanatics declare 'tolerance is no Jewish virtue'. Did we tolerate Hitler, they provocatively ask, putting, by a sleight of hand, the advocates of civilised tolerance on the same level as the partisans of Hitler.

We may be dissenters par excellence in the world at large; we must defy any totalitarian aspiration trying to 'convert' us. Yet among ourselves we respect no dissent. A kind of thought police is at large that, in some ways, may well compare with the Holy Inquisition. The memory it left is not to be envied, and yet (writes G. F. Abbott in his now largely forgotten book *Israel in Europe*) 'the Inquisitors were ... no doubt honest, pious and honourable men, most of them; some perhaps amiable, nay even charitable men. Unfortunately they imagined themselves to be something more – ministers of Heaven's will on earth ... Man would less often become a fiend if he never mistook himself for an angel.' Abbott sums up: 'Strong convictions do not of course excuse unscrupulous and unrelenting brutality, but they explain it. Given such a conviction, persecution becomes a duty and toleration a sin.'

The ire of an orthodox Establishment can indeed be deadly, and to know this we need not delve into the far off past. It is not long since an orthodox rabbi denounced dissenters as 'a cancer in the body of our people ... violating and desecrating every commandment known to God'. Others have deplored the fact that Hitler had forgotten to gas the fellow-Jews of whom they disapproved, and the Reform movement has been dubbed 'a greater danger than the Nazis'.

It is characteristic of the revolution of our time that calls for tolerance are now heard in quarters where, even a short while ago, they would never have been expected. An earnest appeal for 'mutual tolerance' was issued by the then President of the Soviet Union, Mikhail Gorbachev, alarmed by the spread of ethnic violence and an embarrassing resurgence of militant nationalism in his country. In terms of history, an even greater irony attached to the plea made by Pope John Paul II when he urged all faiths to live together in peace. A hundred-odd years ago another Pope had solemnly condemned the very thought of tolerance!

I was much intrigued when, some time ago, the President of Portugal, Dr Mario Soares, publicly asked Jews to forgive the crimes committed against them by the medieval Inquisition. He then said: 'The only possible antidote against the horrors of fanaticism, intolerance and inhumanity is an inquiring mind, freedom of thought and tolerance.'

I would slightly vary the idea. I would plead for a general broad approach to life which is not along one single track but along many. For who knows the truth? Though the Prinz Heinrich school taught me many things which I learnt to reject, I also remember with gratitude the fine remark by Lessing, the 18th-century German dramatist, that 'if God held in one hand truth and in the other the search for truth and said "Choose", I would choose the search for truth as truth after all is only for God alone.' The saying greatly impressed me and I have often thought of it when I met those – too many – who claim to know the truth: give me the search for truth every time.

I am reminded also of kindred teachings I took away from school. From one of the lesser 19th-century German authors, Otto Ludwig, I learnt that 'man shall take care not that he get into heaven but that heaven get into him', and I don't know how often I heard these words of Schiller's: 'Happiness is not in the world outside where only fools will seek it: it is within you – you for ever give it birth.'

Too many of us appear unwilling to admit that there are at least two sides to any reasoned proposition, both equally legitimate. The virtues are not all on one side nor the vices all on the other – a truism if ever there was one. It should be possible, especially in the perspective of history, to weigh the two sides. It is self-righteousness that keeps the scape-goat as a domestic animal. An Irish writer, Mary Kenny, once told how it is done by her people: 'We were taught that alcohol was introduced to the Irish by the wicked English as a deliberate stratagem to make the Irish degenerate', etc. A likely tale – but seriously dispensed and sincerely believed. Similarly, on any issue of specifically Jewish concern, many Jews would be inclined to brush aside any 'objective' assessment if not as 'crazy', at the very least as a deplorable 'weakness' offending 'natural instincts', but few would realise that such views were actually held by among others Hitler who boasted of being 'ruthlessly one-sided'.

269

In fact most of us invariably, almost automatically, take the subjective view, insisting that beside it no other authority shall be tolerated.

We only know of the book burnings perpetrated by the Inquisition and the Nazis (past and present); we never think of the burnings of Hebrew books by fundamentalist rabbis. Their intolerance is essentially indistinguishable from that of the medieval Church.

Yet I also like to see some hopeful signs of change. One of the leading orthodox rabbis in Anglo-Jewry discovered 'an Orthodox tradition that is tolerant', proclaiming 'the tolerant message of loving one's neighbour as oneself'. Rabbi Dr Jeffrey Cohen wrote: 'In the absence of considered argument and debate, authoritarian prohibitions or condemnations are counter-productive', making the intolerant appear to be people who 'cannot defend their entrenched position and fear the moral superiority of the opposition.' There was a need, the rabbi said, to 'strip away the superficial differences, to affirm what unites rather than what divides', to 'expand our people and extend its horizons.'

A great deal of myth is still surrounding the thought, and pervading the talk, of a Chosen Race. Those chosen to keep the commandments behave as if they were already keeping them, assuming as fulfilled (if they do not ignore) this basic ideal condition. We tend to fancy we are a 'holy nation', a 'kingdom of priests', when in fact we have been told we *shall* be – if we qualify for the title (Exodus 19:6). We *shall* love our neighbour as ourselves – do we? Shaw, in his preface to *St Joan*, makes this point with regard to the Church: 'The Church Militant behaves as if it were already the Church Triumphant'. There is a philosophy of the As If – there also appears to be a religion of the As If.

This is perhaps the most charitable way in which the malaise can be presented. There is another one which Byron noted in respect of his own country: 'In these days,' he wrote in 1822, 'the grand *primum mobile* of England is *cant*: cant political, cant poetical, cant religious, cant moral, but always cant, multiplied throughout all the varieties of life ... I say cant, because it is a thing of words, without the smallest influence upon human actions.' The remark greatly moved Hazlitt who thought 'these words should be written in letters of gold, as the testimony of a lofty poet to a great moral truth.'

That moral truth was eloquently expressed by Glückel of Hamelin, the German-Jewish writer, in her memoirs (1665) where she laments: 'If, deep down in our hearts we were devoutly religious and not so wicked, I am certain that God would take pity on us. If only we were to keep the commandment "Love your neighbour as yourself". But may God have mercy upon us, seeing the way we go about it. These jealousies and that causeless hatred – this sort of thing can do us no good.' Few Jews would now, like the Hebrew prophets, care to pass similar judgment on their own people if only because they must expect self-righteousness to fob them off as 'self-haters'.

I will quote in this connection another Jewish voice which I recognise as authoritative, 'Ahad Ha'am' ('One of the People'), Asher Ginzberg, the prophet of a 'cultural Zionism'. As he refers to 'the religious dogma that God had chosen Israel "to make him high above all nations"', he writes in 1898: 'It was for moral development that Israel was chosen by God, "to be a peculiar people unto Himself ... and to keep all His commandments"; that is, to give concrete expression in every generation to the highest type of morality, to submit always to the yoke of the most exacting moral obligations ... This consciousness of its moral election has been preserved by the Jewish people throughout its history and has been its solace in all its sufferings.'

At the same time, Ahad Ha'am cannot help noticing 'our failure to justify in practice the potentialities of our election', and in this he sees 'the profound tragedy of our spiritual life'. He explains: 'Since the day when we left the Ghetto and started to partake of the world's life and its civilisation, we cannot help seeing that our superiority is potential merely. Actually we are not superior to other

271

nations even in the sphere of morality. We have been unable to fulfil our mission in exile, because we could not make our lives a true expression of our character.'

Too often 'our character' is clothed in a self-righteousness that insists on us generally appearing 'holier than thou'. Jews must be seen not only as different: they must seem superior though the plain fact is, in the ordinary pursuits of life, they aren't. I was however impressed by the remarkably high standard reached by the Israeli administration of justice dealing with the much discussed case of the Ukrainian Demjanjuk charged with 'war crimes': it first found him guilty and sentenced him to death but on appeal recognised its error and set the man free, boldly defying a highly emotional public opinion. Unfortunately some of the moulders of that opinion (outside Israel) showed themselves only too willing to approve of the original verdict. The *Jewish Chronicle* felt 'justice has reached back over more than four decades', and 'the triumph of justice' moved the then Chief Rabbi of Britain to quote from Proverbs, 'When the wicked perish, there is joy'.

Similarly we do not add to our stature by insisting that the Jewish State is the fulfilment of messianic prophecy; it is not, obviously. The reality is that the state owes its existence to the exertions of a political movement which, in turn, was the product of antisemitism. The state became inevitable as a result of an overwhelming degree of Jewish homelessness, and the allegorical 'prophecy' of the Promised Land was the myth-embroidered flag under which the goal was achieved.

The many myths infesting history are admittedly indispensable – in the words of Thomas Szass, 'the heart and brain as it were of social organism' – and sometimes they are magnificent myths, the 'life lies' by which we collectively survive. They must be counted among the three forces which Dostoyevsky's Grand Inquisitor says 'hold captive the conscience of men for their own happiness' – 'miracle, mystery and authority'. They certainly lend colour and distinction to our often drab and commonplace existence, and only in that sense are they part of reality, however much one may think it a counterfeit reality.

History is very different, and so far as 'the peculiar people' is concerned, in their story the supreme reality, the presence of God, is manifest in a way which all the myths combined cannot reveal. For while the myths presume to explain what the people do, history explains what a greater power does with them. In the myths is the image of man but in history is the hand of God.

Inevitably, myth has also enveloped the story of the Holocaust. Legends have been woven around it; the doomed, degraded victims have been raised to the status of saints, heroes and martyrs. Hopeful myths were invented to relieve the painful, intolerable truth. The ghetto has emerged as a Holy City, writes David G. Roskies, a US Professor of Jewish Literature, as 'a community that has never been so united before, almost messianic in its "ingatheredness"', 'a composite image that was as glorified and as romantic about the ghetto dead as the subsequent literature would be about the Holocaust.'

# 18

# THE HOLOCAUST:
# MYTHS AND HISTORY

I naturally took the greatest interest in research on the Holocaust, and I was particularly intrigued by the attempts of so-called revisionist historians to prove that it never happened and/or if it happened, Hitler never knew of it. I wrote an extensive analysis of the book by one of their leaders, the American Arthur Butz, and another by the Briton Richard E. Harwood (the pen-name of one Richard Verrall). I had more especially a personal encounter with one of their patron saints, the late Paul Rassinier, a Frenchman best known as the author of *The Lies of Odysseus* where he sneers at the survivors of Auschwitz as purveyors of fanciful fiction copying the inventive wily Greek. Now Rassinier was once some sort of a socialist, a disciple of the out-and-out antisemitic Proudhon. Having got mixed up with the French Resistance, he had spent some time in Buchenwald. He was actually a muddled misfit and cock-eyed freak, incapable of handling facts straight, and when a French Jewish leader accused him of having 'made common cause with his new neo-Nazi friends', he took legal action but failed; the Paris court found 'the ideas preached by Rassinier are identical with those proclaimed by the neo-Nazis.'

I took him up in 1965 when he published in the Paris antisemitic magazine *Lectures Françaises* a review of the documentary novel *The Mission*, by the Viennese author Hans Habe, dealing with a possible rescue of Jews at the time of the Evian Conference in July 1938. In this novel an Austrian Jewish physician of international renown (Professor Heinrich Neumann appearing under a different name) is presented as having been blackmailed by the Gestapo into secretly canvassing an alleged Nazi offer (which Habe regarded as fact) to sell Jews at $250 each.

In his review, Rassinier made the following assertion: 'Hitler never suggested to other countries that he would let them have the Jews at $250 per head – on the contrary he *offered* to pay $250 per head to each country prepared to take them.' Rassinier went on: 'Britain and other democratic countries did not think fit to accept this solution. Nor did the international press at the time make any reference to this affair; it was reported only in the German press.'

As I had never heard of any such thing, I wrote to Rassinier asking him to please state the date when the said report was published, also the name of any particular paper in which it had appeared. He replied referring me to the *Ha'avarah* Agreement between the Jewish Agency for Palestine and the German Government in 1933. This, he said, contained an offer by Hitler to pay money to any country willing to receive German Jews; there had been plenty of comment on this, between 1933 and 1939, in the German press though not once in the Western.

He also referred me to the Evian Conference; at that time again, he claimed, nothing was published about the 'offer' in the West but the German and Austrian press which he had read regularly had carried reports. He had quoted from memory, he said, since he did not keep press cuttings, but I had only to look up any German paper, especially the *Völkischer Beobachter*, between 6 and 20 July 1938.

No great effort was required to debunk this nonsense. I explained to him briefly the character of the *Ha'avarah*

275

Agreement which, being concerned entirely with emigration to Palestine, had nothing to do with any 'offer of money to any country willing to accept German Jews'. Since the Nazi leaders were not agreed about its merits, I don't think it was ever substantially mentioned in the German press, but it was of course discussed abroad: precisely the reverse of what Rassinier asserted. As for the equally irrelevant Conference of Evian which *was* reported by the Nazis (only to jeer at it), not a word was said at any time either in, before or after July 1938, that could be interpreted as bearing out the hare-brained allegations.

He came back with a story that the purpose of the Evian Conference was to extend the terms of the *Ha'avarah* Agreement to the whole world! Besides, Hitler had reiterated his 'offer' in December 1938 when Dr Schacht, the *Reichsbank* director, took it to London! Not a shred of evidence, not even an attempt to produce it; but simply insolent repetition of arrant lies, red herrings and more lies. The 'Lies of Odysseus' were really his own.

Now I was beginning to get on his nerves. No, he could not supply chapter and verse; he repeated he had 'quoted from memory', that must be enough. I could read it all up in the memoirs of Dr Weizmann. Who was I, anyway? He adopted the tone of righteous indignation. 'Don't expect me to inconvenience myself just to furnish you with those press cuttings. So far as I am concerned,' he magisterially announced, 'the matter is closed. I am not the call-boy of those who ask me for references. You go and find out for yourself.'

I did, as a matter of fact I had done so even before he so invited me, and I found that his 'evidence' was not 'from memory' but from imagination – an imagination closed to challenge and immune to scruple. Such was one of the star witnesses paraded before us by the defilers and corrupters of the story of the Holocaust. What the lesser stars might be like can safely be left to *our* imagination.

Whenever I thought of these corrupters and perverters of the abundantly documented truth, I was put in mind of the remark by Márya Dmitrievna in Tolstoy's *War and Peace*: 'Perhaps you think you have invented a novelty? You have been forestalled, my dear! It was thought of long ago. It is done in all the brothels.'

But there was another side to the Holocaust debate, one that can never be stressed enough. Understandably, we are mesmerised by the events which must numb rational thought and it cannot be surprising that such early warners as there were found little credence. It was a repetition of the misjudgment that did not, could not grasp the meaning of Hitler in 1933. The point of the future was – certainly in our time – that it was unimaginable, utterly beyond the human ken. If it was so once, we have no reason to assume that it has changed its ways and become amenable to our calculations which may presume we can provide for it. An international conference recently was devoted to the theme 'Remembrance for the Future'. It rejoiced in the assumption that we can know the future which is usually hidden behind seven veils, and also that we do know the many faces of the past which we claim to remember. Clearly it is believed that we can learn from history – a highly questionable and essentially much discredited belief.

Bernard Shaw makes the very true observation (in *Man and Superman*): 'If history repeats itself and the unexpected always happens, how incapable must Man be of learning from experience!' Besides, of course, the past is, like our dreams, open to many interpretations. We remember facts (demonstrable or assumed ones) which we arrange in an uncertain order of cause and effect, as we cannot always know which causes produce which effects, and we transplant our remembrance such as it is mechanically into a future as we imagine it – an extension of the present, while the truth is, as we might have learnt from Edmund Burke, that 'you can never plan the future by the past'. The future is, alas, elusively different, and the categories of our experience will appear irrelevant even if we remember the past aright.

They are almost certain to be irrelevant so far as the Jews

are concerned since their role has been, for 2,000 years, passive and is now active so that they may easily be involved in grave situations – not only suffering as victims. I have always been impressed by the confession of the famous Yiddish author Shalom Asch: 'God be thanked that the nations have not given my people the opportunity to commit against others the crimes which have been committed against it. I say, God be thanked, for had that opportunity been given, who can doubt that it would have conducted itself against strangers in the same manner as the other peoples?'

Not only against strangers either. Not long ago a regular pogrom was perpetrated by London Jews against strictly orthodox fellow-Jews whose behaviour happened to be disapproved by the even more strictly orthodox. The 'most disgraceful incidents' as described in the Jewish press forced the victims to flee for their lives as their ancestors probably did in Tsarist Russia. The only distinctive feature was that the pogromist women were separated from the pogromist men.

Asch's confession was made quite some time ago, but more recently his point was reinforced by a research psychiatrist at Yale University's National Institute of Mental Health, Walter Reich, who remarked: 'Though we didn't participate in the Holocaust, perhaps, under the same circumstances, we could have, or might have, or would have. Not that we're equally guilty because we're equally human: it was the Nazis who mounted the Holocaust, not we. But the fact that somebody did it makes it necessary for us to acknowledge that people *can* do it, people who differ from us not biologically, not even culturally, but historically... So long as we are inclined to forget how bad something can become, we stand in danger of letting it become that bad.'

Nor is memory in itself a reliable guard. It is certainly important to pillory the Nazi crimes in books, on TV, on the stage and in films, but the grand effect of such enlightenment will fall short of great expectations. For crimes, even

278

those unspeakable crimes, will not necessarily be detested, and deterrence is notoriously inoperative – on the contrary, the sight of the crimes more often than not is likely to waken an urge of imitation; like merchandise it will profit from a boon of advertising.

Some such reflections sprang to my mind when I read of Elie Wiesel's address to the Germans. 'Remember,' he told them: 'memory means to live in more than one world, to be tolerant and understanding of one another. Think of the tormentors as I think of their victims . . . Why such obstinacy on the part of the killer to kill so many of my people? Why the old men and women? Why the children? Why an entire people? . . . What human beings did there to other human beings will affect future generations. After Auschwitz, hope itself is filled with anguish . . . Reject any attempt to cover up the past. Remember . . . remember.'

I agree. Yes, let the Germans remember what they did to the Jews who were the victims. Most certainly and by all means. Let all the countries remember what was done to the Jews, for they too were involved and they have little cause to feel proud of their record – not only with regard to Jews.

Many years ago, Americans were shocked when a black militant told them: 'Violence is as American as cherry pie', but when shortly afterwards the US National Commission on Causes and Prevention of Violence took up the point, they found that the United States is a 'bloody-minded nation' whose past was replete with strife and bloodshed. The Commission referred to the 'historical amnesia' of many Americans that 'masks much of their turbulent past'. Such a tendency to 'sweeten memories of their past through collective repression' was thought to be widespread among all nations, while Americans had 'probably magnified the process of selective recollection' owing to 'our historic vision of ourselves as a latterday chosen people, a new Jerusalem'.

An American Christian commentator at the time re- marked: 'We'll all have to learn to live with our violent past and know that it is part of our reality as a nation... Our amnesia is a way of denying our past and, consequently, who we are. When we're not forgetting or obliterating our past, we romanticise it.'

The writer went on: 'They are true patriots who bear for all to see the scars and wounds of our national pathology of violence. The love of one's people, like the love of one's self, comes only after we have faced ourselves as we really are, known the misery and the grandeur, the perversity and the potential, the sickness and the health of our true condition... May God grant us the strength to look honestly at what we have been in our violent past and expect with hope a different kind of future.'

These reflections must apply to us Jews just as much as to any other nation. We must remember not only what we have suffered, like Professor Wiesel who has learnt from his experience 'first of all that a Jew must place his destiny at the centre of his people', and therefore – in contrast to the Hebrew prophets – he will 'never judge Israel', as if his paramount principle must be 'Right or wrong my country', meaning that we must totally identify, show 'total solidarity', with anything our Government may declare to be right, that we must surrender our own moral judgment, and that conscience which Hitler despised as 'a Jewish invention' must be allowed no voice. To fall on such dire, totalitarian philosophy was a grievous fate indeed. Little has been learnt from the 'total', that is totalitarian, experience of this century. There was, alas, too much 'total solidarity', even and especially when wrong was done. What has happened to the righteous indignation at those who then kept silent?

Jews must remember also another thing: not just what was done to them when they were victims but what they did when they were free agents. Their history does not exhaust itself in the much cited 2,000 years of suffering (which can be reduced to 1,000). Such a vision reminds me of the image of Baron Münchhausen when he rides on half a horse. Jewish history stretches back beyond the Christian era, into tidings glad and tidings sad – the glad (and always remembered) story of the Exodus from Egypt and the sad (and rarely remembered) story of the entry into Canaan, when Joshua was told to 'utterly destroy' the inhabitants of the land, 'both men and women, both young and old, and ox and sheep and ass', leaving 'none alive': 'all that breathes' was to be killed, even as the Lord, the God of Israel, commanded. One is almost tempted to remember the question asked by Elie Wiesel: 'Why such obstinacy on the part of the killer to kill so many? Why the old men and women? Why the children?' – and also, in Canaan, the cattle?

Mr Wiesel is a little (as he puts it) 'embarrassed'. 'Why so much brutality?' he asks. 'Why such lack of magnanimity towards the beaten enemy? ... Why, why?' Also 'Why did not one question the justice of the verdict? What happened to the eternal protesters on whom we could – and still can – count to speak up in the name of truth and justice, in the name of conscience?'

Wiesel knows 'Joshua acted on God's orders', but then he wonders 'why was God so cruel?' He explains: 'Showing mercy would have been mistaken for weakness. They had to be ruthless. Kill or be killed: that was the international law, the law of destiny': (though not necessarily Jewish law). This is how Wiesel interprets 'the law of destiny': 'For Canaan to be conquered, its inhabitants had to disappear. That is how God willed it', and who are the Canaanites anyway – or such as survived – to complain? Wiesel tells us: 'Had the natives fled or collaborated, they would have remained alive. In other words, they had but themselves to blame. They had been foolish to resist.'

Can he be serious? He is not known to be endowed with a sense of humour however black or quizzical. He must be serious. But then it is not often that so callous an attempt is made to inflict insult upon injury. Or is he simply – his Nobel prize notwithstanding – an intellectual *schlemiel* incapable of seeing himself in other people's shoes?

The Canaanites of course did not know that, as Wiesel

281

says, 'it was God who gave their land away to Abraham and his children', and that, he adds, was 'when the first injustice was committed'. 'The first injustice'? Does he then suggest that Joshua's conquest was the second injustice? But he himself specifically declares that 'it was Joshua's sacred duty to liberate Canaan', he was fighting 'a war of liberation', 'reconquering' the land (Elie Wiesel, *Five Biblical Portraits*, London, 1981). Ever since Wiesel received the Nobel peace prize he has become something like a cult figure, and we find it difficult to see him as what in fact he is – a great myth-making simplifier and/or simplifying myth-maker.

The simplifying and/or myth-making process, which is by no means confined to Wiesel, is assisted by the tricks that the collective memory will play on us. It may well be true, as I believe Martin Buber remarks, that Jewry is a community based on memory, but what sort of memory? Memory can be wayward and oddly discriminating. In respect of things that please it will operate in one way, but in a very different way when turned on things liable to embarrass. Memory then severely qualifies Marc Antony's observation about the evil that men do and the good they do – the evil living after them, the good interred with their bones. This may be true of others, but where we are concerned memory combines with conscience to reverse the rule: the good we do lives after us, the evil is interred.

It was Nietzsche who then saw the conflict between memory and conscience – memory knowing 'I have done it', conscience whispering 'I can't have done it', and after a struggle, memory gives way while the whisper insists 'I *cannot* have done it'.

We know what we did to the Canaanites: it's down in black and white, even more than once, but the conscience recoiled. We would rather not have done it, and so a defence had to be devised: we obeyed 'superior orders'. God willed it, God commanded it. I was intrigued when I read a Jewish scholar's reference to a 'historiosophy' which seems to me relevant in this connection. 'Whereas in the relatively early, raw depictions of the Israelite wars, the mortal and the divine are concerted,' says Abraham Malamat in a lecture on Early Israelite Warfare and the Conquest of Canaan, 1978, 'the later redactors (especially the so-called Deuteronomist) brought the role of the Lord of Israel to the fore, suppressing the human element... The sacred element increasingly outshines and overshadows the profane: God fights for His people.'

At least the so-called Deuteronomist says so. But God does not always do so. He did in Egypt but he didn't in Auschwitz – with consequences which I have explained in Chapter 2. However the 'sacred element' has indeed survived down to fairly modern times. The Puritans, for example, though 'persecuted in England, forgot the instincts of mercy in their new home' (North America), and 'regarding themselves as favoured Israelites in the Promised Land, proceeded to exterminate a people whose "iniquity was full", like so many Heaven-commissioned Joshuas,' writes John Bonwick, the 19th-century English historian of overseas colonisation. The 'extinction of the lower races,' he says, was seen as 'predestined by Nature', and the white American was thought to be acting as 'an instrument of Providence', fulfilling 'the will of God' – an echo of the Crusaders' cry *Deus lo volt.*

At the other end of the world, a missionary to the blacks of New South Wales felt the virtual destruction of the people supposed to be in his charge was 'from the wrath of God which is revealed from heaven against all ungodliness and unrighteousness of men'.

How could this be? When (according to the Bible in Genesis 6:13) God decided to destroy the world (which he had recently judged to be 'very good') his reason was that it was 'filled with violence'. Very well, but in that case it must seem strange not only that the recreated world bears the same blemish but that God himself went out of his way to order the indiscriminate violence.

A modern, 'progressive' (non-orthodox) Jewish Bible commentator, Günther Plaut, dealing with the violence in

Canaan, finds it difficult to 'make clear how a loving and caring God could be seen to issue such edicts'. He dismisses the argument of 'necessity' which claimed that 'unless the native people were done away with, they could ensnare Israel with their idolatrous practices'. (Oddly enough, it is never envisaged that the Israelites might have the ability and strength to lure the native people away from their idolatrous practices.) However, that necessity, Plaut says, could not be accepted by any student of history because 'all too many humans have fallen victims to inquisitors and crusading warriors who pretended to act out of the highest religious motives.'

Instead Plaut finds relief in the fact that a policy of annihilation 'was never carried out – the Canaanites were *not* annihilated' (his italics). It is literally a poor relief. How relieved would he allow a German to feel at the thought that the Final Solution was *not* final: the Nazis did not kill *all* the Jews. Moreover Plaut's point does not tackle the paramount problem that the annihilation was divinely ordained and there was no want of trying to fulfil the commandment.

Henry Milman, the early English historian of the Jews, is more straightforward as he sums up the melancholy facts: 'To the generally humane character of the Mosaic legislation there appears one great exception, the sanguinary and relentless warfare enjoined against the seven Canaanitish nations. Towards them mercy was a crime – extermination a duty.' Precisely this was the morality of the exterminators in our time (as I have shown in my documentation *The Text of the Holocaust*). This too must be a 'remembrance for the future', however incredible, inconceivable it may appear, for who knows what the unfathomable future will hold?

Fifty-odd years ago, the indications of a Holocaust were fairly clear however unbelievable, and we now know it was virtually a case of drawing logical conclusions. There was only one thing that stood in the way of our logical foresight: our belief, the belief of the 19th century in human progress. We had progressed, we were progressing, and progress seemed irresistible and irreversible. The idea was poignantly proclaimed by Anton Chekhov in *The Cherry Orchard* (1904): 'Humanity is advancing towards the highest truth, the greatest happiness that it is possible to achieve on earth, and I am in the van... Humanity is perpetually advancing, always seeking to perfect its own powers.'

If this belief was proclaimed in Russia, even at a time when it had least prospect of being honoured, it was certainly commonplace in the West. At the height of Hitler's power, a British Jewish author, Louis Golding, wrote emphatically (*The Jewish Problem*, 1938): 'It cannot happen here, I say, for the English are not composed as the Germans are ... and here there is chivalry and there is God.' Fifty years later, another prominent British Jew, Bernard Levin, in his column in *The Times* (29 November 1990), boldly forecast: 'The Jewish Dark Ages will not come again.' The reason was, according to Levin, that 'the holocaust indelibly stained Germany, the rest of the world and the universe itself. That dreadful truth alone means that anyone who speaks casually or lightly, let alone approvingly, of antisemitism, is a fool, if not a scoundrel.' The trouble is antisemitism was recognised as 'the Socialism of the fools' as far back as the 1890s, even in Germany, and the (National) Socialist fools managed to make fools of the very wisest of *Times* columnists.

They had forgotten the story of Israel in Egypt where the enlightened Pharaoh of Joseph was followed by one who 'did not know Joseph' (or rather did not want to know), though of course the succession might also be the other way round. Their view of history was clouded by the 19th-century belief in progress which fortified all of us in our illusions. Now we no longer have this noble, sadly flawed belief. Now we must face the fact which Victor Frankl, the Austrian Jewish psychiatrist, has detected in the line separating a civilised minority from the majority, a separation he says which 'runs through every political party and every other group' – anywhere. Now we cannot, as the generation at the turn of the 19th century did, mistake the cruel prospect: progress is *not* irreversible. Another holocaust is *not* unthinkable, and remembrance of the past will do nothing for our future – a future enacted in quite different, unforeseen and unforeseeable circumstances of which only one thing is certain: that they will vindicate the wisdom of Ecclesiastes which I recalled at the beginning of my story, a few years before the Nazi holocaust, 'Man knoweth not his time...' Is it too early to warn now that, beyond the irreconcilable arguments, the stage is being set for another holocaust?

The crucial issue between Israelis and Arabs is, as it was in the beginning, possession of the land, and the present international debate is little more than a feint to disguise this reality. The land is 'promised' only so long as we do not enter it: the moment we do, the moment the 'promise' appears to be 'fulfilled', it vanishes among the all too humdrum realities and remains what it was all along, an unattainable ideal, the image in the clouds, half myth, half faith, that passes for history.

But of course the basic issue – possession of the land – remains and since the strength of the emotions involved is such that (as I mentioned earlier on) both Arabs and Israelis pleading for a rational, mutually acceptable settlement are liable to be silenced by fanatics, an irrational, violent show-down must be foreseen.

It half has been – and dismissed, its ghost hovering uneasily over the shadows of the past. When in June 1989 he spoke of the Palestinian insurrection (*intifada*), the then Israeli Army's Chief of Staff, Lt.-Gen. Dan Shomron, mentioned genocide as 'one way to end the crisis' though he added: 'Genocide is unthinkable, both morally and in terms of Israel's international standing'. The General was responding to criticism from Israeli 'extremists' who had accused him of failing to crush the then 18-months-old Palestinian revolt.

Genocide must indeed appear inconceivable but it does lurk hidden in the deep shadows of history. When the Israelites arrived at the border of Canaan (writes Heinrich

Graetz) their victory over some powerful kings had inspired them with confidence and determination to drive out the inhabitants who had driven out others before them and were now demoralised by the 'overwhelming terror' that preceded the approaching invasion. Graetz does not specify details of the 'terror' other than the military victories. He only refers to the conditions after the conquest when the Israelites had 'as many enemies as neighbours' and faced the alternative of 'either waging a war of annihilation against the neighbours or establishing friendship with them'. War being found 'impossible', they sought friendship.

More modern Jewish historians have taken up the challenge presented by the story. 'What of the immorality involved in the horrors inflicted upon the previous population?' asks the American Chaim Potok in his book *Wanderings* (1978), and he explains: 'Tribal movements, like earthquakes, appear to have no anxieties about their reputation... If there was any morality in such rearrangements of human geography, it came from the human need to put an end to wanderings.' The ends were to justify the means – without enquiring whether the means were morally warranted.

Another American, Max Dimant (*Jews, God and History*, 1962) seeks refuge in relative cruelties. According to him, 'the Biblical account of the destruction by the Jews of the Canaanite culture may sound barbarous to readers unfamiliar with the history and practices of antiquity. Actually it was far less barbarous than the destruction of the Cretan culture by the invading Greeks in the 6th century BC or the destruction of the Etruscan culture by the invading Romans in the same century.' There is no comment on the destruction of innocent human life.

This point is met head-on by a modern Christian historian who sees the conflict in terms of a holy war. In her 1980 book, *Holy War: The Crusades and their Impact on Today's World*, Karen Armstrong writes the Canaanites 'were in the way of the divine plan; they were also essential enemies of the new Jewish self. Because they opposed values and plans that were "sacred" to the Jews and essential to God's plans for them, they had to be annihilated. The normal human rights that Jews were commanded to extend to other people did not apply to the Canaanites who had become the enemies of God. This absolute hostility is a characteristic of the holy war... When God had saved his people from the Egyptians the ordinary laws of nature had been suspended, so too when the Jews had to establish themselves in the Promised Land, ordinary morality ceased to apply.' Later, Miss Armstrong remarks, when 'God forbade David to build the Temple because he had shed too much blood, albeit at the divine command', we can see 'the first sign of worry about the morality of the holy war.'

At least one Jewish Bible commentator has been troubled by the fate decreed for the people of Canaan. Hertz refers to the 'moral difficulty' presented by what he euphemistically calls 'the ban' which he says is 'found in peoples as far apart as the Romans and the Mexicans' – though with this difference: 'Among them all it was but an exhibition of cruelty for cruelty's sake', while 'in Israel alone it was moralised'. This argument, even if in itself correct, will not greatly impress those who see a relationship between ends and means: questionable means are rarely justified by good ends. Hertz goes far to illustrate the remark of Bertrand Russell: 'The infliction of cruelty with a good conscience is a delight to moralists.'

Nor would it seem a satisfactory gloss that 'the population of nearly every European country today had conquered its present homeland and largely destroyed its original inhabitants.' This may well be true, but if so, what of the claim that Israel shall be 'a light unto the nations'?

I was deeply moved by the dirge of the German writer Günter Grass over the Nazi crimes. They will 'never cease to be contemporary,' he wrote in February 1990. 'Our shame will neither be suppressed nor overcome. Auschwitz, despite being surrounded by all manner of explanations, will never be fully comprehended... It is a permanent brand in our past.'

Has any such Jewish dirge ever been composed over the innocents that were slain, even on so spectacular an occasion as the entry into Canaan? Has any Jew ever then remembered the words of Abraham: (Genesis: 18:25): 'That be far from you to slay the righteous with the wicked... Shall not the Judge of all the earth do justly?' These words, says Hertz, 'have been well described as an "epochal sentence in the Bible"', making 'justice the main pillar of God's Throne' and Israel the 'merciful children of merciful ancestors'. But has any Jew ever thought of confronting the dark side of Jewish history?

Not that the crimes of the Nazis can be compared with these or any other, either in extent or in sophistication. Of course not, especially when they are seen as the mark of an age that took pride in its enlightened, civilised progress. But judgment on the wilful destruction of innocent human life does not depend on conditions like these. We were rightly horrified when the Serbs enforced an 'ethnic cleansing' by callously driving out the Muslims from Bosnia in 1992. Should we not be profoundly moved by the memory of the terrible things that were done, not in the heat of battle, not in self-defence, but as a premeditated, indiscriminate action, even divinely ordained, not once but several times, to 'save alive nothing that breathes'?

Yet this slaughter not only goes unlamented, the 'moral difficulty' involved is not' even part of our conscious mind when we concern ourselves exclusively with what was done to us. As he speaks of the 'sometimes barbarous lapses' that occurred, Cecil Roth, in his *Short History of the Jewish People*, caustically remarks that 'the old monotheistic ideals of Israel were remembered even when they were not obeyed'.

I am stressing this point because it is rarely made by others who keep on repeating the myths that are infesting so much of history. I am not a revisionist, trying to revise history. I believe the Jewish history that is told by the historians who repeat each other is true so far as it goes – only I believe there is more to it than these historians will permit to meet the eye, and this I believe also is true. I believe we do not, because we cannot, understand our history if we pay attention only to one aspect and ignore others, if the light is not allowed to cast any shadows, and if the moral imperatives crowd out the 'moral difficulties'. We are then bound to feel bewildered and frustrated because I think we do not realise the contradiction between what we claim to be and what we are.

Is it perhaps some unconscious force springing from this contradiction that has driven some Jews, labouring to 'explain' the Holocaust, to suspect punishment for their own sins? Of course it is not an 'explanation' that will survive rational scrutiny. For if we were punished for our sins in this awful way, why not others who almost certainly committed sins no less serious? And if there are sins that 'explain' the Holocaust, which are they? Well, according to the fundamentalists beating their own breast, quite a few. In the paper I previously mentioned on 'The Holocaust in Jewish Theology', Chief Rabbi Jonathan Sacks cites those rabbis who see the sin in Zionism which they denounce as 'worse than idolatry', indeed 'the work of Satan', and, on the other hand, those who hold that Jews were punished because they had 'ceased to be Zionists' or opposed Zionism, choosing instead the fleshpots of 'assimilation'. Such Jewish arguments were put by Sacks on the same level as the doctrine of Christians who believe that 'genocide was the punishment for deicide'. No wonder some Jewish theologians like the American Richard Rubinstein have drawn the conclusion that (in Sacks' words) 'the attempt to find Divine meaning in the holocaust leads only to madness.'

# 19

# A LATE VICTIM: HELGA'S ILLNESS AND DEATH

Most of my family eventually managed to escape from the slaughter but Helga my wife lost both her mother and her father. It was a blow she never came to terms with, and in a way she too may be counted among the victims. For the pain and the grief she suffered as a result gravely affected her heart and it was not long after our marriage that the disease began to make itself felt. She was repeatedly in hospital and (we believed) only thanks to her strong constitution was she able to overcome several attacks. One of them actually seemed to be fatal, and the fact that she survived it was regarded by the doctors as something of a miracle, so much so that I feel I must tell the story in some detail.

Shortly after she had the attack, fairly late at night, she was taken by ambulance to the nearby hospital where she was promptly examined while I waited there for about ninety minutes. Then the examining doctor came, with a Sister, to tell me that Helga was 'in a very poor state', in fact he doubted whether she would last the night. I remained calm and while Sister tried to comfort me (for both had decided that Helga was dead), I could only say she had great will power.

After another hour or so (about midnight) I was taken up to a small room where I found Helga laid up on a kind of catafalque, as if lying in state. I was clearly led to believe she was dead or very nearly so. She seemed lifeless, motionless, her looks were ashen but – she also seemed slightly, feebly, breathing, on and off. So there was some life in her still. I stroked her hands and arms and cheeks; she did not in any way react, and her eyes were virtually closed. I remained with her till 6 a.m. Then I went home, having been told that the hospital would inform me of any development – which, as I understood it, would mean that Helga had died.

Of course I could hardly sleep, did not bother to undress as I was so soon to be off again. I made myself some sort of a breakfast. The phone went – Elli, Helga's sister, enquiring. I told her, crying; she said she would come. Then, suddenly, the phone again – a friend, to say her husband had just died. Remembering the moment now, I am amazed I found it possible to take the message in, even managed to express sympathy and offer words of comfort; I also briefly mentioned Helga. I was not able though to concentrate on the conversation for any length of time. I felt mainly relief there was no message from the hospital.

So I went off in the rain, expecting sad news. But instead I found Helga incredibly changed. She was alive, her eyes fairly wide open, while moving her arms and legs. What a contrast from the night before. Soon the same doctor appeared, an assistant to the resident specialist, now with a party of juniors; he said he must admit it was a miracle, for if he thought Helga would not last the night, it was because her heart had stopped beating for some time, and things being equal, he would make the same judgment again.

Now Helga seemed to me in remarkably good shape, considering. Yet I soon realised that while her physical condition had improved, her mental state was greatly worrying. She was apparently unable to speak any coherent sentence. She seemed confused, disorientated. I mentioned this to some of the nurses; they thought that as there had been a physical improvement so there would be a mental one too. I was, in a way, relieved to hear it but wondered what had caused it all.

Charles, the Minister of our congregation, called but he could not see Helga at once. So I spoke to him, explained her sick heart and said: 'But she's got a great heart.' I meant much more, for I thought that of her it cannot be said she loves people – she *is* love. When we went in to see her, she seemed definitely changed for the better, even since the day before. She appeared to recognise Charles and welcomed him. She was cheerful and could utter a few coherent things: an improvement here too. I now understood she had been drugged, and perhaps the drugs were wearing off. If so, it was of course bound to be a very slow process.

After about a fortnight Helga had rallied sufficiently to be discharged, and the homecoming itself was a great tonic. We arranged for help during her convalescence in which Esther and Elli did more than I can say, and it was not long before Helga was able to take a hand in the running of affairs. We spent a lovely holiday together in Alfriston, near Eastbourne, where we had been before and had been since.

Unfortunately the healing, such as it appeared, was shortlived. The heart kept ailing and though struggling valiantly to stand up to the pain, Helga soon was beginning to realise that the end could not be long delayed. It was becoming more and more difficult for her to walk on her own and whenever she wanted to go out, she would rely on my arm. She was still watching her favourite TV programmes – she would never miss *Songs of Praise*, and I shall always remember the poignant moment when we heard 'Abide with me'.

She was resigned to her fate. In spite of her natural cheerful disposition, she never ceased to feel deeply the cruel fate suffered by her parents, yet though God had not been kind to her in this respect, she was at peace with him whose ways she felt were beyond our understanding. On

293

10 April 1994, listening to a *Songs of Praise* 50th Wedding Anniversary Programme, she said to me: 'If I live that long, we'll celebrate our anniversary next year.' She died on 17 March 1995, seven months before that cherished date.

I hope to be forgiven if I dwell a little on her life. I believe I can truthfully say she was a 'woman of worth' of whom the poet of Proverbs says 'her worth is far above rubies', for 'favour is false and beauty is vain but a woman that feareth the Lord she shall be praised'.

Helga believed in the goodness of the human being and as she could not in fairness claim to take care of all mankind she chose the one relationship that was nearest to her loving heart, the relationship between Christians and Jews. This was to her one symbol of the human relationship and it was in that respect that she felt she must never fail.

As a prominent member of our synagogue's Women's Society, she established a close contact with the ladies of the Catholic Grail in Pinner where her devoted interest and practical work were highly regarded. She often told me how as a girl, on her way to school, she noticed in a bookshop window one particular title that immediately caught her attention: it was *A Day in the Life of a Social Worker*. I thought a title like this *would* attract her, for such a life might be hers but the story would be all about a day in the life of a human being with a human heart, a heart of care and concern for others, a heart of compassion for her fellow-men, a heart of human love. This was the book in which she was really interested – a girl, and so she remained to the end of her days.

She had no ambition of being much to the fore. She wanted to be a spade worker, a servant. She felt she was an ordinary human being though with a clear awareness of her bitter experience: yet her faith in God never wavered. It had taught her something that she felt she could pass on to her friends. She was to be the lifeblood through which a greater spirit would create the human relationship in which she believed. Many of her friends, in their messages of condolence, assured me she 'inspired and lifted us up'. This

294

work she did over the best part of a lifetime, defying the ill health that had long beset her.

I for my part shall never forget the almost magic way she would introduce into our home the Sabbath on its eve, on Friday night. She would kindle the two candles, pronounce the Hebrew blessing and in doing so cover her eyes which were supposed to be dazzled by the splendour of the divine light. At that moment something not of this world seemed to have entered the room. It was the Peace of the Sabbath, *Shabbat Shalom,* and we kissed each other.

We were in sight of our Golden Wedding which we were eagerly looking forward to, but alas she was to see it only from afar. Yet even while she was suffering the mere sight and thought of the event seemed to create in her a sense of gratitude for what she had received, not least in our daughter Esther in whose life and achievement she took great pride.

Firmly grounded in her Jewish convictions, she had unqualified respect for the beliefs of her Christian friends, a respect that was after all at the heart of the work to which she stood committed. She loved her friends with the love of which Tolstoy said when he wrote *Resurrection,* it 'ennobles man', and 'in this form of love,' he says, 'lies resurrection.'

Her tombstone bears the words 'Her Life was Love'. Over that love death has no dominion: it remains as the only thing that gives meaning to our lives.

As I glance over her life, especially the years we spent together, I like to send her the message which Emily Brontë put into these lines:

> O wander not so far away!
> O love, forgive this selfish tear.
> It may be sad for you to stay –
> But how can I live lonely here?

295

# 20

# JEWS AND GERMANS

The question how we are to reconcile ourselves to the world in which we are fated to live has of course troubled the minds of men at all times. Nietzsche was not the first to see life as 'this monstrous and terrible thing ... with all its plagues, catastrophes ... weaving some vast unintelligible fabric athwart our puny efforts to create an ordered and happy existence.' But when he considered the solution offered by the 'ascetic religions' teaching that 'our sufferings are an expiation for sin, or a purification for a nobler existence to come', he dismissed it as 'a device of slaves and cowards'. He was preaching a religion that, he claimed, was 'triumphant, uncompromising "yea-saying of life"'.

The idea that we ourselves must always be to blame for the catastrophes that befall us strikes me as the sort of nonsense that G. K. Chesterton has defended as 'faith'. Many rabbis would have agreed with him that 'the well-meaning person who, by merely studying the logical side of things, has decided that "faith is nonsense", does not know how truly he speaks; later it may come back to him in the form that nonsense is faith.'

For after all, the breast-beating rabbis, however contradicting each other, may claim a certain higher authority.

Jews know (and recite with sincerity) the prayer professing that 'we were exiled from our land because of our sins', and the author of Lamentations, beholding the city that 'sits solitary', also believed that if she is 'become as one unclean', it is because 'Jerusalem has grievously rebelled', 'the Lord has afflicted her for the multitude of her transgressions', 'our fathers have sinned and we have borne their iniquity', etc. Oddly enough no one seems to have thought of charging the author of Lamentations with 'self-hatred'.

*   *   *

The morality involved in the self-deprecating dirges has a bearing also on our relationship with the Germans. I refused to side with the majority in decrying 'the Germans' as evil incarnate. How long is it since we extolled them as foremost in the vanguard of progress? Generations of Jews held the name of Germany in the very highest regard, revering German *Kultur* as a fine flower of civilisation. Heinrich Heine who keenly felt the edge of German antisemitism and spent the best years of his life in voluntary exile, yet believed in 'a true elective affinity' between 'Jews and Teutons'. Though in 1834 he foresaw a time (exactly 100 years later) when 'the brutal German lust of battle' would 'stage a spectacle which will make the French Revolution seem like a harmless idyll by comparison', nevertheless in 1838 he thought Jews and Teutons, were 'so much alike that the one-time Palestine could be regarded as an oriental Germany and modern Germany as the homeland of Holy Writ' – a judgment from which his usual mordant irony was astonishingly absent. German and 'cultured', or 'learned', were considered by 19th-century Jews to be virtually interchangeable terms, and the 'People of the Book' felt akin to what a 20th-century Anglo-Jewish historian (Lucien Wolf) called 'the characteristic German genius for patient enquiry and critical study'.

Yet within a few short years that 'characteristic genius' disappeared and all that was left was a mass of evil and a pack of barbarians whose very language, the language of Goethe, Lessing and Heine, was deemed unfit for human society. Some refused to speak it. If the matter were not so desperately sad, one would be reminded of Xerxes, king of the Persians, who, angered by the great storm that stopped him from crossing the Hellespont, ordered the 'treacherous and unsavoury water' (though not the storm) to receive the exemplary punishment of 300 lashes. Anyway, what had gone wrong – was it the 'character' of the Germans or was it our assessment of it, our understanding of people's behaviour generally? And if our assessment of Germany; how far can we trust it in regard to other nations? What is all this talk about a 'national character'? In my experience, it is, more often than not, a shorthand formula used to lend an air of respectability to any odd generalising judgment that may seem to fit a given situation. The 'character' of the Germans as Britain's friends in the 19th century was very different from what it became in the 20th. The Teuton cousin once was a relation to be proud of, and (said *The Times* in 1860) since Germany as a whole was 'not aggressive', it was 'to our interest that this conservative element of a European society should be powerful and therefore that it should be united.' As the German 'character' has changed in respect of Britain, so it has in respect of the Jews.

Or was it not 'character' which is, by definition, unchangeable but rather the circumstances that are open to influence? This truth was demonstrated by a remarkable British Jewish voice at the end of the first war. When the Treaty of Versailles was signed in 1919, the London *Jewish Chronicle*, refusing to join in the chorus of jingoist 'Hun' propaganda, 'deplored the spirit in which the Peace terms had been imposed', and this view was taken 'not by reason of any tender sentiment for Germany or because we contemplate with anything but loathing and horror the misdeeds of which she has been guilty', but because 'we fear that [these terms] must prove the harbinger of further sorrow and trouble to sorely tried humanity and set back the progress of true civilisation.'

The fears of course were only too well founded. I have

already mentioned (on page 70) Churchill's apposite remarks on the victors' short-sighted treatment of Germany in 1918 by which 'in the name of peace', 'the way was cleared for the renewal of war'.

This criticism did not come from one who might be discounted as an apologist of the Germans. Churchill passed some pungent comments on them, but he had a clear sense of the realities. He was not frightened when the combined nationalist right wing in the Presidential elections of 1925 secured victory for their candidate, Field Marshal Hindenburg. The understandably fear-ridden French suspected 'a renewal of the German challenge,' Churchill says, but he adds: 'Always wishing as I did to see Germany recover her honour and self-respect and to let war bitterness die, I was not at all distressed by the news', and he remained of this mind as long as Germany as a democracy however frail.

He was among those who believed that 'Germany as a democracy with Parliamentary institutions' would be security for the West, and he only changed his mind in April 1933 (the month of the Nazis' anti-Jewish Boycott Day) when he said it was a 'most dangerous' thing to concede the *then* German demand for equality in weapons, etc. It was *then* that he fully backed France against (Nazi) Germany.

*　　*　　*

As a matter of historical interest, it is perhaps worth noting that, possibly for tactical reasons, he, even he, was moving on questionable ground. Though the mass murders during the so-called Roehm revolt in 1934 had shown him that Hitler, 'reeking with blood', 'would stop at nothing' and that 'conditions in Germany bore no resemblance to those of a civilised State', nevertheless a year later, at the time of the Nuremberg Laws, he still 'could not tell' whether Hitler would 'rank in Valhalla with Pericles, with Augustus and with Washington, or welter in the inferno of human scorn with Attila and Tamerlane'; it seemed to him that 'both possibilities were open' at that moment. While criticising the Nazi 'treatment of the Jews or the Protestants and Catholics of Germany' late in 1937, he held that these matters 'as long as they are confined inside Germany, are not our business'; it seemed to him possible to 'dislike Hitler's system and yet admire his patriotic achievement', and as late as November 1938 (three days before the *Kristallnacht* pogrom) he thought fit to recall that he had 'always said that if Great Britain were defeated in war, I hope we should find a Hitler to lead us back to our rightful position among the nations.'

So much for the past (and the man who was to lead the West against Hitler). In such circumstances, who can provide for the future? Lord Jakobovits, the former Chief Rabbi, says Jews must 'seek reassurance' that 'the systematic mass slaughter of millions' will not happen again. This stands to reason and few will disagree. The question is how can we be reassured? The Rabbi says 'we need new international guarantees', 'new international contracts', 'a new set of international standards'.

Here he would seem to be on less firm ground, for all those international safeguards were present before Hitler came to power and they proved to be of no avail. 'Never again' was a cry much in vogue in those years, and though the same did not happen again, much worse did. So it would appear that something more and very different is needed – especially in the face of the sorrows caused by the second war.

Be that as it may, we at all events had been warned and for reasons which are all too human and do us credit, we refused to believe the worst. So before we rail at God and the world (which we have every right to do), we might also search for those causes within ourselves which cannot be read in the stars. I believe many of us are still cooped up in the mentality of war when 'only a dead German is a good German'. But the war and the horror that went with it is over and whether we like it or not, whether we can or cannot forgive (not forget), we must behave as if we do.

300

I should like to reproduce here, by way of illustration of some of my views, a letter I wrote to the *Jewish Chronicle* a few years ago in the course of a controversy sparked off by the Chaplain of St John's College, Oxford, the Revd Dr A. C. J. Phillips:

... Dr Phillips' counsel that we forgive does not 'affront the Jewish experience', as you say. The Jewish experience is very different. We have suffered persecution in nearly every country, but never did we show lasting resentment. Jews returned to Spain long before the Edict of Expulsion was repealed and Israel is eager to be in touch with her.

As for England, Cecil Roth, the Anglo-Jewish historian, writes that she 'played an important and unenviable role in the martyrdom of the Jewish people... [Here] the Jewish Badge was enforced earlier and more consistently than in any other country... It was here that the Ritual Murder accusation first reared its head. At no other time in the bloodstained record of the Middle Ages were the English horrors of 1189–90 surpassed.'

Yet, soon after the expulsion (Roth writes), 'across the Channel and the North Sea the victims of persecution sometimes cast longing eyes at this potential haven of refuge forgetting all that they had suffered there before.'

When they did return, under Cromwell, the Banishment Decree was still in force and (says Dean Milman) 'the religious feeling of the country, as well as the interests of the trading part of the community, would have risen in arms at a proposition of its repeal.'

But Menasseh ben Israel, who negotiated the Resettlement, probably possessed no less dignity and self-respect than any of the Jewish leaders who today refuse to 'forgive evil perpetrated against others'.

For the fact is that it was not, neither then nor now, perpetrated against others. It was perpetrated against

301

all of us; we are all the victims; it is only by the unaccountable accident of fate that I am alive, and if I plead for forgiveness, it is not because I need 'authority from the six million'.

I do not know what the dead will say. I believe I must lead my life and make any decisions upon my own responsibility, and the memory of the dead will be honoured by the integrity of my action. They do not praise God, but I must, in accordance with what I consider the best teaching of religion.

We as a people have been told to be different from others, trying to be 'holy' as God is holy, and the supreme quality of God, as I understand him, is that he is merciful. He is a righteous and a zealous God, and his judgment was executed on the wicked.

But there were also many who, however involved, were not wicked, but simpletons or fools, and those who did not know their right hand from their left. They would seem to have a claim on the compassion of forgiveness.

Besides, we are not now dealing with the generation of Hitler. We are dealing with a different generation, and the sons shall not be held guilty for the sins of the fathers. It would be wrong to treat them as if they were: they would resent it, not without reason, and we would appear as pathetically absurd, if not irrelevant, as those who keep (or kept) on crying 'The Jews killed Christ'.

I am not saying we should forget. I do say, emphatically, we must remember ... But just as there is a time when we must go to war, so a time must come when we forgive. The warfare cannot be kept up for ever. When a plaque was unveiled in memory of the Jews murdered at York in 1190, the Chief Rabbi explained that the ceremony did not mean forgiveness. Not after 800 years. So how do we live?

No doubt the Chief Rabbi can marshal many authorities in his support, so, with some effort, can I, and we know the Bible has been quoted in the most surprising quarters. But all the quotations suitably chosen are merely a reflection of our own image of God.

He can be as harsh and unforgiving as, in fact, we may be, or he can be very different, the one I prefer to believe in, the God merciful and gracious, long suffering and abundant in goodness and truth, forgiving iniquity, transgression and sin.

I may well have been one of the first Jews in England after the war to make the point (now fairly obvious) that 'not all Germans are guilty'. An article of mine under this heading appeared in the Zionist journal *The Gates of Zion* as early as July 1954, and I should like to commend the editor who printed it even while declaring himself 'not in agreement' with my views. I produced irrefutable evidence to demonstrate the then largely ignored fact that 'in spite of totalitarian tyranny [many Germans] greatly daring remained captains of their soul, refusing to call evil good.' How many of us would have dared as much? The fact that they were Germans, I said, 'will not by an iota lift the curse that lies heavy on the name of Germany. But they at least have saved their souls. When the Government of Israel publishes as it intends to do, as part of a Memorial to the Six Million, a special Memorial dedicated to the "Righteous among the Gentiles" (*hasidei umoth ha'olam*), it cannot forget, for the sake of strict historical justice, the righteous among the Germans'. And it is good to know it has not forgotten them.

I mentioned the bewildering record of history. England was the first European country to expel the Jews, yet an Anglo-Jewish historian (Gustave Pearlson) extolled 'the amicable sentiments between those brothers in humanity, the Englishman and the Jew' – which was written at the same time (1898) as a German-Jewish historian (Adolph Kohut) was rejoicing in 'the true brotherhood of the Teuton and the Semitic tribe'. Such are the vagaries of fortune.

Ideas like these would not have stood me in good stead at the Institute of Jewish Affairs. I would have been too much of an outsider, a freak, and popular opinion would have had to be considered. When I once, in a BBC interview, voiced one of my opinions, the Director of the IJA promptly received indignant letters denouncing me as a 'pro-Nazi agent' who 'ought to be screened' – what a shame I had not lost my family at Auschwitz, and a peremptory demand was made for my instant dismissal. I remember with regret that it was seriously considered to ask for a 'transcript' though the pathetic idea was eventually dropped, but my experience of intolerance among Jews was (not for the first time) sadly confirmed.

So when I took my retirement to reflect on my fifty-odd years' active life, I felt I had seen enough to be satisfied that but for the great minds of all nations and creeds which have enriched mankind, we, the generality of men, were unlikely to progress far. It seemed to be a built-in disability, going back to our origins.

I explained (on page 130) that after the Flood which was to do away with the original ('corrupt') model of man, the new one was not created. The new man, made in the mould of the old, could not help remaining what he was from the beginning. If the earth was 'corrupt' before, it has remained so, and all the waters that came down for 40 days and prevailed for 150, could not wash away the chief reproach the violence that 'filled the earth'. If anything it has become worse. The scribe who told the story could never have fathomed such outcasts as hijackers, even if he was able to forsee 'fundamentalist' murderers, and the atomic and nuclear bomb was certainly beyond his most riotous imagination. The Flood made no difference. The world is as corrupt now as it was before, as is the explicitly named cause of the corruption, violence. Thus our prospects of progress now would seem to be dim. The hope of entering the Promised Land remains – as does the hope of reaching the Messianic Age and settling in Utopia. That hope will never die. But our destiny is to for ever claw it from the stars that cast a flickering light upon the long, unending trek into the wide open wastes of the unknown.

# APPENDIX

*Dedicated to the memory of all the scientists, scholars in every field of learning, who, having escaped from persecution, degradation and murder, did their duty in the struggle for man's freedom.*

## THE BITER BITTEN
### Hitler's Propaganda that Recoiled on Him

The man recovered from the bite:
The dog it was that died.

Oliver Goldsmith,
*Elegy on the Death of a Mad Dog*

Not the least of their achievements on which the Nazis never ceased to pride themselves, was the emigration, i.e. expulsion or flight, of those scientists, scholars, writers, artists and other intellectuals, many of them Jews, who had been associated with the once universally respected cultural tradition of Germany. The Nazis were pleased to be rid of them. Relieved of this alien burden and purged of the 'non-Aryan' dross, Germany, they were sure, would flourish as she had never done before. The German people, Hitler

305

declared in his first year of power (1933),[1] had 'no cause to envy the rest of the world for having received these unworthy elements'; they were a 'pernicious and inferior rabble' which had 'aroused a world psychosis' by casting 'hysterical' slurs on the Nazi Government's professions of its true 'love of peace'. This was said in the same speech in which Hitler announced the first of his aggressive moves, Germany's withdrawal from the League of Nations (October 1933). Unfortunately, the refugees' efforts to expose the Nazis were by no means arousing the world.

Dr Goebbels, the Minister of Propaganda, revealed the method in the madness behind the attacks on the refugees – their warnings were to be discredited: 'The world will have to understand (he said as early as April 1933) that it does not pay to have one's information on Germany supplied by Jewish refugees'; the world was to listen to what *he* was telling it, for example, that 'the Jewish atrocity campaign' was spreading 'wrong ideas about Germany',[2] etc.

Before long Hitler went further in his attacks on the emigrés. These 'low-down scoundrels' (he ranted in January 1934) had left the country not for any political reasons but because they were 'ordinary criminals' wanted by the police, 'rootless' 'sub-humans' pretending to stand for political freedom while in fact 'indulging their criminal instincts.'[3]

These reckless lies had a twofold purpose. They were not only to reinforce the Nazis' general antisemitic propaganda which in turn was to feed anti-alien antisemitism abroad and so create world-wide sympathy for Hitler: they were also to serve the equally imperialist design of discrediting voices that were revealing the truth about the character of Nazi policy and ambition. In Hitler's jargon, these 'irresponsible criminals' (warning tirelessly against the rising threat) were 'trying to mobilise a credulous world against Germany.'[3]

As he continued on his path of imperialist aggression (clearly mapped out in his book *Mein Kampf*), the attacks grew in stridency, raging at the 'senseless atrocity propaganda of Jews and Bolsheviks' that was 'misrepresenting our will to maintain peace',[4] etc.

A few weeks after the November 1938 pogrom, Hitler sought to disable the now unmistakably stirring resistance to him by threatening the 'unimaginable' destruction of the Jews, a threat which he reckoned would effectively deter all opposition. In his notorious speech of 30 January 1939, 'prophesying' the Final Solution, he ridiculed the world-wide 'hypocritical outcry against this barbaric expulsion of a culturally valuable, not to say irreplaceable, element'. Why, he mockingly exclaimed, 'other countries should be grateful to us for dispensing with these marvellous embodiments of culture and putting them at their disposal'.[5]

Hitler was not ignorant of what the loss of 'culturally valuable, not to say irreplaceable' people might mean. In *Mein Kampf*, referring to 'the young German intelligentsia who met their death in Flanders' (1914), he says they were 'the best of the nation's estate', and the loss of them proved 'irreplaceable in the course of the war'.[6] He was yet to learn the application of this home truth to his own affairs.

But in 1939, basking in the success of his Jew-baiting, he was (he proudly announced) 'happy to be rid of this commodity'.[7] He was indeed rid of that intelligentsia – but not quite. In fact they were clearly getting on his nerves, and he devoted more than usual time to them in his beer cellar speech of 24 February 1940 where he tried to make fun of 'top-hatted Englishmen wanting to do some propaganda', with the aid of 'advisers' – 'people who once lived amongst us when they held the reins of power in Germany'. Today (Hitler went on) 'they only hold the power of their voice – and the voice sounds badly in Germany. The German people don't want to hear it. They are fed up with it. It is quite uninteresting what these people are talking about. No German believes a single word they say. Every German knows that they are lying.'[8]

Well, yes, not every German, in fact lots of them must have listened to the BBC, for Hitler thought it necessary to return to the charge in January 1941, even while he fancied himself on top of the world. In the 'anti-plutocratic' phase of the Nazi-Soviet pact, he sneered at 'the English lords' who had 'borrowed (*sic*) a few helpers from Germany', but these were 'exactly the same people who had failed so pitifully over here. Who are they? We can see it from their pamphlets. We know exactly who did what. The only difference is that whereas before the imprint read *Vossische Zeitung*, it now reads *The Times*.'[9]

This was in the early days of the war when things went well with Hitler. He then twisted the facts further by ridiculing his enemies who he said 'claimed they had not been fully aware of what he was up to'. Well, he sneered, it wasn't *his* fault, *he* had told them: they should not have listened to 'the silly twaddle talked by refugees, they ought to have read what I have written, not once but a thousand times. More often than I no one ever stated what he intended to do'.[9]

For once he was right: he *had* told us, and that was precisely what the refugees had been quoting all along, that very 'atrocity propaganda' which he had done his best to discredit, the facts derived from the revolting effusions of *Mein Kampf* which few ever read and none believed. Precisely because the enemy had 'relied on the polluted sources of the refugees', Dr Goebbels jeered in 1940, they were now 'too late in realising that Germany had indeed achieved predominance.'[10]

Admittedly they were late but not too late, and there was an unconscious and symbolic irony in the fact that the acknowledged experts on propaganda kept harping on the despised emigrés' activities as publicists and informants. Perhaps they felt they were being hit where it really hurt. In his diaries, Dr Goebbels thought some British radio broadcasts were 'exclusively the work of Jews who emigrated from Germany'; he consoled himself with the reflection that 'they lost their idiotic struggle once already in Berlin;

let them try again, this time from London' where they were getting 'more idiotic every day.'[11] At the same time, he could not help paying tribute to 'the very effectively produced pamphlets of the English' who he found were 'greatly superior to us in this area'.[12]

The fact was that as the fortunes of war were turning against them, the Nazis began to realise more and more the valuable aid Britain was receiving from German emigrés. In his diaries[13] Goebbels claimed, on the authority of 'former Berlin Reuter Correspondent Bettany', that the plan for the devastating RAF raid on the Möhne dam in May 1943 'stemmed from a Jew who had emigrated from Berlin' which 'shows once again (the diarist adds) how dangerous the Jews are'. As the French would say, *Cet animal est très méchant: quand on l'attaque il se défend.* The Minister felt 'certain that treason was involved, for the English were so well informed and after the attack had such exact knowledge of what damage was done that it is hardly credible that they ascertained this solely by air reconnaissance'.[13]

It was 'not for nothing (writes a German historian) that time and again Hitler and Goebbels bitterly attacked the emigrés since their expulsion proved to be, for the Nazis, in moral terms, a permanent lost battle'.[14] Another German scholar[15] stresses the refugees' specific contribution – 'their familiarity with German life and general conditions, more especially their command of the fine points of German usage which they knew how to put to the most telling advantage.'

Many too were prominent in Britain's code-breaking centre at Bletchley Park which has been described as 'probably the most successful intelligence agency'[16] where the refugees' efficiency 'though it did not win the war, dramatically shortened it' by such devices as interrogating U-Boat survivors who furnished 'priceless information about new boats, weapons and tactics.'[17]

In their book on *British Intelligence in the Second World War*,[18] the authors F. H. Hinsley and C. A. G. Simkins stress 'the opportunities offered Britain by the large influx of refugees', a point thought to have been badly neglected when Germany, in this respect, 'made no effective preparations' for war in 1939, partly also because of 'the poor performance' of her own intelligence services as well as the 'corruption and disaffection' due to 'bad leadership and the Nazi system of government'.

Undoubtedly emigrés were among those who supplied Churchill with vital data on German rearmament and economic expansion before the war. Hitler must have heard about them when he said in a speech on 6 November 1938:[19] 'If Mr Churchill were to see more Germans and fewer emigrés, i.e. kept traitors paid by foreign governments, he would realise the madness and folly of his empty talk: the man seems to be living on the moon.'

Though the 'two German refugees of high ability and inflexible purpose' are not named in Churchill's memoirs,[20] some are known. Sir Henry Strakosch, the Austrian-born industrialist, for example, was one of them;[21] journalists who did their bit were the Hungarian Stefan Lorant, founder and editor of the widely read *Picture Post*;[22] Emery Revesz, another formidable Hungarian publicist,[23] and (most likely) Leopold Schwarzschild, editor of the Paris weekly *Das Neue Tagebuch* where Churchill's articles frequently appeared. Churchill characteristically praised him for his 'invaluable contributions to the enlightenment of those who care to be enlightened.'[24]

In a wider sense, Churchill paid tribute to the refugees' achievement when he told Parliament in August 1940: 'Since the Germans drove out the Jews and lowered their technical standards, our science is definitely ahead of theirs.'[25] Others praised 'the brilliant sons of Germany, now refugees here',[26] 'masters of science of German universities',[27] 'some of the finest minds of Europe',[28] persecuted by 'countries too stupid to make use of them';[29] their 'inventive genius' had 'greatly strengthened' Britain's defences.[29]

Not only Britain's. An American scholar has drawn attention to the work done in his country by the refugees among the nuclear physicists 'including some of the most gifted in the world'. According to Professor Roger H.

Stuewer, of the Tate Laboratory of Physics at the University of Minnesota, 'by 1933 nuclear physics had become a seedling with sturdy roots in experimental and theoretical soil, and a rapidly increasing number of young physicists of exceptional ability were being attracted to its challenges. And the great majority of those who were forced to flee Germany, Austria and Italy eventually came, sometimes indirectly, to the United States, so that by the end of the decade no other country in the world had within its borders a larger number of emigré nuclear physicists. And no other field within physics would have more momentous consequences for humanity than nuclear physics. Political and scientific currents had become irrevocably intertwined', for 'with the discovery of nuclear fission in 1938 and the outbreak of war in Europe in 1939, the fear that a nuclear weapon might fall into Hitler's hands served as a powerful unifying force among nuclear physicists in America, emigrés and non-emigrés alike, and most placed their talents in the service of the United States Government working on the Manhattan Project and other wartime research.'[30]

While Britain received about 500 scholars, some of them Nobel prize winners, about 1,100 went to the USA, among them not only Albert Einstein but also victims of Italy's race laws (Emilio Segre and Enrico Fermi).[30a] The place where the atom bomb was finally built, Los Alamos, became known as 'the city of foreigners'. None of these scholars ever returned to their country of origin.

An outstanding contribution was also made to American intelligence, chiefly within the Office of Strategic Studies (OSS). Here (it was noted in the history of that organisation) 'a large and influential German refugee contingent in the Research and Analysis Division ... enjoyed a status of special esteem and honor.' With 'their deep reservoir of political, regional and linguistic espertise', they were able to make themselves exceedingly useful. Similarly they were (as in Britain) conspicuous in the section of Army Military Intelligence responsible for the interrogation of German prisoners of war. By way of ingenuous ruses and

311

the skill of speaking the enemy's 'mother tongue', some managed to secure the surrender of whole German units.[31]

As the war dragged on, even Dr Goebbels came to realise the impact of the refugees' contribution to Allied victory. 'Our technical development both as regards submarine and air warfare is far inferior to that of the English and the Americans,' he writes in his diary in May 1943.[32] The reasons are explained to him in a 'very depressing report' by 'the well-known physics expert', Professor Ramsauer, director of the German General Electric Company and chairman of the *Deutsche Physikalische Gesellschaft*.[33] The expert (diplomatically) 'believes we can catch up with the Anglo-Saxon physicists by concentrating our research facilities ... and by increasing the number of scientists both students and teachers', but this of course (Goebbels notes) 'will take considerable time.'[33] Meanwhile, he adds, 'Anglo-Saxon physical science has completely eclipsed us, especially in research. As a result, the Anglo-Saxon powers are very superior to us in the practical application to warfare of the results of research in physics.'[34] Goebbels does not mention the self-inflicted injury when senseless persecution forced distinguished scientists to flee abroad. He merely blames 'the mediocre talents in the Reich Government'.[35]

He is more specific (short of mentioning names): 'We are now getting the reward for our poor leadership on the scientific front who did not show the necessary initiative to stimulate the willingness of scientists to cooperate. You just cannot let an absolute nit-wit be at the head of German science for years and not expect to be punished for such folly.'[36] True enough – though it seems quite unfair to blame an 'absolute nit-wit' when in fact the fault lay with the larger 'poor leadership', not excluding the critic himself and even the Führer whom Goebbels describes as 'an enthusiastic advocate of pure science'[37] – so long as it was pukka 'Aryan' science.

With these 'enthusiastically' held conceptions of 'pure science' it is inevitable for Goebbels to consider it 'very humiliating to see how the enemy is leading us by the nose in air warfare. Every month he introduces some new method which it takes weeks and sometimes months for us to catch up with ... We have to pay very dearly for what we failed to do in air warfare hitherto. But that was to be expected.'[38] Indeed it was and had been but the 'infallible' Leader knew better.

When, at the end of the war, a survey was published in Britain on 'Science and Victory', one of the foremost British newspapers remarked:[39] 'The benefits to be had from exploiting brains which should have been the enemy's have never been enjoyed on such a scale by a country at war as by America and ourselves', and 'to take the most dramatic example', the question was asked: 'Had such leaders of nuclear physics as Dr Niels Bohr, Dr Liesa Meitner and Dr Rudolph Peierls remained at Germany's disposal, perhaps with Professor Fermi still in Italy, what were the odds that the atomic bomb might not have originated in Germany and fallen on London?'

The biter was indeed badly bitten – as had already happened in the field of medicine where the expulsion of the Jewish doctors created, on the one hand, grave health hazards inside Germany and, again, conferred benefits on the countries that received them. The British Home Secretary at the time, Sir Samuel Hoare, bears witness in his memoirs:[40] 'The help that many of these doctors gave to our war effort, whether in the treatment of wounds, nervous troubles and paralysis, or in the production of penicillin, was soon to prove how great was the country's gain, and how much greater it might have been if professional interests had not restricted its scope.'

The political refugees might have achieved even more, long before war broke out, had many more of their warnings been heeded. Of them might (almost) be said what Goebbels confided to his diary (in 1941) about Churchill: 'If he had come to power in 1933 we would not be where we are today.'[41] If careful attention had been paid to the refugees' abundantly and competently documented factual

313

information which Hitler ordered to be decried as 'atrocity propaganda', if more people had refused to be fooled and corrupted by his blatant lies, he might have been stopped in his tracks long before he had the power to provoke war. But few would listen. The character of the Nazi Government was not understood as the organised conspiracy that it was.

Accordingly, the refugee scientists were regarded as unwelcome aliens, either competitors in the face of 'much unemployment among academic people in England' or because 'these Central Europeans' were not considered to be 'entirely reliable from the national point of view'. In fact 'Government sensitivity about employing foreigners' was reinforced by 'racial or religious prejudice' – precisely as Hitler had calculated it would. Distrust of 'Jewish stories of Nazi atrocities' as 'propaganda' helped to disable Britain as effectively as did the Nazi boobytrap called 'a bulwark against Communism'.[41a]

When one of the Nazi leaders, Dr Robert Ley, chief of the Labour Front, reviewed the situation in November 1939, he confessed to 'utter amazement' because 'we simply fail to understand how it was that ever since 1933 England's behaviour should have been so exceedingly stupid.'[42] And again, with supreme cynicism, Goebbels weighed in: 'What would have become of us if the enemies of National Socialism had, from the beginning, taken us as seriously as we deserved? And were there no refugees making frantic efforts to convince the British plutocrats of Germany's failing strength, we should indeed have to invent them.'[43]

He did not have to invent them – they came back to him, those refugees, even with a vengeance, in the guise of his own 'Aryan' Germans. Having turned the Jews into refugees dependent on international charity, the Nazis, towards the end of the war, were faced with millions of their own people who had become refugees within Germany. Those in the East were forced to flee West, often in the most pathetic, pitiful conditions, spending horrible days and nights before reaching safer places – if ever they did – for, according to a German press report of January 1945,[44] 'they all knew that the road from the Eastern danger zone leads into the zone threatened by annihilation from the air.'

In Berlin heart-rending scenes were witnessed at the railway stations where many people succumbed to the strain or to the epidemics that were fast spreading. Nor were people allowed to stay in the capital. The majority were taken to special camps, with nothing but the few belongings they were able to carry away in a bundle. Mothers could be seen bringing their dead children from the trains to bury them in the snow, with wrapping paper as the only shroud.[45]

The Nazis were not amused. Their chief newspaper[46] was seized with righteous indignation, culminating in the avowal that 'the thought of humanity so treacherously betrayed brings tears of shame to our eyes'. No less – and with these 'humanitarian tears' in their eyes – the question is actually asked: 'Is there not in the enemy's ranks at least one feeling heart that will rise in anger against these wicked cruelties?' Yes, such a question was actually asked by those whose gospel according to *Mein Kampf* was inhuman cruelty and 'the utmost brutality'. Now they were tasting their own medicine as they decried the furious blows fast falling upon them: 'What do the enemy care about humanity, about decency, morality, about the code of a gentleman, since the very lowest instincts of a bestial underworld have been let loose against the Germans?'

This 'humanitarian' appeal was made in Hitler's own newspaper after he had sneered at the warning world, in January 1939: 'Don't talk to me about humanitarian feelings.'[47] From the very beginning of his career, the author of *Mein Kampf* had gone out of his way to deride the 'ridiculous so-called humanitarianism' which he said was nothing but 'a mixture of stupidity, cowardice and pretentious ignorance.'[48] It was on the strength of this Master Morality that all pleas on behalf of the victims of Nazi persecution were always brutally rejected.

Now the tables were turned, and the biter was indeed mortally bitten.

## NOTES

1. Speech on 14 October 1933: Max Domarus (ed.), *Hitler: Reden und Proklamationen 1932–1945*, Neustadt/Aisch, 1962–63, i. p. 311. Henceforth quoted as *Domarus*.

2. Dr Joseph Goebbels, in the earliest volume of his diaries: *Vom Kaiserhof zur Reichskanzlei*, Munich, 1934, p. 292, under 2 April 1933.

3. Speech on 30 January 1934: *Domarus*, i. p. 354.

4. *Westdeutscher Beobachter*, Cologne daily, 24 April 1935.

5. Speech on 30 January 1939: *Domarus*, ii. p. 1057.

6. *Mein Kampf*, German standard edition, p. 368.

7. Speech on 1 May 1939: *Domarus*, ii. p. 1185.

8. Speech on 24 February 1940: *Domarus*, ii. p. 1468.

9. Speech on 30 January 1941: *Domarus*, ii. p. 1662.

10. Speech reported in *12-Uhr Blatt*, Berlin, 12 April 1940.

11. *The Goebbels Diaries 1939–1941*, Ed. Fred Taylor, London, 1982, p. 35, under 31 October 1939.

12. Ibid. pp. 97 and 121, under 17 January and 29 April 1940.

13. *The Goebbels Diaries*. Ed. Louis P. Lochner, London, 1948, pp. 302–3, under 19 May 1943.

14. Walter Hagemann, *Publizistik im Dritten Reich*, Hamburg, 1948, p. 297.

15. Bernhard Wittek, *Der britische Aetherkrieg gegen das Dritte Reich*, Münster, 1962, p. 60.

16. Review in *The Daily Telegraph*, 19 September 1993, of a recent book entitled *Codebreakers. The Inside Story of Bletchley Park*. Eds. F. H. Hinsley and Alan Stripp. Oxford.

17. Letter in *The Daily Telegraph*, 17 May 1993, on those who by breaking German Enigma-machine ciphers, 'allowed us to read the enemy's mind ... thus making an invaluable contribution to victory in the Atlantic.'

18. Volume 4, London, HMSO, 1990, pp. 280–81.

19. *Domarus*, i. p. 964.

20. *The Gathering Storm*. London, Cassell (Paperback), p. 199.

21. See William Manchester, *The Caged Lion. Winston Spencer Churchill 1932–1940*. Cardinal Book, 1988, pp. 110 and 304.

22. For Lorant see Manchester, op. cit., p. 426.

23. For Revesz see Manchester, op. cit., p. 339.

24. Quoted on the cover of Schwarzschild's book *World in Trance*, New York, 1942.

25. Speech in the House of Commons on 20 August 1940.

26. General Jan C. Smuts, the South African leader: *The Times*, London, 13 November 1942.

27. *Sunday Express*, London, 20 September 1942.

28. *News Chronicle*, London, 30 September 1942.

29. *The Lancet*, London, 9 May 1942.

30. Paper read at the 21st symposium of the *Gesellschaft für Wissenschaftsgeschichte*, at Wolfenbüttel, Germany, 12–14 May 1983, printed in *Berichte zur Wissenschaftsgeschichte*. vii, 1984, pp. 23–40. A review of this symposium appeared in the *Frankfurter Allgemeine Zeitung*, 25 January 1985, under the title 'The Elite that was deprived of its Citizenship: When scientists emigrated from the Third Reich'.

30a. A Hungarian, Eugene Wigner, a quantum theorist, left Germany to take up a post at Princeton University (which had already received Einstein). In 1939 he learnt that two German scientists had been on the track of a possible nuclear chain reaction and as he feared that this discovery might produce a devastating bomb, he urged Einstein to warn President Roosevelt, with the result that the Manhattan Project was started.

31. See Guy Stern, 'In the Service of American Intelligence: German Jewish Exiles in the War against Hitler'. Year Book xxxvii (1992), published by the Leo Baeck Institute, London, pp. 461–77.

32. *The Goebbels Diaries*. Ed. L. P. Lochner, op. cit., p. 298, under 14 May 1943.

33. Ibid., pp. 299–300, under 15 May 1943.

34. Ibid., p. 300.

35. Ibid., p. 295, under 12 May 1943.

36. Ibid., p. 298, under 14 May 1943. The 'absolute nit-wit', according to Lochner, was the Minister of Education, Bernhard Rust, who he says 'as a young man had been in an insane asylum'.

37. Ibid., p. 295, under 12 May 1943.

38. Ibid., p. 404, under 7 November 1943.

39. *Manchester Guardian*, 9 April 1946.

40. *Nine Troubled Years*, London, 1954, p. 240.

41. *The Goebbels Diaries 1939–1941*. Ed. Fred Taylor, op. cit., p. 354, under 8 May 1941.

41a. See *The Times Higher Education Supplement*, London, 21 October 1983: 'How Britain lost the physics war', by Paul Hoch.

42. Article in *Der Angriff*, Berlin, 29 November 1939.

43. Article in *Das Reich*, Berlin, 11 May 1941.

44. *Deutsche Allgemeine Zeitung*, Berlin, 28 January 1945.

45. *Morgontidningen*, Stockholm, 27 January 1945.

46. *Völkischer Beobachter*, 13 January 1945.

47. *Mein Kampf*, p. 30. The book teems with calls for 'extreme ruthlessness' (p. 392), 'ruthless brutality' (p. 44), 'brutal determination' (pp. 29, 188, 564).

48. *Mein Kampf*, p. 148.

# INDEX

322